WHEN
THE GOING
WAS GOOD!

WHEN
THE GOING
WAS GOOD!
American Life in the Fifties

Jeffrey Hart

CROWN PUBLISHERS, INC.

New York

ACKNOWLEDGMENTS

It would be impossible to thank properly all of those who have provided invaluable assistance to the author of this book. However, I must mention here the assistance with photographs by Leonard Donato of King Features and James Katz of *Columbia College Today*. Linda Stevens of *The New York Post* educated me on many aspects of the popular culture and popular music of the Fifties. Margot de L'Etoile provided inspiration and meticulous criticism. No editor in the profession is superior to Alan Cross in aesthetic taste and creative suggestion. Lisa Healy was absolutely indispensable in bringing the book to a—I hope—successful conclusion.

"The Camera Eye: Four Poets" from National Review. Copyright © 1981 by National Review. Reprinted by permission.

Excerpts from "White Flannels, Grass Courts" from New Republic. Copyright © 1976, 1977 by New Republic. Reprinted by permission.

Inquiries should be addressed to Crown Publishers, Inc., One Park Avenue, New York, New York 10016

Printed in the United States of America

Published simultaneously in Canada by General Publishing Company Limited

Library of Congress Cataloging in Publication Data

Hart, Jeffrey Peter, 1930–
    When the going was good!

    1. United States—Social conditions—1945–1960.
I. Title.
HN58.H26   973.92   81-20654
ISBN 0-517-54831-3   AACR2
            00- 214064 (24A)
            # 8798897
        10 9 8 7 6 5 4 3 2 1
                First Edition

for
Margot de l'Etoile

Contents

Preface

This is a book about the Fifties, a fascinating period in American life, and one which in retrospect seems to grow ever more attractive.

As I wrote this book and became deeply involved in that period, I also saw the importance of continuities stretching before and after this decade. No period, however distinctive, exists in isolation. Dwight Eisenhower became a global figure during World War II. His presidency is central to the whole post-war period and is part of a story that has not yet ended in 1982. The roots of the great Dodger teams of the Fifties lie in the colorful Macphail Dodgers of the Forties, and there is a majestic Yankee continuity that moves from Ruth to DiMaggio to Mantle. The New York art renaissance of the Fifties had long been prepared for, and both manners and morals have vital connections with what went before and after.

In these and other areas, the focus will be on the Fifties, in many ways a golden era, but also on the Fifties in their wider time frame.

WILLIAM F. BUCKLEY, JR.

Introduction

Jeffrey Hart has undertaken here a most difficult assignment—to make comprehensible, and interesting a synoptic account of a decade. It is wonderful news that he has succeeded. This he accomplished by the universality of his knowledge, by his eclectic enthusiasm, and by a high-spiritedness which other decades, unaddressed by him, weep in envy over.

In order to be done with it, let me confess that I find unconvincing one strain that catches Mr. Hart's attention in a number of the episodes written about here. This is the notion that the great sexual liberation of the Sixties, adumbrated in the Fifties, was a transforming agent responsible for great advances in energy, creativity, and felicity. My own view of the phenomenon is different. This is not the space in which to explore those differences, but rather to remark that whatever it is that has given to Jeffrey Hart the energy to conceive and execute this book is something to rejoice over—animal, vegetable, or mineral.

One guards, in such enterprises, against phoney synthesis or integrations. Many years ago I ceased reading Marxist history, as any other adult should, because of the labored neatness of the explanation of any phenomenon—much as the grassy-knollers will explain any missing document, human being, or historical event—as the subtle working of the same conspiracy that labored

to assassinate John F. Kennedy. Hart is capable of integration, and
of seeking links between apparently disparate events. But he
recognizes also the spontaneity of human action, and is prepared to
note trends without linking them. Thus he fosters confidence
where he does see interrelatedness, and we show this confidence in
him as we would to a skiing guide, who from time to time tells us
we are not permitted to descend this area or that one, giving us in
other situations clearance to proceed.

Inevitably a reader is more suspicious, and appropriately grate-
ful if the experience is successful, of the writer who drags him to
fields in which he is explicitly uninterested, in my case sports.
Jeffrey Hart is an enthusiastic sportsman, indeed it is the problem
of sport that most people are *aficionados*. Even so, it is difficult to
think of anyone who brings greater color or innocent pleasure than
Hart does, e.g., to telling the story of tennis during the Fifties. In
doing so, it is appropriate to add, he does not hesitate, as necessary, to reach back into history if doing so makes his account more
intelligible, or more interesting. The dominant figures, in tennis,
in boxing, and other sports, therefore appear. But the culmination
is that of the Fifties. Here Jeffrey Hart describes, and exploits in
the greatest detail, events that took place during that decade falsely
held as unremarkable—until now. By the same token, where
appropriate to do so, Hart goes past the Fifties, so as not to keep
from us that final satisfaction we may need in order to experience
consummation.

This book is so rich in detail, and in analyses, that it is a purely
subjective indulgence to single out any particular treatment for
attention. But having said this permit a word about theology, and
another about the intellectuals.

Jeffrey Hart is one of those few generalist intellectuals who are
interested in theology as a broad field of learning, quite apart from
any presumption that it has been touched by special historical
grace. Accordingly he treats such men as Paul Tillich, and
Reinhold Niebuhr, as though they actually existed, and as though
what they said actually made a difference. In this respect he tends
to depart from the academic tradition of so many of his peers, who
will notice the fly-by of a theologian, even as monitory radar will
dutifully record the passage of a Pan American clipper on a
regularly scheduled run. It is expected that theologians will exist,
that they will write, and even that what they say will sometimes
prove provocative. What isn't expected, really, is that what they

say should make any difference—in the sense that presidential pronouncements or the movements of the stock market make a difference. Jeffrey Hart is as interested in tergiversations by Reinhold Niebuhr as he is in a hitting streak by Joe DiMaggio. His excitement, in analyzing the findings of theologians, is instantly communicated, and one greets it with a keen sense of pleasure and intellectual satisfaction.

I shall be happy, moreover, to hear what the answer is to the question he addresses to the community of historians, particularly those of them who are Sinologists. This because Mr. Hart takes the work of Owen Lattimore and asks questions that are not easy to answer. Mr. Lattimore will be remembered as a principal target of Senator Joseph R. McCarthy, who said that he was a most important Soviet agent. The charge was not proved, and the general disgrace of McCarthy after the Senate censure tended to have the corollary effect of vindicating Mr. Lattimore. Jeffrey Hart's view of the controversy asks the profoundest question about the nature of academic responsibility in such situations, and is itself worth the cost of this volume.

But there is so very much more—about music, the theater, ballet, song, atom bombs, Aquarius, Estes Kefauver, the Catholic Church, Hemingway. . . . For those who lived through the Fifties this volume is not merely a reminder of what happened, but a course in the importance of what happened—with the perspectives keen, sharp, and compelling. For those who didn't live through this decade, or weren't aware of having done so, this is the liveliest trot they could imagine. One finishes the book genuinely grieved that such volumes do not exist for every decade one cares to know about. Yes, the effort has been made to treat the Twenties, the Thirties, and the Sixties in such a way. But to do right will require that someone as keen, as accessible as Jeffrey Hart to the humor, pathos, piquancy, and flavor of events, accost these other decades. Perhaps after the predictable success of this volume, Jeffrey Hart can be persuaded to lay down one of his other heavy loads, to do for decade after decade what he has done for this one. You're skeptical? You wait and see.

**

. . . to put down what really happened in action; what the actual things were which produced the emotion you experienced.

Ernest Hemingway, *Death in the Afternoon*

Overlord

Perhaps the Fifties really began on June 5, 1944, when General Dwight D. Eisenhower uttered three words.

They were three words that made the Fifties possible, the Fifties as they really were.

At 4 A.M., the General strode into the library of Southwick House, a spacious country mansion not far from the great Portsmouth naval base. The outer rooms bustled with military activity. Southwick House was Eisenhower's headquarters for the invasion of Europe.

The rain and wind crashing against the black windows of the library defined Eisenhower's problem. Minutes earlier, he had driven along the blacktop road and turned up the long access road to Southwick House. Sometimes the wind was so strong the rain blew sideways in horizontal lines. It was the worst June storm in living memory.

The English Channel is always choppy. Since June 3, powerful waves had been battering the cliffs of Dover, crashing over the breakwater at Calais, punishing the coast of Normandy. On June 4, at a 2 A.M. meeting, with hurricane-force winds lashing the countryside and whipping the English Channel into an unmanageable frenzy, Eisenhower cancelled the June 5 invasion date, postponing it one day. If it had to be further postponed, past June 7, it would have to wait another two weeks for favorable tides.

Driving to this meeting of his top commanders, Eisenhower passed miles of waiting tanks, trucks and artillery pieces, jamming all roads leading to the coast. In every southern and eastern English harbor, landing craft and troop ships were jammed with soldiers on the fine edge of combat readiness. In English rivers, the elements of the artificial harbors looked like huge floating crates. Someone had remarked to him that the weight of metal in England was so enormous that only the hundreds of barrage balloons with their cables prevented the island from sinking out of sight altogether.

Eisenhower entered the library looking trim in his tailored battle jacket. He also looked tense to those who greeted him. General Montgomery wore baggy corduroy trousers and a sweat shirt. Vice Admiral Sir Benjamin Ramsey and his aides wore immaculate Navy blue and gold. Eisenhower's chief of staff, General Walter Bedell Smith, greeted him tersely. A roaring fire on the hearth fought the gloom outside. Eisenhower crossed the room and sat on a sofa. The meteorologists were immediately brought in.

Group Captain Stagg, a tall Scot, smiled through his tiredness. "I think we have found a gleam of hope for you, sir," he said. Eisenhower looked at him intently. "The mass of weather fronts coming in from the Atlantic is moving faster than we anticipated. We predict there will be rather fair conditions beginning late on June 5 and lasting until the next morning, June 6, with a drop in the wind velocity and some break in the clouds. Ceiling—about 3,000." His charts showed, however, that the bad weather would then recur, with high seas and low visibility. Otherwise, predictions were hazardous. At best, the meteorologists were telling Eisenhower, he might expect about twenty-four hours of passable weather.

Air Chief Marshal Leigh-Mallory wanted to know about cloud conditions. Could his planes operate? Admiral Ramsey asked about conditions at sea, the wind velocities.

When all the questions had been asked, there was complete silence in the room. It lasted for five minutes. Eisenhower sat quietly on the sofa, saying nothing. Then he looked up. He said, "Well, we'll go."

CHAPTER ONE

Only Yesterday

The 1950s were an extraordinary period in American life.

Not since the 1920s had so much been happening, both in popular and in high culture. Extraordinary books, movies, Broadway shows burst like meteors. Faulkner and Hemingway both won Nobel Prizes at the beginning of the decade. *The Catcher in the Rye* appeared in 1951, *The Old Man and the Sea* in 1952. A spirit of literary ambition was in the air. Norman Mailer had published *The Naked and the Dead* (1948), John Horne Barnes' *The Gallery* (1947) had been felt to be major—Hemingway thought it was, and it was—and John Aldridge's *After the Lost Generation*, a study of these and other postwar novelists, made conscious reference to the 1920s literary renaissance.

The Fifties were a distinctive period in sports: Mickey Mantle, Jackie Robinson, Dick Kazmaier, Pancho Gonzales. For the first time in history, New York was the art capital of the world. Politics seethed with controversy over all the issues connected with communism, at home and abroad. The Fifties saw an extraordinary burst of musical activity. In philosophy and theology, important things were happening. And the nation as a whole experienced an unprecedented burst of prosperity, of home buying, car owning and, of course, television. Mass air travel began. President

Eisenhower inaugurated the greatest national project in history, the interstate highway system.

And yet, despite all this and more, the decade of the Fifties has a bad name. We are instructed that it was apathetic, the decade of the "Silent Generation," a time when nothing much happened.

Of course, that is nonsense. It is, moreover, a tendentious falsehood serving particular cultural interests, which will be specified as we make our odyssey through the extraordinary years of the Fifties.

The historical past is constantly changing before our eyes. It is not static. It is refracted through an unfolding present. Details that were once important fade like the inscriptions on old tombstones. As Eliot wrote in *Little Gidding,* his masterly reflection on time, "See, now they vanish,/ The faces and places." Thus once prominent figures become footnotes, or disappear altogether. Who now gives much thought to Charles Wilson or Neil McElroy, Secretaries of Defense around whom fierce controversies once swirled? And does Sputnik now loom as large as it once did in those distant days when it seemed to presage a huge Soviet lead in space?

In 1958, the old President, Dwight Eisenhower, plagued by ileitis, stroke and heart attacks, was on his way out. At the time, he seemed used up, part of the past. In his presidential campaign, John F. Kennedy would work that perception into his political rhetoric: ". . . the torch is passing to a new generation. . . ." But from our present perspective, from the perspective of history, Ike is growing in stature, Kennedy diminishing.

Eisenhower has been popularly regarded as a do-nothing president, yet he was the dominating political figure of the Fifties. He presided over the arguing out of the issues raised by Senator Joseph McCarthy, the end of the Korean War, military actions in Guatemala and Lebanon, the launching of the federal highway program, and the period of sometimes violent adjustment that followed the *Brown vs. Board of Education* decision.

His recently published *Diaries,* superbly edited by Robert H. Ferrell, make clear that he had a shrewd historical economic sense—under Ike, inflation "raged" at an annual rate of less than 2 percent, as the nation entered a period of unprecedented affluence. Eisenhower was a complex figure who masterfully manipulated his consciously crafted public image. "Since Roosevelt," writes columnist George Will, "seven presidents have struggled with the modern presidency Roosevelt created. Of these, Eisenhower was the most successful. Only the power of ideological prejudice prevents many people from even considering the possibility that Eisenhower did better because he was a better politician. Robert Lowell wrote that 'the elect and the elected' come to Washington 'bright as dimes,' and remain until they are 'soft and dishevelled.' Not Ike. He left with a reputation that grows brighter as years pass." The historical scholarship of recent years is more and more regularly confirming Will's judgment.

During those 1950s, a time when "nothing happened," we saw the birth of a communications revolution the consequences of which have yet to be fully appreciated or absorbed. The Eisenhower campaign of 1952 introduced the first large-scale hiring of skilled advertising men, through Batton, Barton, Durstine and Osborne. The radio and the Model T had revolutionized American culture in the 1920s. You could actually *listen* to Los Angeles, music from the Coast in the stillness of a Cincinnati night. With your flivver, you no longer had to sit decorously with your date on the living room couch. In the early Fifties, that decade when nothing was supposed to be happening, the first widespread viewing of television was changing America even more than had radio or the Ford car. Eisenhower's 1952 TV spots were primitive by today's standards, but revolutionary in their own time. By 1956, research into "image" for all sorts of products had entered its period of sophistication. A decade of middle-class affluence was ushered in by an advertising genius, an Englishman named David Ogilvie, who had gone to Oxford, and moved on to invent Commander Whitehead of the Schweppes ads, the Man in the Hathaway Shirt, and the Marlboro Man. And the image makers created a mystique around themselves. Most people did not know the name Batton, Barton, Durstine and Osborne; but they were aware of an almost mythical power called B.B.D. & O.

The popular culture of the 1950s has dwindled to a couple of foolish stereotypes. During the Eisenhower decade, when everyone was presumably conforming, and nothing was supposed to be happening, there were many diverse and exciting popular cultures. Today, in myth, John Travolta's *Grease* has won the stereotype race.

But I have a confession to make, no doubt somewhat unrepresentative: As a young man growing up in the 1950s, I never knew anyone who wore a black leather jacket. I never knew anyone in middle-class Forest Hills, Long Island, who had long, greasy hair swept back over his ears. Ever-present TV ads, in fact, condescended to such styles with the famous campaign against "greasy kid stuff." In the summer, my friends and I usually wore polo shirts or regular white shirts open at the collar, plus slacks or chinos, plus sneakers or loafers. In the vicinity of the beach, we normally wore the same outfit, minus socks. In the winter, we normally wore slacks, mostly grey flannel, and either a sweater or a sports jacket, and, almost inevitably, a regimental-striped tie. Far from sporting greasy hair, most of us wore crew cuts. Princeton undergraduates were remarkable for brushing the crew cut forward, and they favored glasses with dark tortoise shell rims. Yale freshmen were notable for joining at least thirty campus organizations, especially singing groups, as soon as they arrived in New Haven—and I half-consciously considered Fielding's Tom Jones to have been the first Yale Man. Harvard undergraduates developed funny accents, a sort of Cambridge cockney.

Out at the Hungry i cafe in San Francisco (it stood for "Hungry intellectual"), the Kingston Trio was doing something new in music, singing to crowded small groups ballads of genuine historical interest and musical power. They would give brief informative comments on the background of these songs. The Kingston Trio looked like Ivy Leaguers and wore crew cuts and striped shirts, but they were expanding the range of popular music, and before long they were playing all across the country to wildly enthusiastic audiences. Both culturally and intellectually, they were reaching out to both American and foreign ballad traditions, and providing their audiences with brief but highly informed commentaries on musical traditions. They both demanded more of their audiences and helped to create a more sophisticated sense of history and musical possibility.

Elvis Presley, in this ambience, was a dim and marginal figure. We—people like me—had no notion of what deep currents were stirring under the surface out there, or what energies he would come to represent and express. His flat, almost Frankenstein-like cheekbones, his over-full lips, and the way his hair grew straight across his forehead ruled him out completely. No one I knew cared about Elvis Presley. But backed up by the new music of Buddy Holly, and the national adolescent cult of James Dean, Elvis Presley changed the emotional temperature of America.

My own friends did not move to the rhythm of "Hound Dog."

Our musical heroes fell into two categories. There were the "good" dance bands that would play in the summer at beach and tennis clubs on Long Island. When I first read Scott Fitzgerald's great 1922 story "Winter Dreams," I saw instantly that the mood he had captured was also the mood of the early 1950s: "There was a fish jumping and a star shining and the lights around the lake were gleaming. Over on a dark peninsula, a piano was playing the songs of last summer and of summers before that—songs from 'Chin-Chin' and 'The Count of Luxemburg' and 'The Chocolate Soldier'—and because the sound of a piano over a stretch of water had always sounded beautiful to Dexter he lay perfectly quiet and listened.

"The tune the piano was playing at that moment had been gay and new five years before when Dexter was a sophomore at college. They had played it at a prom once when he stood outside the gymnasium and listened. The sound of the tune precipitated in him a sort of ecstasy and it was with that ecstasy he viewed what happened to him now. It was a mood of intense appreciation, a sense that, for once, he was magnificently attuned to life and that everything about him was radiating a brightness and a glamour he might never know again."

In the early 1950s, the tunes were not from *Chin-Chin* or *The Chocolate Soldier,* but from Rodgers and Hammerstein. We listened and sang and danced to the songs of *South Pacific,* in which Mary Martin and Ezio Pinza were breaking all attendance records, tunes like "Some Enchanted Evening" and "This Nearly Was Mine."

Also there were the new jazz pianists who emerged in the late 1940s and had passionate followings among young people—Cy Walter, Errol Garner, Bill Clifton, Earl Wilde, Oscar Peterson, George Shearing. They played in small clubs and hotel lounges. The Drake Room in New York, where you could not only hear but actually talk with Cy Walter, was a big adolescent hangout. We danced in the Cub Room at the old Stork Club, and sometimes you ran into Ernest Hemingway in the adult headquarters downstairs.

It thus seems to me that the image of the 1950s current today is in very important ways false. I have reached the firm conclusion that when people say the 1950s were apathetic and not "political," they really mean that there was not much *left* politics, or rather that the *Left* had been seriously disabled. In fact, ferocious political debates marked the beginning of the decade. You only have to cite the names Hiss, Chambers, Rosenberg, Fuchs, Gouzenko, Coplon, McCarren, McCarthy, Lattimore to begin to recall the political intensity of the period. What was at issue there was no "witch-hunt," but the question of just how a free society ought to deal with demonstrable conspiracy, and reflection upon this issue gave rise to some of the most profound writing in political philosophy of our time.

It was during the leftist revival of the 1960s that the myth was generated of a nonpolitical and apathetic Eisenhower era, though from our present perspective, that of the 1980s, there are indeed aspects of the Fifties that render the decade, in Hemingway's phrase, "another country." This has to do chiefly with manners and morals. A recent evocation, for example, recalls the following:

> In Rapid City, South Dakota, right next to the "Shrine of Democracy," where Mount Rushmore's four stonefaced Americans look dignified, 90 percent of the town's bars and 30 percent of its restaurants and motels refused to accommodate blacks. "We don't serve colored people," hat-check girls said defiantly. One restaurant owner exclaimed: "The only thing we're scared of is the young ones [blacks] coming in and trying to intermingle."
>
> In Los Angeles that year a college student named Kenneth Young, going to summer school, sported a beard for the occasion. His family was angry and ashamed. "What would people think?" they asked. His aunts and uncles called him a beatnik, a Castroite, an anarchist, a communist. His crime actually lay not so much in being leftist, but in being different, in not fitting in.
>
> The high school in Cohasset, Massachusetts, suspended four students because their hair was too short.
>
> A school in Springfield, Ohio, actually expelled the 16-year-old daughter of a part-time pastor for refusing to wear bloomer-type shorts to gym. Judy Rae Bushong's objection was not that the shorts were ridiculously dowdy and Victorian but that they showed her knees. Judy Rae was very moral. "I would like to convert heathens in Mexico or Germany or something like that," she said.
>
> Nor was she alone. In Lubbock, Texas, a high school suspended two girls who did not want to wear sleeveless blouses and Jamaica shorts and participate in "immodest exercises."

Of course, these represent extreme cases, out of the mainstream of Fifties feeling. Yet the sexual attitudes of a given period are important to its identity. History does not really show a continuous development from more to less restrictive attitudes. Rather, there seems to be a more complex dialectic: indeed, the sexual landscape of the Fifties themselves was complex.

On the one hand, it is instructive to go back to the 1950s and read *Seventeen* magazine, or *Mademoiselle,* or such an etiquette book as *On Becoming a Woman* by Mary McGee Williams and Irene Kane, which went through seventeen printings and sold hundreds of thousands of copies. Throughout all of these popular and influential publications, the assumption reigned that marriage and motherhood were every woman's sole destiny and reason for existence. The etiquette book contained lists of things girls were supposed to do to please their adolescent dates. There was no suggestion that a boy had to make an effort to please the girl. She was supposed to steer the conversation toward automobile engines and baseball and such subjects, and defer to his interests and knowledge. A typical chapter is called "It's Not Too Soon to Dream of Marriage." The image of the desired girl in this literature is almost entirely a passive one. Under no circumstances was a girl to phone a boy and ask him out. "In dating, like dancing," we read, "a boy likes to take the lead: a girl's role, traditionally, is to follow." On a dinner date, the girl was supposed to tell the boy her choices, and he would then tell the waiter. Chastity was a constant theme. "Boys," we are instructed, "will only respect you if you say no." At no point in this culturally official literature do you get the impression that sex is something people might enjoy doing under varying conditions and assorted understandings.

I've wondered about the roots of this—what would one call it?—partial neo-Victorianism. In their intellectual and artistic brilliance and in the richness of their popular musical culture, the Fifties in some ways resembled the Jazz Age of the 1920s, but in their sexual aspect, officially at least, they did not.

Here's a tentative speculation. The real basis of the racial and sexual changes that are customarily associated with the 1960s seem to have been prepared during the war years of the 1940s. World War II had a tremendous impact on the American domestic scene, introducing social and moral changes to a greater extent than any event since the Civil War. Hundreds of thousands of women went to work in the defense plants—Rosie the Riveter—or served in the women's branches of the armed services, the WACs and the WAVEs. For the first time since the 1920s, we witnessed a widespread and aggressive assertion of female sexuality, an assertion, indeed, far more widespread than anything in the Twenties. Frank Sinatra was one lightning rod. Virtually single-handedly, Sinatra displaced the Big Band and subordinated it to his virtuoso eroticism. Sinatra not only sang; he made love to the microphone, as if it were a symbolic woman. His fans, dressed in sweaters, skirts and white tennis socks, were called "bobby-soxers." I recall one performance by Sinatra in the fall of 1944 when mobs of these women practically demolished the Paramount Theater in Times Square in an orgy of erotic frenzy.

While all this was taking place, the social position of the blacks was also undergoing a profound change. They began the great migration out of the South, seeking wartime jobs. Many achieved an unprecedented degree of affluence. American blacks were ceasing to be a largely agricultural and rural population, a demographic fact of immense social and political consequence, to which adjustments in due course had to be made. Blacks also fought alongside whites in the war. They became "visible men," alongside ethnic soldiers like those portrayed by William Bendix in the war movies.

Thus, although the women's movement and the black power and civil rights movements are usually associated with the turbulent 1960s, I would argue that both revolutions began during the 1940s and were unstoppable thereafter.

If that is true, perhaps the neo-Victorian aspect of the Fifties, in manners and morals, represents a temporary reaction against the far-reaching social convulsions of the war years. The settled life of family and suburb, of middle-class respectability, acquired a new aura of desirability. Like those who had voted for Warren Harding, Americans after World War II wanted a "return to normalcy." The difference was that in 1922, Americans, or an influential segment of them, were also engaged in rejecting Victorianism—boop-boop-adoop—not indulging a quasi-desire for it.

You can hear these changes in the popular music representative of the successive eras. The Jazz Age of the 1920s, when blacks were anything but invisible in the entertainment world, gives way to the Swing Era of the depression and the Big Bands. During the war, Frank Sinatra and his counterparts displace the Big Bands. But Rodgers and Hammerstein own the early Fifties. The overtly erotic gives way to the romantic and lyrical, and then, in the late

1950s, this gives way to the early Rock stars like Buddy Holly, who ushered in the Rock Era of the 1960s.

And yet. Despite the neo-Victorianism of much Fifties morality, there are some important facts that ought to be borne in mind. Dr. Alfred Kinsey's *Sexual Behavior in the Human Female* appeared in 1953, complementing his earlier study of male sexual behavior. In contrast to the official attitudes of the time, and setting aside cavils over Kinsey's methodology, he showed convincingly that there was a lot of sexual activity going on. Of the 6,000 women questioned, half admitted to having intercourse before marriage and a quarter to intercourse outside marriage. This second Kinsey Report shattered the notion of the passive "good girl" of the etiquette books and the women's magazines. Women were as interested in sex as men, maybe more so. In a related phenomenon, consider the most powerful female movie stars of the Fifties, Marilyn Monroe and Brigitte Bardot. Both expressed an entirely unashamed female sexuality. Their every wiggle made it crystal clear that they would enjoy sex whenever they wanted to. They expressed a sexuality as aggressive and independent as that of any male.

These phenomena, only touched on in this chapter, make it clear that the Fifties was a much more complex period than is generally realized, its official attitudes coexisting with powerful countercurrents of feeling, not to mention actual behavior.

In the accepted stereotypes, the Fifties were a period of intellectual stagnation. It is time to demolish that notion. For me, a sophomore in college in the year 1950, it was a period of extraordinary intellectual excitement.

I was aware that F. R. Leavis, a wild and brilliant don at Cambridge University, was consummating one of the great intellectual and academic rebellions, and also producing some of the most trenchant and combative literary criticism ever written. Leavis was changing the ways in which we see the past, and changing the education of his time. He was a colorful character and a formidable intellect.

At my school, Columbia College, Columbia University, the youthful partisans of F. R. Leavis lined up against the equally youthful partisans of the local champion Lionel Trilling, whose recently published volume of essays, *The Liberal Imagination*, staked out a position different from that of Leavis. The issues were complex, but they were passionate issues, and they had significance far beyond literature.

The great literary figures who had roared out of the American provinces and into the center of the modernist movement were at their apogees: Allen Tate, John Crowe Ransom and the rest. Ransom was teaching at Kenyon, Cleanth Brooks at Yale, R. D. Blockmur at Princeton. T. S. Eliot was at the pinnacle of his international reputation, though he had already written all of his best poetry, and Robert Frost was challenging his preeminence. In New York, in 1950, as I watched the rehearsals of his hit play, *The Cocktail Party*, Eliot showed such an extravagant appreciation of the pretty young actresses that make, to me, the recent speculation about his possible homosexuality seems preposterous. In 1958, Eliot recited his poems to a large audience at Columbia—he was an absolutely dominating stage presence—and later that night proved to be a prodigious consumer of Kentucky bourbon. I later heard from Allen Tate that one evening in Greenwich Village during the early Thirties, Eliot had drunk both Tate and e. e. cummings under the table at a local bistro.

During the 1950s, that period of "stagnation," New York replaced Paris as the art capital of the world, because of the dominant Abstract Expressionist school. The Cedar Tavern, a few blocks north of New York University on University Place, replaced the cafes of the Left Bank as the place where art was discussed intensely by those actually producing it. Willem de Kooning, Jackson Pollock, Robert Motherwell, and others were engaged in a great intellectual and artistic enterprise. On the one hand, they were in full revolt against the Stalinist "social realism" of the Thirties and the war years, with its workers and tractors and sharecroppers; on the other, they were testing the very boundaries of the idea of art. What, actually, *was* art? American artists no longer went to Europe—the Europeans came here. At the same time, the very different but towering figures, Edward Hopper and Andrew Wyeth, were painting their masterpieces. Hopper, that great painter of American space and light and loneliness, did not frequent the Cedar Tavern, but he could be seen sometimes with his wife around the Village.

Just before the decade of the Fifties began, the critic Malcolm Cowley saw something until then unrecognized: he saw that William Faulkner was a great novelist, possibly the best since Henry James, and Cowley proved it with his *Viking Portable Faulkner*, which was a major critical event. At about the same time, a number of critics, including Edmund Wilson and Lionel Trilling, were discovering the same thing about a writer whose novels had been neglected for years, F. Scott Fitzgerald. The Fitzgerald boom was on, all his books back in print. Things were stirring in San Francisco, with Kerouac and Ginsberg prominent on the scene. Can this be intellectual stagnation?

The intellectual life of the nation was greatly enriched, too, by the flood of refugees from Hitler's Germany. Hannah Arendt, for example, and Paul Tillich. At Union Theological Seminary in New York, Tillich and Reinhold Niebuhr were at the peak of their influence. Niebuhr had worked out a political critique of liberal optimism based on the theological doctrine of original sin: he was anti-totalitarian and democratic. Tillich was exploring the area between traditional Christianity and modern culture, even as Eliot was in his poetry. His most interesting books and lectures dealt with the theological significance of paintings and poems. As the title of his *Travel Diary, Between Two Worlds* (1936) nicely suggests, he lived in the tension between two perspectives on existence, both valid. And there they were, offering courses at Union Seminary. I doubt that many readers of this book could name a single present-day faculty member of that institution.

This dynamic American society has seen several great surges of affluence. During the Coolidge prosperity, the purchasing power of American wages actually increased at a rate of 2 percent per year. The federal budget shrank, taxes were cut, and consumer prices fell 2.3 percent. There was next to no inflation. The terse Vermonter in the White House summed up his views on inflation succinctly: "Inflation is repudiation." Prosperity transformed the social landscape. Radio, automobiles. In 1926, the somber black of earlier Ford cars gave way to a rainbow of colors due to the invention of pyroxylin finishes. The number of people paying taxes on incomes of more than $1 million jumped from 75 to 283. No wonder people went around whistling the hit tune "It Ain't Gonna Rain No More."

The decade of the 1950s saw another postwar surge of affluence, if anything, more widespread than the boom of the Twenties. It had been dramatically foreshadowed by the New York World's Fair of 1939–1940, which rose out of Flushing Meadow, Scott Fitzgerald's "valley of ashes," and treated its stream of visitors to a central vision of The World of Tomorrow. It was there that the public saw its first very primitive TV set, its first glimpse of the super-highway automotive future, the possibility of organ transplants in the Charles Lindbergh-Alexis Carrel machine-operated chicken heart. But the lights were going out globally for an extended period, powerfully symbolized at that World's Fair by the closing of the Finnish Pavilion to the heart-breaking strains of "Finlandia." The future had to wait.

It arrived, after the war, with the 1950s. The suburb—average house price in 1950, $25,000—became the home of thirty million Americans. Not only the age of television, but the age of mass air travel dawned for ordinary people. To speak of a "blue collar" or "proletarian" class became a joke: factory workers were buying Ivy League shirts and "topsider" shoes. A revolution occurred in household utensils. Tailfins grew on automobiles, and their radiators soon looked like a variety of jukeboxes. America was the most powerful and also the richest country in the world, and everyone knew it. The depression and the War were OVER.

Between the Fifties and the present there intervened, of course, the 1960s.

While I myself was undergoing the 1960s, I greatly resisted them. The decade was ushered in by a stylistic and political struggle between two dramatic and contrasting figures: John F. Kennedy and Fidel Castro. Stylistically, I much preferred Kennedy, who came to power determined to overthrow the Cuban dictator—"ninety miles off our shore," as Kennedy put it in his 1960 campaign. But Castro first won the military battle, and then, for the decade of the 1960s, the stylistic one. Castro created the style of the New Left, the Bohemian Revolutionary. Che Guevara's angry visage glowered from posters on the walls of college rooms. Hair had defeated irony and vigor. Castro was fortunate that he did not have to deal with Eisenhower.

But from our present perspective, the turbulent Sixties were also creative, or at least had their creative side. Contrary to appearances at the time, they were not politically radical in any Marxian way. As far as institutions are concerned, the only valuable Sixties invention was the boutique—a fact that Marx, I think, would enjoy in his sardonic way.

But the Sixties did complete a revolution in sexual attitudes begun, as I have said, in the Forties. Some conservatives today argue as if *Playboy* and pornography caused the change toward greater openness and "permissiveness" in these matters, but that is hardly the case. Kinsey, the Pill, and penicillin—plus the changing role of women—were the more profound causes, along with ideas, energy, and affluence.

The changes that were crystallized during the Sixties rang a historical bell for me. Something very much like this sexual revolution had happened during the 1920s, at least among the educated upper-middle class. "Very shortly," wrote Scott Fitzgerald in his great essay, "The Jazz Age,"

> people over twenty-five came in for an intensive education. Let me trace some of the revelations vouchsafed them by reference to a dozen works written for various types of mentality during the decade. We began with the suggestion that Don Juan leads an interesting life (*Jurgen*, 1919); then we learn that there's a lot of sex around if we only knew it (*Winesburg, Ohio*, 1920); that adolescents lead very amorous lives (*This Side of Pardise*, 1920); that there are a lot of neglected Anglo-Saxon words (*Ulysses*, 1921); that older people don't always resist sudden temptation (*Cytherea*, 1922); that girls are sometimes seduced without being ruined (*Flaming Youth*, 1922); that even rape often turns out well (*The Sheik*, 1922); that glamorous English ladies are often promiscuous (*The Green Hat*, 1924); that, in fact, they devote most of their time to it (*The Vortex*, 1926); that it's a damn good thing, too (*Lady Chatterley's Lover*, 1928); and finally, that there are abnormal variations (*The Well of Loneliness*, 1928, and *Sodom and Gomorrah*, 1929).
>
> In my opinion the erotic element in these works, even *The Sheik*, written for children in the key of *Peter Rabbit*, did not one particle of harm. Everything they described, and much more, was familiar in our contemporary life. The majority of the theses were honest and elucidating. . . . The married woman can now discover whether she is being cheated or whether sex is just something to be endured. . . . Perhaps many women found that love was meant to be fun. Anyhow, the objectors lost their tawdry little case, which is one reason why our literature is now the most living in the world.

We will see further swings of the pendulum, back perhaps, but back in a different way and not all the way back. As a college professor, I now find that many of my students are more socially conservative than I am. But I don't think that the honesties achieved by Fitzgerald's Twenties, by Kinsey and others during the Fifties, or the large-scale shift in attitude which took place during the Sixties can be entirely reversed. Certainly the multiple possibilities now opening for women cannot somehow be withdrawn.

There have been enormous gains since the Fifties, but also some corresponding losses. The Fifties ended with a sense of promise betrayed. Sometimes I hear like distant music a voice dry-edged and with a Boston accent. "Can the world exist half slave and half free? . . . The enemy is lean and hungry, and the United States is the only sentinel at the gate. . . . Extraordinary efforts are called for by every American who knows the value of freedom. . . . We must prove to a watching world that we are the wave of the future." That was John F. Kennedy campaigning for the presidency at the end of the Fifties. Kennedy, alas, had the stirring words, which he could unfold like a cavalry banner. He had the stunning public image. But Kennedy lacked the Shakespearian "readiness," which, as Hamlet tells us, is "all." The old president, Dwight Eisenhower, who dominated the entire decade, looked like your grandfather, but was razor sharp mentally and possessed of steel nerves. He handled things peremptorily in Korea, Lebanon, Guatemala, Iran. He built the hydrogen bomb and created a formidable missile program. It now seems clear that when Eisenhower decided that Patrice Lumumba had to go, Lumumba shook hands with his own mortality.

Kennedy, in contrast, left 1,500 men and his own reputation on the beach at the Bay of Pigs. He submitted to the Berlin Wall but decided that Castro had to go. Despite schemes involving poisoned wet suits, exploding cigars and booby-trapped seashells, Castro very much stayed. To add injury to insult, Kennedy was murdered by a fervent Castroite, Lee Harvey Oswald. Kennedy also flubbed the Laotian crisis, in effect cutting the ribbon that opened the Ho Chi Minh Trail. Kennedy was superbly attractive, but we paid a high price for his insubstantiality.

Often in thinking about the past that I have experienced, I find I slide out of the judgmental and into the purely aesthetic mode. The period of World War II and then its aftermath—the 1950s—was complex and contradictory, as all times perhaps are; we should not mythologize it. Let it be; let us see it as it was. It also had great beauty at times. In my own mind now, Kennedy's stirring cadences are replaced by the achingly elegiac sentences Hemingway wrote as the conclusion to his *Death in the Afternoon* (1932): "Pamplona is changed, of course. . . . I know things change now and I do not care . . . and if no deluge comes when we are gone it still will rain in the summer in the north, and hawks will nest in the Cathedral at Santiago, and in La Granja, where we practiced with the cape on the long gravelled paths between the shadows, it makes no difference if the fountains play or not. We will never ride back from Toledo in the dark, washing the dust out with Fundador, nor will there be that week of what happened in the night in that July in Madrid. We've seen it all go and we'll watch it go again. The great thing is to last and get your work done and hear and learn and understand. . . . Let those who want to save the world if you can get to see it clear and as a whole."

Let us, then, return to the world of the 1950s, and try to see it clearly, see it in its whole significance, as a remarkable and often beautiful, and very important period in American life.

FOUR POETS

Robert Frost strode onto the stage at Carnegie Hall to a standing ovation from an overflow house, Frost looking exactly like Frost, with his lined face and strong white hair, the quintessential American Elder. He had always been a very popular poet, "readable" was the word, but for most of his career he had struggled under the enormous shadow of T. S. Eliot. Now, in the Fifties, he was beginning to get serious critical acclaim, and he was becoming not only a national but a world figure. A few years later, Kennedy would ask him to read at the inaugural, then send him to Russia as his personal cultural ambassador. Frost bantered with Yevtushenko in Moscow, was sought out by Khrushchev.

At Carnegie Hall, he read his poems, interspersing witty and homely remarks, telling anecdotes—usually with a bite to them. He read "Stopping by Woods on a Snowy Evening." He ridiculed critics and academics who thought it a "death poem." "They must be Freudians or Jungians or something," he sneered. The crowd loved it, knowing that they, in the audience, weren't Freudians or Jungians. He read "Mending Wall," and "The Pauper Witch of Grafton," and the darkly prophetic "Once by the Pacific." The old poet seemed to get stronger as the long performance went on.

He finished up with the famous poem "The Road Not Taken." "I took the one less traveled by," Frost said with triumph in his deep and gravelly voice, "and that has made all the difference."

Another standing ovation, rebel yells even. Frost held up his arms like a heavyweight champion. The audience understood Frost to be saying that he had courageously taken the lonely road of poetry . . . and triumphed!

The trouble was that the poem itself had *said the opposite*. "Though as for that the passing there/Had worn them equally about the same." Frost was diddling his cheering audience. The poem is about the tragedy and difficulty of choice, and how later bombast obscures all this. The audience was cheering the bombast, and Frost grinned with pleasure over his secret triumph.

.   .   .   .

One night in 1957, T. S. Eliot was reading his poems to an overflow audience in Columbia's McMillin Theater. Even faculty members had difficulty getting tickets, and people were crowded into the windows and doors, and listening outside to Eliot over loudspeakers.

No modern writer has possessed an authority comparable to Eliot's in the Forties and Fifties, not Joyce, not Hemingway. Eliot had an authority backed up by his poems but also by his criticism, the most influential in English. His authority was backed by his intellectual and emotional career, a journey toward God. He was a modern Dante. His mere presence was overwhelming.

Eliot that night was no longer the cadaverous young man of the Twenties and Thirties. He was not only tall but large, his wide shoulders looking still wider in his tuxedo. Someone said he looked like George Sanders.

Lionel Trilling introduced him. Trilling was a major intellectual in his own right, and a local hero at Columbia, but when he noted, in his introductory remarks, that he had not always agreed with Eliot, it sounded ridiculous. So what if Trilling did not like Eliot's Christianity? This was *Eliot,* the author of *The Waste Land*.

"April is the cruelest month," Eliot boomed, "Breeding

lilacs out of the dead land." Eliot had always had the reputation of being a highly intellectual poet, but this was witch-
doctor stuff, mysterious, reaching way back to primitive emotion through sound, powerful in its mysteriousness. All the resurrected gods of myth and the resurrected God of history
seemed present in McMillin Theater. Eliot *was* the West that
night.

.   .   .   .

Dylan Thomas stood at the podium in a hall in Manhattan's
Young Men's Hebrew Association, the scene of frequent poetry readings. This was his third American tour in two years.
That day, as on every other day, he had been drinking since
morning, and he had been on an all-afternoon pub crawl up
Third Avenue. Then he had gone to a prereading cocktail party
in Midtown. Bored by the sexual autograph-hunters of the past
weeks, spreadeagled from coast to coast, he made obscene
propositions to respectable matrons. Then he opened a window
and urinated into the street ten stories below.

Standing there behind the podium, Dylan Thomas was an
absurd figure. He was short and had a huge belly, a red face
with a bulbous nose, bulging eyes and tangled curly hair. A
clown who did not need a clown suit. You had to keep re-
minding yourself that this fellow had written some great and
passionate poetry.

But when he began to read, there came out of him an extraordinary voice, a voice like the ocean, better than Richard
Burton's, a voice with full range and crowded with dancing
vowels and consonants. Thomas was certainly an alcoholic,
but he was also drunk on words. He read his own poems, and
poems by Hardy, Auden, Eliot, Yeats. He was reading his
great poem on the death of his father:

> And you, my father, there on the sad height,
> Curse, bless, me now with your fierce tears, I pray.
> Do not go gentle into that good night.
> Rage, rage against the dying of the light.

In November 1953, at the beginning of another American tour,
Thomas died at age 39 in St. Vincent's hospital in Greenwich
Village of alcoholism and pneumonia. Much later it came out
that there had been serious mistakes in medication, the wrong

sedative. The hospital spokesman stated that Thomas had sustained an "insult" to his system. Poet Donald Hall called it a public suicide.

.   .   .   .

One afternoon in the late Fifties, W. H. Auden arrived at Dartmouth College to read his poems and deliver a public lecture on Romanticism. In the afternoon, Auden read his poems and held a literary "conversation" with his audience in the sumptuous library of Sanborn House, which houses the English Department. Auden was tall, and by that time he had that extraordinary bloodhound face, deeply lined, and his manner was gentle and highly civilized. As he spoke, Oxford was pervasive. He might as well have been at High Table in Magdalen College. He was impressively learned, not only about literature but about music, theology, history, yet he seemed to take it all very lightly, almost as a joke. That was the Oxford manner. He was deprecating about his leftist phase during the Spanish War, speaking about it as if it had happened to someone else, someone who was very young, and knew nothing, a long time ago. Auden was now much under the influence of Reinhold Niebuhr and his sense of sin and difficult historical options.

That evening, Auden had a disaster, but he triumphed over it with his Oxford aplomb. First there was a cocktail party for Auden given by the faculty, at which he drank too many martinis. Then there was a long dinner, at which he drank too many martinis. Then they escorted him to the auditorium, which was full.

Ascending the half-dozen stairs to the platform, Auden tripped over the top stair, and his typed-out lecture fell in scattered pages across the stage. Auden scooped them up with some difficulty, but he was too drunk to reassemble them in the right order, so he read them in just any order, without explanation, without batting an eye. The audience thought the lecture had a lot of good things in it. They also thought it was weak on organization.

CHAPTER TWO

God's Country and Mine

By and large, Americans felt good about themselves and their country during the Fifties. An economic boom that began in the late Forties was interrupted briefly by shortages and controls due to the war in Korea, but the boom resumed full blast in 1953, and from then on the graphs rose steadily, sometimes surprisingly. Looking abroad, Americans found ample reason to appreciate their own nation. They saw abroad the baleful figure of Stalin glowering from behind the Iron Curtain, they saw the more inscrutable figure of Mao, presiding over an ant-hill society, and they also saw a Western Europe reviving under American auspices. As the decade of the Fifties unfolded, Americans had good reason to feel confident and celebratory.

During the Fifties, Jacques Barzun was an influential, even preeminent professor of history at Columbia. He had helped to launch dozens of significant intellectual and academic careers, and he had written important books on just about everything under the sun: Berlioz, Romanticism, Race, Darwin, Marx, Wagner. In 1954, he published a book which now strikes us as possessing a startling title, *God's Country and Mine*. This was a forthright celebration of America, and I have taken from it the title of the present chapter.

Two important things should be noticed about Barzun's book:

first, that as you read it, you find that it is both correct and persuasive in its observations about America; but, second, that it probably could not even have been published during the Sixties and Seventies, let alone have found a substantial audience, especially among intellectuals. But in the Fifties it was different.

Barzun is certainly not uncritical about America. Even in his detailed criticisms, however, what strikes you today is his tacit assumption that even the flawed aspects of American civilization are worthy of intellectual interest. There is present here no reflex of total rejection, such as dominated so much writing on America during the Sixties and Seventies—when, indeed, the name of the country was often spelled Amerika, or even Amerikkka. Barzun criticizes our assembly-line medicine, our misperceptions about science, an American tendency to lose sight of the richness and contradiction of experience because of an addiction to abstractions; he has a sharp eye for the discomforts of urban living, for the shallowness of advertising; he notices a tendency to trivialize sex, and he despises the flaccidities of much American education. But the deep groundswell of the book is affirmative: this *is* God's country, something genuinely new, and it is also, straightforwardly, Jacques Barzun's country.

Barzun knows—and, above all, he says right out—that "New York is a skyline, the most stupendous, unbelievable manmade spectacle since the hanging gardens of Babylon." He *comes right out* and says that America is, well, *better:* "To begin with, we have here a complete Europe—Swedes cheek by jowl with Armenians, Hungarians with Poles, Germans with French, English with Italians, Jews with Christians, Orthodox Greeks with Baptists, and so on ad infinitum. No one can say that all is love and kisses in this grand mixture. In many a town there are two sides of the railroad tracks and on one side the poorer group, very likely ethnic in character, is discriminated against. But at what a rate these distinctions disappear! In Europe a thousand years of war, pogroms and massacres settle nothing. Here two generations of common schooling, intermarriage, ward politics and labor unions create social peace." Barzun is well aware of the blacks, Chinese, Hispanics, and American Indians, but he sets against the darker spots the larger panorama. "But the dark shadows are not all there is to see. We often overlook the real sweep of our democracy because we fail to add together what we know in fragments." Like Gertrude Stein, Barzun sees America as *the* modern nation, and he wonders aloud whether it is "possible that modern civilization is something new, incommensurate with the old, just like the character of the American adventure itself."

God's Country and Mine begins with a dramatic evocation of our sheer continental space.

> The way to see America is from a lower berth about two in the morning. You've just left a station—it was the jerk of pulling out that awoke you—and you raise the curtain a bit between thumb and forefinger to look out. You are in the middle of Kansas or Arizona, in the middle of the space where the freight cars spend the night and the men drink coffee out of cans. Then comes the signal tower, some bushes, a few shacks and—nothing. You see the last blue switch-light on the next track, and beyond is America—dark and grassy, or sandy, or rocky—and no one is there. . . . It's only ten, fifteen minutes since you've left a thriving town but life has already been swallowed up in that ocean of matter which is and will remain as wild as it was made. . . It is a perpetual refreshment to the soul to see that the country is so large, so indifferent to the uses we have put it to, so like a piece of the earth's crust and unlike any map. No names on it, no lines, no walls with guns through them. . . . Europe is lovely, but it looks like a poodle-cut—the trees are numbered, the flat parts divided like a checkerboard, the rivers as slim and well-behaved as the mercury in a thermometer."

And *God's Country and Mine* ends with lyrical-factual passages worthy of Walt Whitman about American names and places.

> Everybody knows Tombstone but they ought to know Barstow, about which Henry Patch has written a great song, and they ought to go to our Western Sacrobosco [Hollywood] and see for themselves that though larger than Midwestern cities, it is not uglier or more deplorable: the contempt is a cliché. Wilshire Boulevard breaks out into hills and ocean that make one forget the art of photography and acknowledge that there is more ugliness between New York City and Bivalve, New Jersey, than between Vine Street and the sea.
>
> San Francisco I will not name. It is loved and praised on principle because it is cramped like a European town, and Fisherman's Wharf smells of the Old World. I like it well enough, but Palo Alto more, and Raton, New Mexico. . . . One has to reach Aspen to be cool and think of Goethe, whose bicentennial was honored there—fittingly, since almost his last words were: *Amerika, du hast es besser.*

By association with him, who wanted to cut a Panama Canal, the great dams come to mind—Norris, Shasta, Grand Coulee—the only architecture that truly merges with the landscape and measures with it.

Unlike other peoples we do not only name for killers and saviors: we have Cattleman Corners, and Helper, Utah. . . . South again to Greenville, S.C., where another, the unique Bob Jones University, sits a hundred yards off the four-lane highway, all modern buildings, all fundamentalist teaching, plus a picture gallery full of old masters. Next to Williamsburg, the town restored by the Rockefellers and declared by Mr. Lewis Mumford to 'smell of embalming fluid,' yet all the same one of the first towns in the United States where Mumfordian principles of city technics and civilization were carried out two centuries ago. . . . One has to smell Cape Cod to value it; even Thoreau, magician that he is, cannot bring up its image from cold print, though he makes Walden and Concord visible enough. Walden is now a swimming park, but Concord is the same—the bridge, the manse, the burying ground; no movie house for little men and women, but a big white building which people will tell you is "Mr. Emerson's church."

Vermont is greener, Peacham gay. William James would say "One loves America above all things for her youth, her greenness, her plasticity, innocence, good intentions, friends, everything." Another quarter century, and Scott Fitzgerald put the meaning in an epigram: "America is a willingness of the heart." After his death, a hundred thousand more Europeans, forlorn, fleeing wanderers, found out what he meant.

To us who came before them, the meaning is not fainter, though more familiar, and we scarcely need Emerson's gentle reminder and advice: "The ear loves names of foreign and classic topography. But here we are, and if we tarry a little, we come to learn that here is best."

God's Country and Mine was a tremendous valentine to America, written by a major scholar and intellectual who had, in fact, been born in France. The funny thing is that in the Fifties, America deserved it, and practically everyone knew it.

Let us now locate ourselves in the exact middle of the Fifties—in January 1955. Shortly after noon on January 6, President Eisenhower delivered his State of the Union Address to a packed and ebullient joint session of Congress. The president's speech radiated total self-confidence, a mood which permeated the hall and extended to the vast national audience which watched him on television. The speech contained no surprises, but it had sweep, balance, calm. The nation was at peace and enjoying prosperity the limits of which could only be guessed at. The economic boom was historically unprecedented in its scope. It reached deeply into the lives of ordinary Americans. The president expressed firmness toward the Communists abroad, but did not sound bellicose. He had a sublime confidence regarding the economy at home. The great strength of the speech derived from the fact that what he had to say was in a sense completely obvious to everyone. An unsympathetic reporter, when the president had finished to prolonged applause, sourly commented "Uh-huh."

But *Time* magazine reflected a broad national consensus when it commented: "Perhaps that was precisely what the nation needed. After years of insecurity, anxiety, drift and desperate expedients, Eisenhower in half a term has brought the U.S. to the confidence and agreement symbolized by that 'Uh-huh.' "

The president's own demeanor that day dramatized exactly that sense of broad consensus. At precisely 12:31, the doorkeeper of the House of Representatives, William Moseley "Fishbait" Miller, rose and announced in stentorian tones, "Mistah Speaker, the President of the United States." To standing applause from the senators and representatives, a beaming President Eisenhower strode to the rostrum. Standing behind him were his vice-president, Richard Nixon, and the Democratic Speaker of the House, seventy-three-year-old Sam Rayburn, a national political institution. Eisenhower began: "The district where I was born has been represented in this Congress for more years than he cares to remember, I suppose, by our distinguished Speaker. Today is his birthday, and I want to join with the rest of you in felicitating him and wishing him many happy returns of the day." Then Eisenhower turned and shook the hand of Sam Rayburn of Bonham, Texas, twenty-five miles from his own birthplace in Denison. Thunderous cheers echoed through the House. It was a moment of high politics, and high civility.

In that year, 1955, Americans had caught the LP record habit. The records had been on the market for seven years, but by 1955, Americans were buying them at a volume ten times that ever reached by the old 78s. This apparently almost trivial fact had far-reaching consequences. The new recording techniques were energizing a musical revolution, a quantum leap in musical taste. You could hear the whole of *South Pacific* conveniently. Among the ten best-selling concert LPs that year were Vaughan Williams' *Pastoral Symphony,* Cherubini's *Symphony in D,* Prokofiev's *Symphony No. 7,* and Beethoven's *Ninth.* Because of the LP record, Americans were becoming musically educated on a mass basis, and this would affect the entire culture of popular music. In 1955, popular and classical, music was in the American air.

That January, when Eisenhower gave his State of the Union Address, the Grand Ballroom of Manhattan's Waldorf Astoria was hung with white-dipped smilax with pink lights twinkling among the leaves. This was the nineteenth annual Debutante Cotillion and Christmas Ball. On stage, young ladies dressed in white and escorted by young men in formal dress moved between rows of tall candles, and curtsied to the jovial audience. The hostess was Jacqueline Cochran, pilot and cosmetics magnate. Meyer Davis' orchestra struck up "The March of the Toys," as each couple walked through the row of candles, bowed and curtsied, and then descended some velvet stairs. The band was playing "The Most Beautiful Girl in the World," and then it played "Shining Hour." Then, clutching white candles, the debutantes sat on the floor, while everyone sang "White Christmas." That was the end of the ceremony. For the next three hours, the Grand Ballroom rocked to the beat of mambos, sambas, waltzes. When a photographer approached Charles Coburn to take his picture, the portly actor asked a debutante to please hold his cigar, and twinkled at the camera through his monocle. By three in the morning, most of the revellers had dispersed to places like the Stork Club or El Morocco. Some people danced until dawn.

Of course, there was the eternal genre of the campus riot, which took on a period style during the Fifties. The riot at Yale began when a Good Humor man and an ice cream vendor known as Humpty Dumpty began fighting over a parking space. A cop tried to mediate, but students by the hundreds flowed into the street, where they let the air out of automobile tires, shot off firecrackers, and mocked the police. The Harvard riot began after 15,000 students gathered turbulently in Harvard Square to nominate Pogo for President of the U.S. For several hours, they battled a hostile force of local Cambridge police. The "panty raid" appears to have been invented at the University of Michigan, where a mob of males rampaged through the women's dormitories, stealing underwear. Following that, panty raids occurred almost immediately on sixteen campuses, then spread like wildfire. At the University of Miami, a mob of panty raiders battered down a heavy wire fence and threw tomatoes at the cops. The girls screamed, "Come on up." At Columbia, a mob of male undergraduates swirled through the fenced-in compound of Barnard College across Broadway from the Columbia campus. The girls waved panties from their windows.

This was the exuberant froth on the surface of the heaving sea of American society during the Fifties. Underneath, the economic boom was changing the whole American society to its depths, all of the changes interlocking and reinforcing one another. To pick one: the Eisenhower administration undertook the largest public program in the history of the world, the 41,000-mile interstate highway system. Overseeing construction under the Highway Act was a Mormon from Utah, Ellis Leroy Armstrong, who had previously worked on the Aswan Dam project in Egypt. "This," said Armstrong, "is a job of coordination and cooperation on a giant scale." It also represented one aspect of an American social and economic revolution.

Highway construction, not surprisingly, helped energize the boom in automobile sales, but also, to cite one spin-off effect, created a boom in motel construction. No longer did Americans on the road spend the night in those clapboard tourist cabins with cold water and bumpy mattresses and desk clerks who looked like Tony Perkins. By 1955, some 53,000 new motels had been built along the great motorways. They provided comfortable baths and beds, TV, swimming pools, room service, children's play areas, telephones in every room, sometimes barber shops and beauty parlors. One North Carolina motel kept its free soft-drink machine open all night. Many motels had first-class restaurants. In New Orleans, the new $2 million redwood and glass Motel de Ville had a pool, a cocktail lounge, a restaurant, and room service twenty-four hours a day.

In 1955, spokesmen for Chevrolet and Ford engaged in an unseemly dispute over which company ranked Number One in automobile sales. According to R. L. Polk and Company, the industry statistician, Chevrolet led Ford 1,417,453 cars to 1,400,440. Not so, said Robert Strange McNamara, Ford Vice President. Chevrolet, he said, had rigged the statistics. Its own dealers had registered 56,802 cars in their own names—phony sales.

By 1980, it had become commonplace among political and social commentators to observe that the so-called Sunbelt states were now pivotal in the American equation. We have come a long way from the impoverished Hookworm Belt of the 1930s to the powerful Sunbelt of the 1970s. For this transformation to take place, two things were absolutely necessary, and they were provided by the Fifties: water for the parched Southwest, and mass air conditioning for the homes, offices, and cars of the entire region.

From the governor's office in the state capitol in Sacramento, Democratic governor Edmund G. "Pat" Brown, a meat-faced pol of the old school, guaranteed the future of his state and region by pushing through the state legislature a water bill that linked the resources of the North to the needs of the parched South, and which involved the most elaborate aqueduct system in the world. The enormous scheme drew upon the waters of the surging Feather River, collected the water behind an earthen dam higher than Hoover Dam, and channeled the supply through the Central Valley to a new reservoir near Los Angeles. Without this scheme, the growth of Los Angeles, San Diego, and the beach cities all along the coast, would have been inconceivable. Pat Brown's water network helped to create the population, real estate, and political explosion of Southern California, whose favorite son, Ronald Reagan—there is irony here—rolled to a million-vote landslide over Brown in 1966, and a national landslide over fellow-Sunbelter Carter in 1980.

In the year we are focusing on, 1955, American private corporations spent $5 billion on research. In a building on the South Side of Chicago, three miles from the University of Chicago football stadium, where the world's first atomic pile went into action in 1942, a ringing alarm bell sounded the birth of the domestic atomic age. A scientist wearing a white smock turned the knobs on a control panel, and a lighted dial flashed: REACTOR ON. The world's first nuclear reactor designed for industrial research went into operation at the Illinois Institute of Technology's Armour Research Foundation. At the same time, research by the Bell laboratories into the nature of matter resulted in the development of the silicon transistor, a flea-sized element that amplified an electric signal and opened up major industries: synthetics, hydraulic pumps of new design, an emerging computer technology, and revolutionary fertilizers. Standard Oil of New Jersey estimated that every dollar invested in research returned five dollars. IBM, with an annual research budget of $19 million, said that all of its present products were the result of research investment.

Not at all surprisingly, the boom of the Fifties produced stresses and strains. The dawning age of mass jet passenger travel arrived before the airports were ready for it. "Unless some of these people get busy and fast," remarked a United Airlines pilot, "I can see the day when the sky will be full of planes all looking for a place to land." Washington, D.C., had no commercial field adequate for the new passenger jets, and Chicago was still dependent on Midway Field, which had been built for the canvas-covered planes of the Twenties. The city had authorized an expenditure of $25 million for the new O'Hare Airport, fifteen miles from the Loop, but suitable access highways and other facilities were lacking. Kansas City and Denver were stalled in their airport construction projects, though Boston, New York, and San Francisco were ready with the necessary long runways and large terminals. All across the country, America was scrambling into the jet age.

Other problems were created by the postwar housing boom and the mass migration to suburbia and exurbia. The rapidly increasing commuter traffic began to strain railroad facilities. The New Haven railroad announced $15 million in passenger deficits for 1956, while the New York Central reported that it was losing $30 million annually on commuters. The Boston and Maine told Massachusetts authorities that it would go broke unless it could cut commuter service to save a minimum of $3 million per year. The Southern Pacific said that it spent 57 cents for every 48 cents of revenue from its 14,200 San Francisco commuters. Passenger losses ate up 52 percent of the Pennsylvania's freight profits. And so it went all across the country, as the railroad executives argued, plausibly, that if some method were not found to meet the commuter bill, the only alternatives would be steadily poorer service or no passenger service at all.

But these were only shadows on a brightly tinted canvas. As the great economic expansion of the Fifties surged forward, editorials asked nervously "How High Is Up?" The financial pages printed stock market graphs labeled "Bull Run." Next to aircraft stocks, the best performers were a group of issues connected with the new electronics boom. Thus, in one nine-month period during 1954, General Electric rose 68 percent and Westinghouse 73 percent. The average rise in all electrical equipment stocks was 59 percent during the same period. Some companies were diversifying so rapidly that they did not have time to change their old names. Minnesota Mining had gone into Scotch tape and recording tape as its stock rose 55 percent. The American Machine and Foundry Company, which started out making cigar machinery, was now producing everything from bowling pin setters to tie stitching machinery and pretzel twisters. Its stock rose 38 percent. Oil and rubber stocks rose 37 percent on the thrust of the automotive and air travel booms, and companies going into the uranium business were striking it rich, such as the Vanadium Corporation, up 83 percent, and Climax Molybdenum, up 44 percent. Wall Street had not seen anything like this since the heady days of 1929, a reflection which produced some quiet nervousness, but on the Big Board the figures went up, up, and then up again, and there seemed to be no end in sight.

William Levitt, president of Levitt and Sons, described his company as the "General Motors of the housing industry." Out on a thousand acres of former farmland near Hicksville, Long Island, a steady stream of trucks sped over new roads. Every hundred feet, the trucks stopped and dumped identical shipments of lumber, pipe, brick, tubing, shingles, all neatly packaged. Earth-moving equipment took thirteen minutes to dig a four-foot trench around a twenty-five-by-thirty-two-foot rectangle. As soon as this was done, cement mixers poured the foundation for a house into the rectangle. As soon as the cement hardened, construction crews of two or three men went to work, laying bricks, raising studs, nailing laths, painting, shingling. The new development, called Levittown, grew to be larger than Poughkeepsie, New York. In the early years of the Fifties, Levitt and Sons was completing a new home every fifteen minutes, and selling them as fast as they could be built for a uniform price of $7,090.

Levittown in the early Fifties would not win any aesthetic prizes, but it, and developments like it elsewhere, were providing hundreds of thousands of Americans with the opportunity to own their own home for the first time in their lives, and to escape the congestion of the cities. The houses in Levittown had a sharply angled roof and a picture window, radiant heating in the floor, a twelve-by-sixteen-foot living room, bath, kitchen, two bedrooms on the first floor, and an attic which could be converted into two more bedrooms with a bath. The kitchen came equipped with a refrigerator, stove, and Bendix washer. The living room had a fireplace and a built-in Admiral television set. Levittown had community swimming pools and playgrounds, and strict rules about mowing the lawn and keeping the property neat. Up in Massachusetts, similar mass-production housing was struggling to keep pace with the demand, only there the uniform model was a Cape Cod cottage. Variations on the Levittown idea were going up from Philadelphia to Los Angeles and at numerous points in between. By 1953, new construction of all kinds hit $16 billion for the first half of the year, the highest level in history.

When Levittown was going up, even as people praised it as a revolution in low-cost housing for average Americans, they worried about its uniformity. There was something depressing about all those identical houses. But Levittown changed over the years. If you visit it today, you see surprising variety. Homeowners have added new wings, dormer windows, planted a variety of shrubs, shaped their property to their own needs and personalities. We should have known at the time Levittown was being built that this kind of thing would happen, and that American individuality and creativity would improve upon William Levitt's invention.

Between 1951 and 1955, the United States entered the world of the computer, a quantum leap in automated data processing. In principle, before the Fifties, sophisticated business machines did not differ from the mechanical calculator designed by Blaise Pascal in 1640. They operated on moving metal parts. But at the beginning of the Fifties, the metal parts gave way to electronic circuits, cathode ray tubes, and transistors. Remington Rand hit the computer market first in 1951 with its $1,125,000 UNIVAC, placing 26 of the big machines at various locations around the country. By 1955, IBM had moved into a dominant position in the field, with orders for 129 of its big computers, which cost more than $1 million to build, but which produced more than $50 million per year in rental fees from the industrial and military users. The Atomic Energy Commission had three IBM 701 computers and used them to figure out solutions to the incredibly complex problems of its nuclear production line. IBM, in 1955, delivered its new NORC computer to the U.S. Navy. The machine cost $2.5 million to build and could perform one billion calculations daily. Computers were on order for the Air Force. They could calculate the course, speed and altitude of incoming bombers and fire guided missiles to intercept them. Computers were at work solving problems of aircraft design, assembly line coordination, weather forecasting, and medical diagnosis.

The great economic expansion of the Fifties produced a Renaissance in American architecture, guided both by European masters such as Walter Gropius, Mies van der Rohe and Le Corbusier, and native talent such as Eero Saarinen, Wallace Harrison, Paul Rudolph, and the giant New York firm of Skidmore, Owings and Merrill. Living and working in the Michigan countryside, about eighteen miles from Detroit, with a relatively small office staff of forty-three, Eero Saarinen produced a remarkable succession of prize-winning designs. His cylindrical brick chapel at M.I.T. won the Grand Architectural Award from the Boston Arts Festival, and his design won first place in the competition for a new U.S. embassy building in London. He designed the new T.W.A. terminal at Idlewild Airport in New York and was architectural consultant to the new Air Force Academy in Colorado.

Skidmore, Owings and Merrill, a giant firm with 7,000 employees, nevertheless performed with consistent excellence and flair, and created a distinctive style. Its top architect, Gordon Bunshaft, designed the breathtakingly beautiful Lever Brothers building on Park Avenue and the Fifth Avenue branch of the Manufacturer's Trust Company. Park Avenue, between Grand Central Station and Fifty-Ninth Street, was reinvented by the new architects, becoming a glittering avenue of glass and purity of line, fountains and courtyards. Le Corbusier, the only major twentieth-century architect who did not live and work in the United States during the Fifties, designed the glass-slab U.N. headquarters. Walter Gropius, founder of the famous Bauhaus school in Germany, taught at Harvard and was head of the department of architecture there. Richard Neutra, Buckminster Fuller, Wallace Harrison, and Frank Lloyd Wright produced an apparently unlimited flow of architectural inventions during the Fifties, a decade during which, we were later instructed, nothing much interesting occurred.

Naturally, not all of these new buildings were triumphs. Many were banal, imitative; but that has been true of every new style in all modes of art. The best will survive.

Of course the auto industry was a prime force in the great

economic boom. In 1950, you could buy a new economy model Plymouth, Ford or Chevrolet for a little over $1,000, and the prices ranged upward to a $32,000 Cadillac yellow convertible with upholstery of leopard skin and grey nylon satin and leopard skin floor rugs. In 1950, Henry Ford announced that he anticipated his best year ever and planned to step up production to 5,000 cars per day during April, May, and June, and he bought a 200-acre tract in Cleveland on which to build a new $80 million engine plant. Chrysler projected a production schedule of 7,100 cars and trucks per day.

It is part of the saga of the Fifties that as the decade unfolded, automobile design entered its baroque period. By 1957, the new cars were arriving in the showrooms accompanied by advertising campaigns talking about "jet intakes," "bubble windshields," "flight-pitch transmissions," "Marauder engines," and an "ICBM look." The cars had snouts that looked like a missile, or else colossal chrome grilles, sweeping tailfins, giant taillights, with chrome ornamentation applied wherever an excuse for it could be found, and sometimes where no excuse could be found. In 1957, Ford had passed General Motors in sales for the first time in twenty-one years, and much of the credit for this feat went to Ford's chief designer, or "stylist," as it was then called, vice president George William Walker, whom *Time* magazine called "The Cellini of Chrome." A former pro football player and part American Indian, George Walker had firm theories and a taste for the flamboyant, and Ford paid him $200,000 a year to fight GM for the car market. Walker thought that women made the decision on purchasing the family car, and he thought that women based that choice on style. "It is the women," theorized Walker, "who like colors. We've spent millions to make the floor covering like the carpet in their living rooms."

Walker's 1958 Ford retained from his 1957 model the tube-like rear and the flaring tailfins, but it added a honeycomb jet intake grille, dual headlights, and spreading horizontal taillights. Ford also came up with a restyled four-seater Thunderbird designed to give a car designed for the family a special sporty look. To fight the Cadillac for the luxury car market, Walker came up with a new and longer Lincoln.

But General Motors did not give up the lead easily. The 1958 Chevrolet was completely restyled, featuring the latticework grille and gently curving rear fender lines. Two new models, an Impala hardtop and a convertible, went forth to compete with the Thunderbird. The Pontiac had a new rocket-motif body, a double-barrelled taillight, and a more powerful 300 horsepower engine. The new Buick had a waffle-iron grille with 160 square nubs, and sold for $4,663. American car buyers were not much interested in small cars, and the major automakers left these to foreign manufacturers and to outfits like Kaiser and American Motors. The Hillman Minx, the MG, the VW and the Renault fought over the market for small cars, which grew significant only at the end of the Fifties, when a reaction against Detroit baroque began to set in.

Perhaps George William Walker will go down in automobile history as the man who designed the Edsel—a mechanically superior car that flopped because of its styling. To make the Edsel distinctive, Walker designed a new oval grille which became the subject of much merriment. Some said it looked "like an Oldsmobile sucking a lemon." Earthier types noted a similarity to the female sexual parts. Anyway, the buyers were not entranced, and the word "Edsel" entered the language as a synonym for absurdity and failure.

Perhaps not surprisingly, advertising techniques underwent a process of refinement during the Fifties. On television, the radio-style hard-sell rapidly gave way to ads that entertained, amused, or kidded themselves. The Burt and Harry Piel's beer ads signaled the new approach in the early Fifties, and one of the most successful ads of all time featured Baron George Wrangell in a black eyepatch for Hathaway shirts. For a mere $300,000 over four years, Hathaway boosted sales by 65 percent. Philip Morris made a key decision to turn the ladylike Marlboro cigarette into a he-man item, and did so with a succession of tattooed "Marlboro Men." The cigarette moved up to number three in the filter field after one year of that ad campaign. Spaceship cartoons sold Standard Oil products, and comedian George Gobel's sophisticated humor launched Dial soap on a climb to third position in the market. On his "Toast of the Town" television show, master of ceremonies Ed Sullivan introduced a new and effective wrinkle: the celebrity who flacks for a single product. Sullivan's sponsor was Lincoln-Mercury, and Sullivan not only moved easily between his roles as entertainer and salesman, but gave blood in San Francisco, landed on Boston common in a helicopter, and went down in a diver's suit, all for Lincoln-Mercury. Betty Furness travelled from coast

to coast for Westinghouse; James Mason, on "Lux Video Thea-
ter," sold a lot of soap; and Douglas Fairbanks, Jr., and Adolphe
Menjou went down the line for, respectively, Rheingold and
Schaefer beer.

A decade, then, of unprecedented prosperity, of an affluence
widely spread, and, on any reasonable estimate, of enormous
improvement in the standard of living of the average American.
But what of the life of culture; what of the books, the movies, the
theater? Was it there that the Fifties were boring?
It would be impossible, of course, to discuss every important
book, movie, and play that appeared between 1950 and 1960. But
let us, instead, try to enter into the cultural existence of a representative American, a person who liked to read the new books and
see some of the new movies and plays, a person of some education
but not a professional critic or academician. How was this American treated by the culture of the Fifties? Was he bored to death, as
he sampled the wares of his bookstore or movie theater? In a later
chapter, we will have a chance to consider some of the towering
intellectual achievements of the Fifties—but here, what of the
daily experience, the culture met, so to speak, on the run?
In the year 1950, that alert American was certainly not aware of
being bored. In fact, things seemed pretty lively. It was a year in
which a Coke or a cup of coffee cost five cents, *Time* magazine
twenty cents, and in which a televised puppet show called "Kukla,
Fran and Ollie" built up a Milton Berle-sized audience. Clark
Gable suddenly eloped with Lady Spencer as a chorus of sighs
went up from Broadway to Sunset Boulevard. Paulette Goddard
commented, "That's that. So long, sugar." Rita Hayworth gave
birth to Yasmin Khan in Lausanne, and on Broadway, Lili Palmer
and Sir Cedric Hardwicke were starring in Bernard Shaw's *Caesar
and Cleopatra,* while the ninety-three-year-old playwright bom-
barded them with transatlantic advice and criticism. Katharine
Hepburn played to packed houses in *As You Like It,* and Mary
Martin and Ezio Pinza sang for audiences that had bought their
tickets a year in advance for *South Pacific*.
Our American found that a lot was happening at the bookstore.
At long last, Ernest Hemingway, who had been promising "the big
book" ever since 1940, brought out his first novel since *For Whom
the Bell Tolls*. All of a sudden, everyone realized that there was a

serious Hemingway problem. Though John O'Hara, reviewing it in *The New York Times,* pronounced it the greatest piece of writing since Shakespeare, *Across the River and Into the Trees* was a disaster. Despite the public bravado of that bearded bear of a man you could see from time to time at the Stork Club or Abercrombie's, a serious deterioration had set in. This was underscored by a profile of Hemingway that Lillian Ross wrote for *The New Yorker.* The scene is Hemingway's suite at the Sherry-Netherland. Though it is still morning, Hemingway has killed a bottle of champagne and is working on another one:

"Papa, please get glasses fixed," Mrs. Hemingway said.

He nodded. Then he nodded a few times at me—a repetition of the sign for attention. "What I want to be when I am old is a wise old man who won't bore," he said, then paused while the waiter set a plate of asparagus and an artichoke before him and poured the Tavel. Hemingway tasted the wine and gave the waiter a nod. "I'd like to see all the new fighters, horses, ballets, bike riders, dames, bullfighters, painters, airplanes, sons of bitches, cafe characters, big international whores, restaurants, years of wine, newsreels, and never have to write a line about any of it," he said. "I'd like to write lots of letters to my friends and get back letters. Would like to be able to make love good until I was eighty-five, the way Clemenceau could. And what I would like to be is not Bernie Baruch. I wouldn't sit on park benches, although I might go around the park once in a while to feed the pigeons, and also I wouldn't have any long beard, so there could be an old man didn't look like Shaw."

He stopped and ran the back of his hand along his beard, and looked around the room reflectively. "Have never met Mr. Shaw," he said. "Never been to Niagara Falls, either. Anyway, I would take up harness racing. You aren't up near the top at that until you're over seventy-five. Then I could get me a good young ball club, maybe, like Mr. Mack. Only, I wouldn't signal with a program, so as to break the pattern. Haven't figured out yet what I would signal with. And when that's over, I'll make the prettiest corpse since Pretty Boy Floyd. Only suckers worry about saving their souls. Who the hell should care about saving his soul when it is a man's duty to lose it intelligently, the way you would sell a position you were defending, if you could not hold it, as expensively as possible, trying to make it the most expensive position that was ever sold. It isn't hard to die." He opened his mouth and laughed, at first soundlessly and then loudly. "No more worries," he said. He picked up a long spear of asparagus with his fingers and looked at it without enthusiasm. "It takes a pretty good man to make any sense when he's dying," he said.

Two years later, this major American writer would rescue his reputation with the superb novella, *The Old Man and the Sea,* and he would win the Nobel Prize. But no one could say for sure when he had actually written *The Old Man,* maybe as early as 1936. Between 1952 and his suicide in the summer of 1961 in Ketchum, Idaho, Hemingway had deteriorated badly.

During 1950, an enormous revival of interest in Scott Fitzgerald was under way. Edmund Wilson had edited Fitzgerald's notebooks, Malcolm Cowley had brought out a *Viking Portable* collection of Fitzgerald, and in 1949, Arthur Mizener had published the first serious critical biography, *The Far Side of Paradise.* In 1950, Budd Schulberg's *The Disenchanted,* a novel based on Schulberg's acquaintance with Fitzgerald, became a bestseller. In many ways, people sensed similarities between the year 1950 and the year 1920, when Fitzgerald had first burst upon the scene with *This Side of Paradise,* a golden youth just up from Princeton with his golden bride Zelda. The war was over. The depression was over, prosperity was at hand, and the possibility of romance loomed large indeed.

ALMOST TO MANCHURIA

The initial rush of four North Korean columns had sent the South Korean army reeling backwards. President Truman named General Douglas MacArthur commander in chief in the Korean theater, and MacArthur established a defense perimeter around the port of Pusan at the southern tip of the Korean peninsula.

Then, on September 15, 1950, MacArthur executed a maneuver of Napoleonic daring. His Tenth Corps landed far to the north at the port of Inchon, completely outflanking the enemy. They went ashore despite thirty-foot tides and a difficult sea wall. Seizing the capital of Seoul, they cut north-south communications, and the North Korean forces in the south disintegrated before the Eighth Army as General Walton Walker broke out of the Pusan perimeter.

At Inchon, MacArthur, tactically speaking, had fought the last battle of World War II—an amphibious attack perfected in a hundred Pacific landings. The script had been written, long before.

Under General Walker, the army fought its way rapidly up the peninsula and then established a defensive position at the Chongchon River, a broad and shallow stream which flows through northeastern Korea and into the Yellow Sea. North of the Chongchon, the Americans knew, a large, but undetermined number of Communist Chinese had moved down into Korea from jump-off points in Manchuria. It was Thanksgiving, 1950.

At a temperature of 15 degrees, the night was brisk and clear, with a full moon illuminating the hilly terrain. The Americans of the Eighth Army, deployed along the Chongchon, could see tracer bullets streaking in different directions north of the river. Light patrol action. They could hear the rumble of artillery fire.

At 0400, Baker Company of the Ninth Regiment was on combat alert. Corporal Walter K. Crawford, a seventeen-year-old Virginian, was wide awake. Private John Howard was dozing in his foxhole a few feet away. Suddenly Crawford saw a figure standing at Howard's foxhole. It said: "Don't shoot. South Korean GI. Enemy come! Many! Many! Hubba Hubba!" Master Sergeant Herbert Seeger jumped up with his M-1 and fired from a distance of six feet. The single shot blew the man's face away.

Looking down the slope in front of their position, the men of Baker Company could see a skirmish line of perhaps eighty soldiers moving toward them through a corn field. Some of the Chinese ran, but others walked. They fired rifles and light machine guns as they came forward. The men of Baker Company could hear the sounds of fighting all along the Chongchon.

Able Company moved forward in a patrol action, encountered stiff Chinese resistance, ran low on ammunition, and returned to the supply dump and loaded up with grenades and bullets. Major Hinkle ordered tank cover for the Company, plus artillery. Able Company knew the Chinese were there, but not just where. When they passed some boulders a dozen potato-masher grenades came crashing down on them. Able Company moved steadily forward, throwing grenades as they went. When they came to a small rise, a few Chinese stood on top of it with their hands in the air. They were close enough for the Americans to see the buttons on their uniforms. The shooting stopped. The American skirmish line was only twenty feet from the enemy.

A Korean soldier known to the Americans as "Moonshine" spoke to the enemy in Chinese: "If you want to quit, you must come down." One Chinese soldier answered: "No, you must come up and get us." More Chinese appeared on the top of the small rise, their hands in the air.

Suddenly, as if at a signal, the hands jerked forward and grenades showered down on the Americans as the Chinese disappeared into their foxholes. The Americans fell flat. Moonshine lost part of one hand in a grenade explosion. The Americans exchanged grenades with the Chinese until they ran out of them and returned back down the road to the supply base.

Army Intelligence had tried to come up with an estimate of the strength of the Chinese forces north of the Chongchon. Prisoners were carefully interrogated. Most were "volunteers" who had been ordered involuntarily into Korea. The first nasty surprise came when Intelligence determined that the 54th, 55th, and 56th Chinese Special Units were not regiments but full divisions. On the basis of what could be ascertained, Intelligence informed General Walker that somewhere between 30,000 and 60,000 Chinese had already been deployed in northern Korea. In fact, the number was 100,000, and other Special Units were moving across the Yalu from Manchuria, marching by night, and preserving absolute camouflage during daylight hours.

Baker Company of the Ninth Regiment was the last unit to pull out of the line and begin the retreat south. Seoul fell again. MacArthur plunged from the pinnacle of confidence to the depths of gloom. He wanted the bridges over the Yalu bombed, and they were, but the river froze, and the Chinese were crossing everywhere. MacArthur knew that the war could not be won on the peninsula by waging a battle of attrition against a Chinese army. Truman wanted "no wider war," and replaced MacArthur with Matthew Ridgeway. General Walton Walker died in a car crash.

In the first open confrontation between American and Communist forces, the first military battle of World War III directly involving the United States, we settled for a stalemate.

CHAPTER THREE

More Is Better

In 1950, contemporary writers were conceding nothing to Hemingway and Fitzgerald, and in 1950, Robert Penn Warren, who had published a major novel in *All the King's Men,* returned with *World Enough and Time.* Thor Heyerdahl tried to solve the mystery of Easter Island in *Kon-Tiki.* John Hersey's novel about the Warsaw ghetto, *The Wall,* became a bestseller, as did Henry Morton Robinson's *The Cardinal.* In a curious way, the fates of these two books were linked. Both the Jewish and the Catholic ethnic groups had prospered in America by 1950, had become mainstream and often suburban. Two years later, large numbers of Catholics would desert their ancestral Democratic party and vote for Dwight Eisenhower. The popularity of *The Wall* and *The Cardinal* in 1950 reflected the mainstream debut of these two potent ethnic groups.

A lot of readers in 1950 were fascinated by the verse plays of the British playwright Christopher Fry, who that year published *Venus Observed* and *The Lady's Not for Burning.* Ezra Pound, who was locked up in St. Elizabeth's mental hospital in Washington, brought out *Seventy Cantos.* A year earlier, Pound had been at the center of a furious literary and political controversy, when the Library of Congress awarded him the Bollingen Prize for his *Pisan Cantos.* While they were great poetry, the *Cantos* were anti-semitic and pro-Mussolini. This precipitated a great debate about whether great poetry could express views widely held to be outrageous, whether art and morality could finally be separated.

A major bestseller of 1950—or of any other year, for that matter—turned out, unexpectedly, to be *The London Journal* of James Boswell, biographer of Samuel Johnson. Readers were fascinated by the immediacy of Boswell's diary of life in eighteenth-century London, the color, the violence, the beauty, and, of course, Boswell's astonishing candor about his sex life: "I was really unhappy for want of women. I thought it hard to be in such a place without them. I picked up a girl in the Strand; went into a court with intention to enjoy her in armour. But she had none. I toyed with her. She wondered at my size, and said if I ever took a girl's maidenhead, I would make her squeak. I gave her a shilling, and had command enough of myself to go without touching her. I afterwards trembled at the danger I had escaped. I resolved to wait cheerfully till I got some safe girl or was liked by some woman of fashion."

The appearance of *The London Journal* and the subsequent volumes of Boswell's diary marked the climax of one of the great romantic stories of literary detection. It had been known during Boswell's lifetime that he kept a journal, but after his death in 1795, whatever material did exist seemed to disappear. In fact, it must have been shipped, with his other effects, to the family castle at Auchinleck, in Scotland. No trace of them appeared until the year 1840, when a Major Stone of the East India Company was making some purchases in Boulogne. He found that they were wrapped in letters by Boswell, which the merchant had evidently bought as waste paper. But, once again, silence descended on the hypothetical journal.

In 1873, Boswell's great-granddaughter, Emily Boswell, married into the Irish nobility, the Talbott family, whose family seat was Malahide Castle, outside Dublin. The Talbotts inherited Auchinleck and moved a lot of its furniture and other things to Malahide Castle. During the 1920s, a young Yale professor, Chauncy Tinker, was working on Boswell and projecting a biography, which eventually appeared as *Young Boswell*. Tinker advertised in the *London Times Literary Supplement* for any additional information or manuscripts concerning Boswell. He received an anonymous postcard with three words on it: "Try Malahide Castle." He journeyed to Ireland and was shown some Boswell papers in a mahogany cabinet. Lord Talbott, however, was uninterested in Boswell and uncooperative with the scholar. He rejected a collector's offer of £50,000 for the papers, and they remained unavailable.

The man who finally acquired the papers was a legendary American collector named Colonel Ralph Isham. He managed to invite himself to Malahide Castle in 1926 and won the favor of Lady Talbott. Together they went over the papers in the mahogany cabinet, which proved, in the opinion of Lady Talbott, to be frequently obscene. She wanted to cut out the offending passages with a pair of scissors. Isham persuaded her to merely ink them over, knowing that modern techniques could recover the passages. Isham bought all the papers then known to be at the castle, the mahogany cabinet and two chests. But that was only the beginning. In 1930, opening a croquet box, the Talbotts found more Boswell papers. Isham bought them. In 1937, Isham searched the castle and found still more. In 1940, the British government sought remote refuges for art treasures which might be damaged by air raids, and workers cleaning out a stable at Malahide found two more large chests of Boswell material. Isham bought it. A Scottish scholar named Claude Abbott ran across bags and bundles of Boswell material at the estate of a descendent of one of Boswell's executors. Isham bought that, too. All of this material arrived at Isham's New York house in 1948 and was the occasion of an elegant party and opening ceremony. Fortunately for Isham's bank balance, the Mellon family donated to Yale enough money to buy the enormous mass of material. McGraw-Hill bought the publishing rights, and in 1950 made a financial killing with *The London Journal*.

For our interested American reader, then, the first year of the Fifties was not exactly barren of literary appeal. And, if this reader had a taste for more specialized things, one of the most important and influential books of literary criticism was also published that year, Lionel Trilling's *The Liberal Imagination,* an intellectual event to which we will return later. The British novelist Joyce Cary published *The Horse's Mouth* that year, and William Carlos Williams brought out the third part of his epic poem *Patterson.* T. S. Eliot's important verse play, *The Cocktail Party,* opened on Broadway. And not only Eliot, Williams, and Pound were writing then, but Auden, Robert Frost, Wallace Stevens, Theodore Roethke, and Marianne Moore. If you had already taken in *The Cocktail*

Party and *South Pacific* and *The Lady's Not for Burning,* you might want to see the new opera by Gian-Carlo Menotti, *The Consul,* which was playing to sell-out crowds at the Ethel Barrymore Theater. Some pretty good movies had appeared, too, such as Vittorio De Sica's *The Bicycle Thief; The Third Man,* a chiller about postwar Vienna starring Joseph Cotton and Orson Welles and featuring the famous "third man theme"; and also *All the King's Men, The Heiress, Cyrano de Bergerac,* with Jose Ferrer, *The Asphalt Jungle, Devil in the Flesh,* and *Tight Little Island.*

Despite the richness of the first year of the Fifties, things actually seemed to get still better as the months unfolded. During the next couple of years, our American reader had a lot to choose from.

If you had to pick out the single most important novel published in 1951, it would be J. D. Salinger's *The Catcher in the Rye,* a work of lasting value by an author as much identified with the Fifties as Scott Fitzgerald or Edna Millay had been with the Twenties. But *The Catcher in the Rye* had plenty of competition that year. James Jones published *From Here to Eternity,* and Herman Wouk *The Caine Mutiny.* Both became important movies, the latter the basis for a Broadway play. William Faulkner, considered by many to be the best American novelist of the twentieth century, published *Requiem for a Nun;* and a young southern writer who had learned much from Faulkner, William Styron, published *Lie Down in Darkness.* From abroad came Graham Greene's *The End of the Affair* and Nikos Kazantakis' *The Greek Passion.* Rachel Carson's *The Sea Around Us* would become a minor classic. W. H. Auden brought out a fine volume of verse, *Nones,* and George Santayana brought his long and major career as a philosopher to a close with his majesterial *Dominations and Powers.* On Broadway, audiences were flocking to the new plays *A Tree Grows in Brooklyn* and Tennessee Williams' *Rose Tattoo.* Robert Frost published his *Complete Poems* and Dylan Thomas tumultuously toured America.

But if one were forced to choose the book of the year, it would probably have to be *The Catcher in the Rye.*

J. D. Salinger burst upon the national consciousness with a novel that has since become required reading in every prep school and high school, but which is also both a technical masterpiece and a book with a very disturbing and idiosyncratic consciousness at its center. "'Holden!' she said. 'It's marvelous to see you! It's been *ages*.' She had one of those very loud, embarrassing voices when you met her somewhere. She got away with it because she was so damn good looking, but it always gave me a pain in the ass." That is the voice of Holden Caulfield, sixteen years old, a flunk-out from several prep schools, and on the edge of a nervous breakdown. *The Catcher in the Rye*, technically, is a very sophisticated piece of work. Holden's colloquial language makes us recall Huck Finn.

Salinger also means us to understand that he is writing a *truer* book about adolescence than Dickens did in *David Copperfield*: "If you really want to hear about it, the first thing you'll probably want to know is where I was born, and what my lousy childhood was like, and how my parents were occupied and all before they had me, and all that David Copperfield kind of crap, but I don't feel like going into it, if you want to know the truth." The name Caulfield derives from Copperfield—Copperfield, of course, having been born with a caul. But *The Catcher in the Rye* also stakes out some claims against *The Great Gatsby*. At the end of *Gatsby*, Nick Carraway revisits Gatsby's now deserted mansion. "On the white steps an obscene word, scrawled by some boy with a piece of brick, stood out clearly in the moonlight, and I erased it, drawing my shoe raspingly over the stone." Toward the end of *The Catcher in the Rye*, Holden goes to his sister Phoebe's elementary school. "I saw something that drove me crazy. Somebody'd written 'Fuck you' on the wall. It drove me damn near crazy. I thought how Phoebe and all the other little kids would see it." Holden rubs away the offending words, but then he sees them again, scratched into a wall. "If you had a million years to do it in, you couldn't rub out even *half* the 'Fuck you' signs in the world. It's impossible."

Not only, through this allusion to *Gatsby*, is Salinger demonstrating the greater verbal latitude possible after World War II, but he is, I think, claiming for his book a truer vision as against *Gatsby*. But the odd thing about its vision is that it centrally asserts that it is a tragedy to grow up. With very few exceptions, the adults in this novel are ghastly—"phonies," in Holden's language, or worse. The best people in the book, besides Holden himself, are Phoebe, his kid sister, and his dead younger brother Allie. Holden even dreams of "catching" the little children as they run through the field of rye—and preventing them from falling over a cliff, out of childhood. No doubt this vision of an almost entirely corrupt adult world is one source of the book's congratulatory appeal to adolescents, but it is a weird vision to lie at the center of a literary classic.

Each successive year during the Fifties came up with at least one book, and usually several, which would achieve the status of literary classic. In 1952, Ralph Ellison published *Invisible Man,* which was immediately recognized as a great novel, but Hemingway came out with *The Old Man and the Sea* that year, and it was serialized in *Life* magazine. It was widely believed that he had recovered his powers after the disaster of *Across the River and Into the Trees.* From England came Evelyn Waugh's *Men at Arms,* which would form the first part of his great World War II trilogy, *Sword of Honor.* John Steinbeck published *East of Eden,* and both Marianne Moore and Dylan Thomas brought out their collected poems. Truman Capote published *The Grass Harp,* which opened on Broadway with music by Virgil Thomson and sets by Cecil Beaton; and Samuel Beckett published *Waiting for Godot.* Flannery O'Connor's *Wise Blood* appeared, and Eleanor Clark's exquisite *Rome and a Villa.* Thousands of readers were moved by Anne Frank's *Diary of a Young Girl.*

The American also could choose among a remarkable assortment of movies and plays that year. Humphrey Bogart and Katharine Hepburn were starring in *The African Queen,* Alec Guinness in *The Lavender Hill Mob,* and *Rashomon* from Japan was delighting American audiences. Eartha Kitt made her Manhattan debut at The Blue Angel, slim in a tight satin dress, a sultry and beautiful blues singer: "Bury me where he passes by. . . ." Rodgers and Hammerstein had two musicals on Broadway, *South Pacific* and the new *The King and I,* with Gertrude Lawrence. You could also see a revival of Rodgers and Hart's *Pal Joey,* or *The Moon Is Blue, Guys and Dolls,* or *The Male Animal.*

The year 1953 produced a new popular hero, 007, James Bond, as Ian Fleming published *Casino Royale,* but the big literary event was another major novel, this time Saul Bellow's *The Adventures of Augie March.* Heretofore, Bellow had been a gifted and promising writer, but with *Augie March* he arrived in the first rank. Simone de Beauvoir foreshadowed the rise of women's issues and causes with *The Second Sex,* but the second sex to many Americans meant Marilyn Monroe and Jane Russell in *Gentlemen Prefer Blondes,* a revival of Anita Loos' 1925 hit about Lorelei Lee, who believed that diamonds are a girl's best friend. *From Here to Eternity* came memorably to the screen, starring Burt Lancaster and Montgomery Clift, and Frank Sinatra, making a big comeback on the screen. *Three Coins in the Fountain* was a big hit that year, and so was *Men of the Fighting Lady,* starring Van Johnson.

Hemingway got the Nobel Prize in 1954, and in the acceptance speech, read in Stockholm by the American ambassador, used the old fisherman, Santiago, as his symbol of the modern artist. Like Santiago, the artist goes "far out," goes alone, perhaps too far out. He always presses forward into unexplored territory. Hemingway was through as an artist by 1954, but William Golding published *Lord of the Flies,* a chilling parable about human evil as it surfaces among a group of stranded schoolboys. Golding's novel provided a nice complement—indeed, an "answer"—to the "innocent" sincerity of Holden Caulfield in *The Catcher in the Rye.* Theodore Roethke won the Pulitzer Prize with *The Waking: Poems 1933–1953,* and J. R. R. Tolkien published *The Lord of the Rings,* a vast Victorian-Christian fairy tale that soon became the icon of an expanding Tolkien cult. In *The Doors of Perception,* Aldous Huxley reported on his experiences with hallucinogenic drugs, seeming to claim for the visions induced some objective validity. The book had a brief vogue, but it foreshadowed the drug experiments and the drug culture of the Sixties. Kingsley Amis published his hilarious satire of a rising young academic hustler, *Lucky Jim,* and Francoise Sagan's *Bonjour Tristesse* poignantly raised the banner of independent female sexuality. Charles Lindbergh won the Pulitzer Prize for his autobiographical *The Spirit of St. Louis,* and Time Inc. launched a new publication called *Sports Illustrated,* which few people at the time thought would amount to much. In fact, it became one of the great success stories of journalism, riding on the boom and a tremendous consequent rise in American interest in sports.

During the month of May, television viewers were glued to the Army-McCarthy hearings, but they also had time to roar at a hilarious movie called *Beat the Devil,* a parody of the Casablanca-style film, which starred Humphrey Bogart, Jennifer Jones, Robert Morley, and Peter Lorre. On Broadway, *Teahouse of the August Moon* won a Pulitzer, and Bruce Catton won one for *A Stillness at Appomattox,* the third volume of his superb history of the Army of the Potomac. In November, Dylan Thomas died in St.

American troops in action in Korea, 1951. The last old-style war with a fixed front. (*U.S. Army*)

Eisenhower and Dulles, 1954. These men knew who they were. (*Wide World Photos*)

Nixon poses as a sleuth, but there was a lot on the Chambers microfilms, as
Alger Hiss found out. (*King Features*)

Nixon played to win.
(*Eisenhower Library*)

Jack Benny with his
violin, and another show
business personality.
(*Hearst Newspapers*)

Grace Kelly (1954, *The Country Girl*) and Brigitte Bardot (1956, *And God Created Woman*), two sides of the Fifties— both real.

[Kelly (*International News Photograph*)]

[Bardot (*Tony Crawley*)]

Ebbets Field in the glory days of baseball. Dem Bums. (*Keystone*)

[Mantle (*King Features*)]

[Di Maggio (*Acme News Pictures*)]

The Yankees had a great succession: Babe Ruth, Joe Di Maggio, Mickey
Mantle . . .

Jackie Robinson signs his contract with the Dodgers for the 1952 season. Shhh, no one notices.

Jack Kramer, the dominating tennis player of the postwar period, was the man who revolutionized tennis. (*Steve Kaplan*)

Ernest Hemingway, a major Fifties presence, in his last phase at a bullfight. (*International News*)

Vincent's Hospital in Greenwich Village of alcoholism, pneumonia, and a botched medication. Across the street from the hospital, Marlon Brando was starring in *On the Waterfront*.

In 1955, at mid-decade, the top ten TV shows were: (1) Jackie Gleason; (2) "Toast of the Town," with Ed Sullivan; (3) "I Love Lucy"; (4) Milton Berle; (5) "Dragnet"; (6) "Disneyland"; (7) Martha Raye; (8) "Max Liebman Presents"; (9) Groucho Marx; and (10) Jack Benny. The Gallup Poll reported that 96 percent of Americans believed in God, and enrollments reached an all-time high in both Protestant and Catholic secondary schools.

The literary level continued to be very high. MacKinlay Kantor won the Pulitzer Prize with his novel about a Buchenwald-style confederate prisoner-of-war camp, *Andersonville*. Evelyn Waugh published the second volume of his trilogy, *Officers and Gentlemen,* and Graham Greene a small masterpiece about American innocence amid a very ancient and corrupt Vietnam called *The Quiet American*. Taking advantage of a relaxation in state censorship following Nikita Khrushchev's denunciation of Stalin and Stalinism, Ilya Ehrenburg published *The Thaw*.

Two books, however, books of very different quality, indicated a certain restlessness. In *The Man in the Gray Flannel Suit,* Sloan Wilson satirized and attacked the programmed and conformist life of the corporate man; and in *Lolita,* which was written in America, published in 1955 in Paris, and then in 1958 in New York, Vladimir Nabokov portrayed the obsessive love of Humbert Humbert for Dolores Haze, called Lolita, a twelve-year-old schoolgirl. Prior to its American publication, the novel circulated widely from hand to hand in the manner of *Ulysses* or *Lady Chatterley's Lover*.

Clearly, Nabokov intended to shock. By 1955, certainly in literature, and to a considerable degree in society itself, pre- and extra-marital sex had lost their capacity to produce moral outrage. But the prohibition against sexual relations with children retained all of its traditional force. But what happens when we read *Lolita* is that we find our moral objections being undercut, subverted, no doubt in part because although Humbert sets out to seduce the girl, she in fact ravishes *him*. We come, as Lionel Trilling put it, "to see the situation as less and less abstract and moral and horrible, and more and more as human and 'understandable' . . . Humbert is perfectly willing to say that he is a monster, but we find ourselves less and less eager to say so. . . . Psychiatry and the world may join in giving scientific or ugly names to Humbert's sexual idiosyncrasy; the novel treats it as a condition of love itself." The excitement of *Lolita,* its power to fascinate and disturb, lay in the collision between the power of Nabokov's art and the most deeply held prohibitions. Though Nabokov was by no means recommending paedophilia, he had searched out a key taboo and taken it on artistically. The extraordinary vogue of *Lolita* shows clearly that in the mid-Fifties, Americans were more adventurous intellectually and aesthetically than the stereotyped concept of that extraordinary decade would suggest.

A related measure of the complexities of American emotion in the Fifties may be grasped by considering for a moment the four big new female movie stars of the period. Audrey Hepburn and Grace Kelly embodied a widespread middle-class desire for aristocratic style, for elegance. At the other end of the emotional spectrum, Marilyn Monroe and Brigitte Bardot expressed in complex ways the sexual revolution which had been under way since World War II, which was recorded statistically by Kinsey in 1953, and which would peak in the Sixties. There was even a Lolita-like aspect to Monroe and Bardot: they were both femmes fatale and enfants fatale, sensuous women and self-indulgent children.

Audrey Hepburn broke through as a super-star with her leading role in MGM's 1953 film, *Roman Holiday.* Combining royal aplomb with hints of underlying mischief, the slim actress with the huge limpid eyes and heart-shaped face suddenly found herself a nation's sweetheart. Humphrey Bogart called her "elfin" and "birdlike." Director John Huston spoke of "those thin gams, those thin arms, that wonderful face." Billy Wilder, who directed her next hit film, *Sabrina Fair,* predicted that "this girl, single-handed, may make bosoms a thing of the past."

Hepburn was a brunette, Grace Kelly a blonde, but the stylistic meanings were similar—aristocratic and refined. In a feature article on Kelly in 1955, an anonymous *Time* magazine reporter was inspired to write a sentence worthy of Scott Fitzgerald: "For in her low-heeled shoes, and horn-rimmed spectacles, actress Grace Kelly is all but indistinguishable from any other well-scrubbed young woman of the station-wagon set, armored in good manners, a cool expression, and the secure knowledge that whatever happens, Daddy can pay." But on the screen, with her blonde hair, chiseled features, blue eyes, and refined Philadelphia diction, Grace Kelly was not to be confused with anyone else. "Her peculiar talent," said one Hollywood wit, "is that she inspires licit passion."

During an eighteen-month period, Kelly was cast in roles opposite six of the most important male stars in Hollywood—Gary Cooper, Clark Gable, Ray Milland, Jimmy Stewart, William Holden, and Cary Grant. Her pictures were major: *High Noon, Mogambo, Dial M for Murder, Rear Window, The Bridges at Toko-Ri, The Country Girl.* Kelly's presence on the screen was so stunningly refined that it actually seemed a social comedown when she married Prince Rainier of Monaco.

But Monroe and Bardot were as powerful at the box-office as Hepburn and Kelly, and they expressed another and opposite aspect of the culture of the Fifties. Both combined a sense of innocence at the core with a blatant child-whorish sex appeal that represented something genuinely new on the screen. They sometimes wore as little on the screen as the censor would permit, and the kinds of clothes they wore on other occasions were more erotic than the quasi-nude shots. Monroe, all wiggling buttocks and breasts, was the Himalayas of sex appeal, while Bardot, with her baby face, large pouting lips, and tousled blonde hair, represented some ideal dream of French eroticism. Nor was there any hint in their wriggling, jiggling comportment that one lover would be enough. The amply documented private life of both made that message clear. Monroe had a succession of lovers and husbands that included Joe DiMaggio, Arthur Miller, and Jack Kennedy, while Bardot, after her early marriage to Roger Vadim, had a succession of open love affairs stretching from Paris to St. Tropez. These women represented a powerful new expression of female sexual freedom, of a female claim to freedom comparable to that of males. Roger Vadim, who had married Bardot in 1952, shrewdly assessed this revolutionary nature of her sexual appeal in his comments on her film *Et Dieu Créa La Femme* (1956): "The reason people thought she was naked all through the film was because she displayed a different attitude to sex from the one that prevailed in films at that time. She was not submissive. Neither was she a whore. She was not like Deborah Kerr, Grace Kelly, Michelle Morgan. For the Americans it was the first declaration in a film that love for pleasure is not sin. Even in France, which had been permissive over books and plays, films were treated surprisingly strictly. The difference between the way we saw life as young people—especially the amoral attitude toward sex—and the conventional way of portraying it on screen was so great that I knew we were on the verge of a big change. After *Et Dieu Créa La Femme* they accepted the idea that love could be filmed without being pornographic. . . . That was the end of the cinematic euphemism for making love—the misty dissolve, the rocketing fireworks or rearing waves which had been the director's equivalent of the novelist's three dots."

Much was thus happening in the mid-Fifties culture that surrounded our alert American. Kinsey's 1953 *Sexual Behavior in the Human Female* had indicated that one-fourth of married women had sexual relations outside of marriage by the age of forty, and the percentages were markedly higher among better educated women. He found that 50 percent of women had intercourse before marriage, and, of these, that one-third had done so with from two to five men. In 1957, the Searle pharmaceutical company brought out Enovid, which immediately became widely known as "the Pill," and reinforced trends that had been powerful for at least a generation. In 1953, Hugh Hefner caught the spirit of the time with *Playboy* magazine, whose circulation neared the 1 million mark within three years. It is important to realize that *Playboy* was not selling only or even mainly sex but what later became known as "lifestyle." The image of the with-it male that comes out of its pages involves not only the nude beauty in the centerfold, but digital watches, classy sport cars, Beefeater gin, casually elegant clothes, and posh resorts. The *Playboy* male also has some culture. The magazine featured pieces by Mailer and Sartre and Baldwin along with its nudes and bawdy cartoons and high gloss advertising.

In view of all this, it is not at all surprising that the runaway best seller of 1956 was *Peyton Place,* a first novel by an unknown from Gilmanton, New Hampshire, population 750. The book instantly acquired a lurid reputation and was consumed, coast to coast, as a sex novel. Rereading it today—it has been reissued on the twenty-fifth anniversary of its publication—that seems a little odd. There is a good deal of explicit sex in *Peyton Place,* and the characters have sex on their minds a good deal, but it all seems realistic and quite persuasive. Perhaps the striking thing for American readers in 1956 was the fact that author Grace Metalious located this material in a small New England town with a typical white church and steeple. Sex, abortion, violence, degeneracy—these might be fitting subjects in New York or Chicago. The novelty was to find them in rural "unspoiled" America.

But there was a lot of other good reading around for alert Americans during the last few years of the Fifties. John F. Kennedy won a Pulitzer Prize in 1956 for his *Profiles in Courage* and strengthened his image as an "intellectual" preparatory to his open bid for the presidency. Edwin O'Connor's *The Last Hurrah* was also related to the rise of Kennedy and a growing interest in things Irish and Catholic. On Broadway, John Osborne's *Look Back in Anger* was the latest in the succession of works by Britain's Angry Young Men, and soon we also had John Braine's *Room at the Top*. The great and underrated American novelist James Gould Cozzens brought out *By Love Possessed* in 1957, and William Faulkner, now at the pinnacle of his reputation, published another volume of stories about the remarkable Snopes clan, *The Town*. Bernard Malamud's *The Assistant* appeared that year, adding yet another distinguished work to the lengthening list of first-rate work by postwar Jewish authors. And, signalling something new in American culture, a young drop-out from Columbia named Jack Kerouac published *On the Road*. The "Beat" movement waited in the wings of the American scene.

As the Fifties drew to a close, we had a cascade of diverse and interesting work. Boris Pasternak won the Nobel Prize for *Dr. Zhivago*. Graham Greene's *The Potting Shed* and T. S. Eliot's *The Elder Statesman* were successful on Broadway, where Rex Harrison was starring in *My Fair Lady* and Siobhan McKenna in Shaw's *Joan of Arc*. Archibald MacLeish won a Pulitzer Prize for his verse play *J. B.*, which was based on the *Book of Job,* but he stimulated a theological controversy over his handling of the biblical story. His critics believed with some justice that he had downplayed the biblical concept of God.

In the final year of the Fifties, Saul Bellow published *Henderson the Rain King* and Norman Mailer *Advertisements for Myself,* which included the sensational story "The Time of Her Time," as well as the pamphlet urging the reader to be a "White Negro," that is, more instinctually alive. Faulkner brought out more Snopes stories in *The Mansion*. A beautiful piece of historical reconstruction, Columbia professor Garret Mattingly's book about the Spanish Armada, *The Defeat of the Armada,* climbed onto the bestseller lists. Another Columbia professor, sociologist C. Wright

Mills, author of *The Power Elite,* foreshadowed some of the radical themes of the Sixties with a book called *The Causes of World War III,* and the philosopher-priest-anthropologist Teilhard de Chardin produced innumerable theological controversies with *The Phenomenon of Man.* Allen Drury won the Pulitzer Prize for his political novel *Advise and Consent,* Philip Roth published *Goodbye, Columbus,* about the stresses and strains of Jewish assimilation, and Ian Fleming weighed in again with *Goldfinger.* As John F. Kennedy advanced toward the presidency at the end of the decade, it was possible to make connections between James Bond and the tough, sexy, unillusioned style of Kennedy and the young men around him.

The end of the decade was marked by the quiz-show scandals associated with a young Columbia English professor named Charles Van Doren, son of Mark Van Doren, the poet and critic who was a leading professor in the Columbia English Department. Week after week on NBC-TV's high-rating quiz show *Twenty-One,* the young professor, standing in a glass booth, would apparently wrack his brain and come up with an astonishing amount of arcane knowledge in answer to the questions he was asked. Week after week, he raked in the dough, and his potential stake rose dizzyingly. Back at Columbia, his fan mail was prodigious—requests for loans, proposals of marriage. One day, he walked into his Columbia classroom carrying a briefcase containing an examination he planned to give. He asked the class what they thought was in the briefcase. The class answered as with one voice: "Money!" But then some of the participants talked, and it turned out that the show was rigged. He had known the answers all along. Though Van Doren had lied under oath at one juncture, he escaped prosecution, but he had to resign at Columbia. By a peculiar coincidence, the last lecture he gave in his Columbia course on seventeenth-century literature concerned the charges of financial corruption that brought down the brilliant public career of Sir Francis Bacon.

In this chapter, an attempt has been made to survey the general literary cum entertainment culture of the Fifties, and to give some impression of its interest, variety, and richness. Such books and plays and movies have been mentioned which might plausibly be supposed to have come into view for an average literate and alert American. Naturally, hundreds of other books and movies and plays could have been mentioned and discussed, but no one person could have read or seen that many. Our alert American missed *The World of Suzie Wong,* and he did not read Lawrence Durrell's *Justine* and *Balthazar.* He somehow missed the brilliant movie made from Stendahl's *Le Rouge et Noir.* He missed *The Rebel* by Camus, even though Camus won the Nobel Prize. He intended to read—but somehow never got around to it—major works by Wittgenstein, Ludwig von Mises, Eric Voegelin, and Karl Mannheim. But as he looked back on what he had read and seen, he was not disappointed. It seemed to him that the Fifties were clearly superior in general culture to the Thirties and Forties, and that to find anything comparable you had to go all the way back to the Twenties.

ERNEST

Ernest Hemingway sat at a corner table at the 21 Club, one of his favorite Manhattan haunts during the Fifties. You also ran into Hemingway at the Stork Club and at Abercrombie and Fitch, where he patronized the hunting and out-of-doors department. Sitting there in the 21 Club, Hemingway was unmistakable with his beard and bear-like body, the *Papa* of the final phase.

By the Fifties, Hemingway had become a world figure, a legend, an American Byron who had gone to the wars of the twentieth century, who had hunted, deep-sea fished, fought bulls, had four wives and innumerable mistresses, besides writing several American classics. Hemingway had not only invented Jake Barnes and Brett Ashley, he had invented Humphrey Bogart, Lauren Bacall, Edward R. Murrow, and John O'Hara. By the Fifties, Hemingway was supposed to be finishing the Big Novel that would also be his culminating masterpiece. He stood at the pinnacle of contemporary American writing, its dominating presence.

Michael Arlen and his Harvard undergraduate son had been having a drink at another table. They noticed Hemingway, who seemed to be giving an interview. Hemingway was never alone. Arlen had been born Dikran Kouyoumdjian, but he changed his name to sound more English, and in 1924, he published *The Green Hat* in England, a tremendous best-seller—sex, glamor, the Twenties—but he had not written in recent years.

His son had serious reservations about much of this. The name change to "Arlen" seemed a betrayal of the family's Armenian heritage. His father had once been a famous writer. But was he a writer any longer? It did not look like it. He was an exile from the republic of letters. Arlen and his son got up and prepared to leave.

"Michael!" Hemingway shouted. Arlen and his son went over to Hemingway's table. "Sit down, sit down," Hemingway said. Arlen demurred. Hemingway insisted. Arlen sat down. His son recalls that Hemingway seemed to ignore everyone else at the table. He recalls a kindness that seemed to exist between the two writers, though Arlen was no longer a writer and maybe Hemingway no longer really was either. Hemingway had just published *Across the River and Into the Trees*. The reviews were awful. Hemingway had been getting over a skin disease, and he kept rubbing his face with his hand.

"I wrote the bloody book for $25,000," he said. "I don't think it's too bloody bad. I could have written five hundred pages just about Cantwell."

"Cantwell is a marvelous character," Arlen said. "You really did him very well, Ernest."

"They've been tearing it all to pieces," Hemingway said.

"You don't have to worry, Ernest," Arlen said.

Hemingway chatted with Arlen's son. He mentioned his own son, Patrick, who was in Africa. Hemingway and Arlen talked about John O'Hara. Arlen and his son got up to leave. A lot of handshaking, shoulder clapping. Hemingway towered over the small and dapper Arlen.

"I still owe you a favor, Michael," Hemingway said. The two men laughed loudly.

"Goodbye, Ernest," Arlen said.

Arlen and his son walked down Fifty-second Street in the dusk. Arlen's cane clicked on the pavement.

"What did Mr. Hemingway mean about the favor?" the boy asked.

"Oh that," Arlen said. He laughed happily. "An old private joke," he said. "One autumn in Paris I introduced Ernest to a girl I was with. Duff Twysden. Ernest later made that book around her. You know: Lady Brett."

Arlen and his son turned left on Fifth Avenue and headed uptown toward the St. Regis, where Arlen lived.

"At some time or other," Arlen said, "everybody was in love with Duff Twysden."

Arlen's son looked upon his father freshly. A small gesture from Ernest Hemingway had readmitted Michael Arlen to his identity as a writer in his son's eyes. Hemingway was that powerful in the early Fifties.

CHAPTER FOUR

"I Like Ike"

I suppose I have always been a conservative of some sort. At the Republican Convention of 1976 in Kansas City, I sat in the press gallery at the Kemper Auditorium and watched tanned, articulate Alf Landon deliver an address, and I suddenly had almost total recall of the first presidential election I was actually aware of—Landon's, in 1936, when he carried Maine and Vermont, period, against FDR. During that campaign, in a bitter depression year, I wore a brown Landon button. It had a beautiful orange border made of felt, designed to suggest a Kansas sunflower. The Democrats among my classmates in kindergarten called me an economic royalist, a mysterious phrase being bruited about by FDR that year. Actually, my father was an out-of-work architect forced to teach in the New York City public high schools.

During the years of my Republican adolescence, the two words "President" and "Roosevelt" might as well have been one. My parents were middle-of-the-road Republicans, and they resignedly voted for Wilkie and then for Dewey, certain losers. Those elections very much resembled the heavyweight fights that were also being conducted during the same years by Joe Louis. Against Roosevelt, Wilkie and Dewey corresponded to the "Bum-of-the-Month." The election was always over rather quickly, with the South automatically Democratic, and then the big industrial states weighing in to put FDR, once again, over the top. The GOP fought from its electoral trenches in the Northeast and Midwest, but the thing was pretty hopeless. It is not at all surprising that the political perceptions of Richard Nixon were lastingly affected by those Roosevelt years. One afternoon in 1970, as I sat chatting with President Nixon in the Oval Office, he suddenly remarked, as if meditating on one of the permanent truths: "You know, when the Democrats unite, and come at you all at once, they are a formidable power."

It is against this background that the excitement surrounding the emergence of Eisenhower can be understood. The idea that Eisenhower might one day run for president was born early. As he recalls in his recently published *Diaries,* "The possibility that I might one day become a candidate for the presidency was suggested to me about June 1943. My reaction was of course completely negative. . . . Actually the hard military campaigns of the war were at that time obviously still ahead of us, and any diverting of our attention to political matters would have been more than ridiculous." The "completely negative" as regards the presidency was probably disingenuous, written for the record, but in 1943 the time was certainly not ripe.

After the victory in Europe, which Eisenhower then considered the climax of his career, the pressure on him to run for the presidency increased. He was a global figure. His charismatic smile was known everywhere. He resisted the pressure, and President Truman named him chief of staff of the Army, a crucial post, with responsibility for organizing the postwar occupation of Europe. Nevertheless, as he says in the *Diaries,* "By mid-1947 the pressure brought to bear upon me to secure my consent for seeking the presidency had many times intensified. No longer was the matter completely personal; it now began to involve governmental philosophy. . . . The whole affair became more difficult. At a Republican dinner, which I had supposed to be entirely social and non-partisan, an attempt was made to portray me as an extreme New Dealer. The purpose of this was to show me as unacceptable as a Republican candidate. Whether traveling outside Washington or in my office in the Pentagon, every day brought some new recommendation, conviction, or opinion. The purport of each was that I simply had to run for the presidency."

In January 1948, Eisenhower received a telegram from a newspaper publisher named Finder with the news that he was going to enter the general in the New Hampshire primary. He declined. He had accepted an offer to become the President of Columbia University, which he did in May. "Strangely enough," he recalls, "a new flurry came from the Republicans during the course of their national convention, held that year in Philadelphia. Numerous telephone calls came into the office to the effect that certain individuals wanted to come over to New York at once to urge me to reconsider my decision and, as reported to me, to stop the trend toward Dewey. I refused to receive any calls or to discuss the matter further."

In the election of 1948, the old FDR coalition creaked to yet one more victory. President Truman, who had succeeded Roosevelt upon his death, was widely regarded as the weakest candidate the Democrats could put up. His intelligence and his abilities were lightly regarded, and his closest associates appeared largely to be political hacks. Truman's reputation has been greatly enhanced by the passage of time, but in 1948 he looked to be a pushover. Nevertheless, Dewey managed to lose narrowly—and this, in retrospect, and though Eisenhower continued to resist the idea, virtually made an Eisenhower presidency inevitable. The *Diaries:* "With Dewey's failure against Truman, who was then popularly supposed to be the weakest candidate that the Democrats could put into the field, the cry began to be heard that 'We must find some new faces in the Republican party if ever we are going to win a national election.' Since we were again in the beginning of a presidential cycle, most of the suggestions and arguments could be pushed off without trouble. But before many months the campaign began to intensify. When Mr. Dewey ran for re-election to the governorship of New York, he stated, in order to answer a charge that he was running again merely to enhance his standing as a candidate for the presidency, that he favored me as the Republican candidate in 1952. This really put fresh fuel on the fire—and every day contributed something new to its heat."

President Truman saw the urgency of postwar consolidation of the Western position in Europe. With the Marshall Plan and Point Four and the organization of NATO, Truman and his secretary of state, Dean Acheson, laid claim to their place in history. In December 1950, Truman called upon Eisenhower to undertake the duty of commanding the Allied Forces to be established under NATO. "I was in complete agreement with the president," writes Eisenhower, "that collective security arrangements for Western

Europe had to be worked out in the least possible time and that America had to participate in the effort. . . . I felt that the European post was of such importance that, so long as he thought me best fitted for the job, I should have to undertake it, at least until we had worked out its programs of raising, organizing, training, and deploying troops. It was a demanding task."

It is difficult to recall, now, the dark atmosphere of 1951, when Eisenhower took over command of NATO at the request of President Truman. The Korean war had begun in June of the previous year with a North Korean assault upon the South that initially carried all before it. General MacArthur in Japan had few forces to deploy in Korea. He sent several hundred men, named for their commander "Task Force Smith," in the hope that American uniforms, however few, would give the North Koreans pause. But the invaders, who possessed tanks and planes, which the defenders did not, refused to pause. South Korean forces rapidly disintegrated. By the end of July, the Americans and the remaining South Koreans had established a perimeter around the southern port of Pusan, which everyone hoped would not prove to be a Dunkirk. Early in September, General Douglas MacArthur staged his brilliant amphibious landing high up on the west side of the Korean peninsula at Inchon, and at the same time the U.S. Eighth Army, under General Walton Walker, broke out of the Pusan perimeter and sent the overextended North Koreans reeling backward.

What all of this meant for Europe and NATO was highly problematical. NATO existed as an alliance, but without much military muscle or coordination. When the North Koreans attacked down the peninsula, menacing Japan strategically, the guess in Washington was that the Soviets had egged their satellite on to launch the attack as a diversionary operation which would draw U.S. forces, already stretched thin, away from the real theater, which was Europe. The Soviets had exploded their first nuclear device in August 1949, and, on the ground, they seemed capable of taking Western Europe whenever Stalin threw the switch.

In January 1951, the domestic political power of the Truman administration was at a low ebb. The Defense Department, under Secretary Louis Johnson, had presided over a decisive cutback in our forces. The administration was on the defensive against charges of venality, but more seriously against vulnerability to subversive penetration. A series of spectacular revelations had demonstrated that, indeed, this charge had substance. Truman's own stature was negligible. He was not at that point perceived as the man who had given the go-ahead to the Marshall Plan and Point Four, who had held Iran, Turkey and Greece, as the man who, however plain, had had the courage to put his foot down. He was regarded as a testy little clerk.

In that dark January of 1951, with the West itself possibly at stake, Eisenhower flew to Washington to support President Truman. The political requirements were clear. The European alliance had to be reassured, and NATO divisions had to be deployed against the looming Soviet threat on the ground. The U.S. commitment to NATO had to be rock-hard. Eisenhower made a reconnaissance of the NATO capitals, returned to the U.S. and, in the words of *Time* magazine, did "for the President what Harry Truman could not do for himself." In speech after speech, Eisenhower convinced American leaders that the Europeans, so recently devastated by war, would do what was necessary to meet the Soviet threat, but that they would need American support, not only with money and equipment but also with troops.

In this national tour, Eisenhower actually was campaigning for Truman's crucial decision to commit U.S. forces to Europe. He spoke to senators and congressmen assembled in the Library of Congress auditorium. He spoke to the nation on national television. He spoke in major cities and on the radio. With his great prestige and his overwhelming persuasiveness, he was winning the assent of the nation to Truman's valid goals in Europe. In the words of an editorial in *Life* magazine, he had "once again shown himself to be a foremost symbol of all that is right and good and strong in American policy and purpose." What Truman and Acheson, with diminishing political power had willed, Eisenhower made politically possible. The nation had also seen him again. He was not only, now, the historic conqueror of Hitler. He stood between the West and the aggression of Stalin.

It was at this point that Mr. Republican, Senator Taft, threw away whatever chance he had to become president. He wrecked himself, in a momentous interview, on Eisenhower's commitment to a strong Europe and a viable NATO. The *Diaries* may not, perhaps, be taken at face value. If Eisenhower was moving toward the presidency, he here showed great political skill in attacking Taft's vulnerabilities:

I called in a couple of members of my staff and told them that I was going to make a personal move and a statement which, if successful in its preliminary parts, would take me forever, and beyond any question, out of the political scene. [One must interpolate here that politics does not work that way, and that nothing Eisenhower did or said in 1950 could have had that effect. However, he might have changed the Republican equation somewhat.]

My purpose was to invite Senator Taft to come to my office to discuss what we were trying to do in Europe, and I told my associates that if Senator Taft would pledge his support to the idea of collective security in Europe, I would immediately make a statement to the effect that my return to active military service precluded any further speculation about the possibility that I would enter the political arena and that my answer, in advance, to any further importuning along this line would be a flat negative.

I invited the Senator to my office in the Pentagon, and he came one evening around five or five thirty. My conversation with him was exclusively on the subject of NATO. I went through the whole history of the war and later developments in Europe, the operation of the Marshall Plan, the responsibilities and opportunities now lying before the Western world, and how necessary it was that we strengthen European defenses by welding them together in one machine. I thought also that American contingents and troops would have to be employed in Europe but as to their number I was not certain.

It happened, at that moment, there was an argument going on between the president and Congress as to the president's unrestricted right to station American troops wherever he decided they should go in the world. Congress was further preoccupied with a debate as to whether there should be four or six divisions sent to NATO.

I told the senator that with the details either of the constitutional question or with the amount of forces to be sent abroad I had no interest at the moment. I said that until I could survey the situation more closely, I would not have any recommendation as to the size of the American forces that should come to Europe. I simply asked the senator whether he could not agree that the collective security of Western Europe, with some American help, had to be assured. He declined to commit himself on the matter, repeating words to the effect that he was not sure whether he would vote for four or six divisions. I argued that this was of no interest whatsoever. I simply wanted to get his assurance of support in the work for which I was called back to active duty. He repeated his refusal to make the point clear, and so finally we parted and, of course, I did not go through with the part of my plan that would have depended upon his affirmative reply.

At that moment, Senator Taft no doubt was in a tough political spot. A substantial part of his political support in the country and in the Congress had isolationist roots. Even in 1950, many of these people deeply distrusted the idea of peacetime American involvement in Europe. But what we also notice about that conversation, so momentous for both men's careers, is the clarity of Eisenhower's objectives, and the tenacity with which he pursues them. On other important political issues, his differences with Taft were not very great. He and Taft had similar attitudes about the Democratic opposition.

"I think," writes Eisenhower, "that the argument that began to carry for me the greatest possible force was that the landslide victories of 1936, 1940, and 1944 and Truman's victory over Dewey in 1948 were all achieved under a doctrine of 'spend and spend and elect and elect.' It seemed to me that this had to be stopped or our country would deviate badly from the precepts on which we had placed so much faith—the courage and self-dependence of each citizen, the importance of opportunity as opposed to mere material security . . . and that instead we were coming to the point where we looked toward a paternalistic state to guide our steps from cradle to grave." Senator Taft would have agreed with all that. Taft, "Mr. Republican," later shocked President Eisenhower with what Ike described as "leftist" attitudes on such matters as old-age pensions. But Taft had flunked the test of the North Atlantic Alliance.

By the autumn of 1951, pressure began to build irresistibly for an Eisenhower candidacy. A Draft Eisenhower movement was launched. Politicians, personal friends, celebrities sought out the NATO commander. There were long conversations at his Marnes-la-Coquette residence near Paris. Senator James Duff of Pennsylvania, a former Princeton football player and political enemy of Tom Dewey, joined the Eisenhower effort immediately, but if he was to be successful in gathering support, he would need, in writing, assurance that Eisenhower would not refuse the nomination if it were offered. On Friday, October 12, 1951, two days before Eisenhower's sixty-first birthday, a mutual friend, General

Edwin Norman Clark, who had served on Ike's SHAEF staff, flew from New York to Paris with Duff's message.

"Duff needs assurance from you in writing," Clark told Eisenhower. "If you don't give it to him, here's what's going to happen. Dewey and Taft will fight it out. And Taft will win; the Republicans can't stomach a Dewey candidacy a third time."

Eisenhower agreed, and struggled with the wording of the message. The next day it slowly emerged. The original has disappeared, but William Bragg Ewald has provided a paraphrase, in his *Eisenhower, the President:* "No man who is an American can refuse nomination to the highest office in the land. If it were offered to me, I would accept, and would resign from the army, because I believe no military officer should seek a place in politics. I consider myself a liberal; I also consider myself a Republican; and through the years whenever I have voted, I have voted Republican. If given the nomination, I will wage an aggressive campaign."

That was it. The Draft Eisenhower movement hit the ground running to round up political and public support.

The words "liberal" and "conservative" mean such different things at different periods that one must be careful about Eisenhower's claiming to be a "liberal" Republican. He essentially meant that he was not an isolationist. He makes this clear in a letter to *Herald Tribune* executive William E. Robinson on March 6, 1951: "There are certainly far greater areas of intellectual agreement between me and Mr. Hoover, for example, than there are between me and so-called New Dealers." But, he continued, he "could not accept the views of Mr. Hoover with respect to the wisdom of attempting to make America a military Gibraltar." On the other hand, "except on this one issue, I do not recall anything in recent years in which I found my own views in direct opposition to his."

In February of 1952, a stunningly successful Eisenhower rally at Madison Square Garden brought Eisenhower into an active role in the movement. As William Ewald puts it in his splendid account of Eisenhower's career, it moved him over the imperceptible line dividing pursued from pursuer.

In 1952, sometime around the first of the year, Jacqueline Cochrane received a phone call from Jock Whitney. Would she co-chair a huge Eisenhower rally to be held in Madison Square Garden? An ardent political amateur, Cochrane enthusiastically accepted. The other co-chairman was John Reagan "Tex" McCrary, of talk show fame, with his wife, Jinx Falkenberg, tennis player and film star. Mr. Arthur Gray, a New York businessman and early Eisenhower backer, recalls the apprehension with which they awaited the rally. If the thing flopped, it might have a negative effect on Eisenhower, maybe even derail the campaign. When the evening's boxing matches were over on February 8, the Eisenhower fans began to pour into the arena, colliding with the crowd trying to exit. After the confusion ended, the Garden was packed.

The organizers of the rally filmed it and rushed the film to be processed; the next day, Jackie Cochrane took off for Paris. At five in the afternoon on February 11 at Marnes-la-Coquette the film was shown, in a long salon with a screen at one end, to the General and several aides. When Eisenhower heard the repeated ovations, he was deeply moved. "He just couldn't believe it," Cochrane said. "As the film went on, I could hear a sniffle once or twice." When the film was over, he said to her: "I want you to go back and see four men." As Ewald explains, the key man of the four was General Lucius Clay, who, along with Dewey, Lodge, Sherman Adams, and many others, had been working for months to make Eisenhower president. A few days after Jackie Cochrane's return from France, Clay flew to Paris and got Eisenhower's firm commitment to the campaign. As soon as he could finish his duties in Europe, he said, he would return to the United States.

And so was born the dominating presidency of the 1950s, the dominating political figure of the decade.

There is no need to recount here the story of the 1952 Eisenhower campaign. It had its remarkable moments, the famous Checkers speech, the moment when Senator Joseph McCarthy, making a pro-Eisenhower speech, referred to "Alger, I mean Adlai, Stevenson." But Ike swept to his landslide with two special assets, beyond his colossal reputation as a war hero.

First of all, he had an extraordinarily attractive and highly mobile face. His smile was almost a philosophical statement. It was a smile of infinite reassurance. It not only reassured the beholder of the benevolence behind it, but it called forth feelings of benevolence. It was a political statement: American was *good;* unlike Hitler or Stalin, America was offering to the world a *good* man. The promise of postwar prosperity and well-being seemed summed up in the Eisenhower smile. And, not least important, it was a defanaticizing smile. Demagogues and ideologues—people who may hurt you—are much more likely to glower at you. In its complex significance, the Eisenhower smile was American, and democratic. It was what sociologist John Murray Cuddihy calls a "civil smile." Understandably, it drove fanatics and the alienated up the wall.

The second major factor in the campaign was the professionalism of the Republican advertising, handled by the firm of Batton, Barton, Durstine, and Osborn. It was the first presidential campaign to make widespread and effective use of television. The Eisenhower spots were primitive by later standards, but they got the message into millions of living rooms. As Eisenhower stared into the camera, seldom blinking, a voice would come in with such a question as: "Mr. Eisenhower, can you bring taxes down?" The candidate would moisten his lips and say: "Yes. We will work to cut billions in Washington spending, and bring your taxes down." Viewers then either saw a printed message or heard a musical refrain. Primitive, yes, but for its time revolutionary.

In fact, Dwight Eisenhower in person did not much resemble the grandfatherly image on the tube and in the ads. He had a quick and incisive mind. He was terse and articulate. He could be hard as nails. He did not tolerate incompetents or fools. The American public voted overwhelmingly for Ike: as the *mot* of the day had it, how could a man named Adlai who was divorced beat a man named Ike who had a wife named Mamie? They voted for Ike, but they got Eisenhower—a lucky thing for them.

Among serious historians at the present time, a sharp revision is taking place concerning Eisenhower's achievement as president. "For all the jokes about golf playing," says one admirer, President Reagan, "he did a far, far better job of handling that office than anyone realized." In a shrewd review of the new Eisenhower scholarship, Professor Stephen Ambrose backs up this judgment: "Since Andrew Jackson left the White House in 1837, 33 men have served as president of the United States. Of that number, only four have managed to serve eight consecutive years in the office—Ulysses Grant, Woodrow Wilson, Franklin Roosevelt, and Dwight Eisenhower. Of these four, only two were also world figures in a field outside politics—Grant and Eisenhower—and only two had a higher reputation and a broader popularity when they left office than when they entered—Roosevelt and Eisenhower. . . . Shortly after Ike left office, a group of leading American historians was asked to rate the presidents. Ike came in near the bottom of the poll. That result was primarily a reflection of how enamored the professors were with FDR and Harry Truman and, I would add, with the new Kennedy administration. Today, those same historians would compare Ike with his successors rather than his predecessors and place him in the top ten, if not the top five, of all our presidents." This assessment appeared in the liberal *New Republic*. Unlike those "leading American historians," the American public has never fluctuated in its regard for Eisenhower, and, no doubt sensing this, President Reagan and his staff have repeatedly invoked the Eisenhower Administration as a political ancestor. It is unimaginable that the Democratic nominee in 1984 would invoke Camelot or The Great Society.

Much of the new pro-Eisenhower opinion is based upon a general sense of the period during which he was president. The annual inflation rate was 1.5 percent, hardly noticeable. Unemployment hovered around 3 percent. Eisenhower succeeded in balancing the federal budget three times, and in holding the deficit down during the other years of his term. He ended the war in Korea, and when forced to intervene abroad did so with complete success. From the perspective of the 1980s, the 1950s are a decade of peace and prosperity, and for this Eisenhower gets much of the credit.

But during the last few years, new sources on the Eisenhower years have become available to scholars, a rich lode, inviting reassessment in more detailed terms. Eisenhower kept a private diary beginning with his service under MacArthur in the Philippines during the 1930s and ending with his death. This has now been published in a superbly edited edition by Professor Robert H. Ferrell of Indiana University. His extensive correspondence is now available for examination, as well as his telephone conversations (many of which were either taped or summarized), a large store of minutes and memoranda from his executive branch, the extensive Eisenhower papers, and the voluminous diary of his former press secretary Jim Hagerty. This material has given rise to the previously cited study of Eisenhower as president by his former aide and speech writer, William Bragg Ewald, as well as to more specialized studies. Out of all this material, a new view of the Eisenhower personality is emerging, and a new historical estimate of his presidency. Here are some of the lineaments of the new portrait, in terms of the principal issues of his presidency.

"The bland leading the bland" was a popular derisive description of the Eisenhower administration. To a considerable degree, this resulted from a deliberate tactic on the part of the president. He never attacked a political opponent by name, not Truman, not Stevenson, not McCarthy, not Rockefeller. Instead, he used, for public consumption, general descriptions of behavior which the audience might, if it wished, attach to the individual in question. For the hard infighting, Eisenhower used subordinates, sometimes used them ruthlessly, knowing that they would pay a price for doing his political work. The object of this tactic is obvious. He wished to protect his above-the-battle reservoir of goodwill, and he succeeded. But as his *Diaries* and other papers show, he could be direct, cutting, and sometimes bitter. After a meeting with Churchill in Bermuda, he privately described him as "childlike," even senile, and as harboring illusions about international relations. He is scathing about leading Democratic figures of the 1950s, such as Hubert Humphrey, Lyndon Johnson, and John Kennedy, but he does not exempt his fellow Republicans. In *Eisenhower, the President*, William Bragg Ewald recalls that when Eisenhower was urged by Republican leaders to persuade Nelson Rockefeller to take second place on the 1960 ticket, the president rather grudgingly did so, and then reported on Rockefeller: "He is no philosophical genius. It is pretty hard to get him in and tell him something of his duty. He has a personal ambition that is overwhelming." Rockefeller, he told Nixon, would agree to take second place only if Nixon promised to step aside in favor of Rockefeller in 1964.

Nor was Eisenhower a part-time president who played a lot of golf and practiced putting in the Oval Office. He in fact worked an exhaustive daily schedule, was concerned with the details of administration, read and wrote exhaustively, and carried on an immense correspondence. He was not an especially elegant *ex tempore* speaker, and much amusement was had at the time over some of his press conference syntax. But Eisenhower was not inarticulate. He was an excellent writer, the *Diaries* and papers show; he carefully corrected the wording of statements and memoranda; he had been a speechwriter for no less an orator than

General Douglas MacArthur in the Philippines; and often his press-conference garbled syntax served a deliberate purpose.

It has repeatedly been demonstrated in recent studies that Eisenhower often confused his opponents and kept his options open by beclouding the issue. For example, when he was asked at a March 1955 press conference if he would use atomic bombs to defend the offshore islands of Quemoy and Matsu, he answered:

> Every war is going to astonish you in the way it occurred, and in the way it is carried out. So that for a man to predict, particularly if he has the responsibility for making the decision, to predict what he is going to use, how he is going to do it, would I think exhibit his ignorance of war; that is what I believe.

Like the audience at the press conference, the Chinese must have had some reflections on the Inscrutable West.

Yet the Chinese could never assume that Eisenhower would *not* use the bomb against them. When the truce talks over Korea bogged down in May 1953, Eisenhower hinted broadly that the atomic bomb might be used if a truce were not concluded. He backed this up by transferring American atomic warheads to our forces on Okinawa. The Chinese, not knowing whether or not he was bluffing, arranged a truce.

One of the major crises of his first term arose out of the Supreme Court's *Brown vs. the Board of Education* decision, which led to the dispatch of troops to Little Rock, Arkansas, to integrate the schools there over the loud protests of Governor Orval Faubus. On the *Brown* issue, Eisenhower, on the evidence, entertained conflicting attitudes. On the one hand, he was a social evolutionist. In July 1953, he had a long discussion with Governor Byrnes of South Carolina about the race issue, and recorded in his diary: "He is well aware of my belief that improvement in race relations is one of those things that will be healthy and sound only if it starts locally. I do not believe that prejudices, even palpably unjustified prejudices, will succumb to compulsion. Consequently I believe that federal law imposed upon our states in such a way as to bring about a conflict of the police power of the states and of the nation, would set back the cause of progress in race relations for a long, long time." He was thus philosophically opposed to a desegregation decision imposed by the Supreme Court. When the decision was handed down, however, on May 17, 1954, he regarded it as the law of the land and obeyed his duty to enforce it.

Eisenhower did refuse steadfastly to speak out in public in favor of *Brown,* and for this Earl Warren excoriates him in his memoirs. He recalls that while the Court was considering the *Brown* decision, Eisenhower had the chief justice to a White House stag dinner, at which he sat Warren next to John W. Davis, the lawyer for the segregationist states. Eisenhower also mentioned to Warren, according to the memoirs, an old segregationist argument, which, according to the *Diaries,* he had heard from Governor Byrnes: Don't put our white girls next to those sexually advanced black boys. Throughout the memoirs, Warren treats Eisenhower with bitter intellectual and personal contempt.

Eisenhower himself explains his refusal to speak out in favor of *Brown* on the grounds of his understanding of the strict separation of powers: it was not the job of the president to speak out for or against the law as handed down by the Court. It was his job to enforce it.

In 1965, Eisenhower was asked by Professor Stephen Ambrose, who is currently at work on a full-scale biography of the former president, what his biggest mistake in government had been. For an answer he got: "The appointment of that S.O.B. Earl Warren." Pressed for his reasons, Eisenhower fumed, "Let's not talk about it." Professor Ambrose concludes that Eisenhower's fury was directed not toward the *Brown* decision but toward the later crime-related decisions of the Warren Court.

One of the early-looming problems in the first Eisenhower administration concerned the junior senator from Wisconsin, Joseph R. McCarthy. Where McCarthy is concerned, Eisenhower's liberal critics make two points: first, that he was inclined to accommodate the senator, beginning in September 1952, when Eisenhower was persuaded on political grounds to delete from a Wisconsin speech a passage favorable to General Marshall, a McCarthy target; and then, second, Eisenhower's failure to take McCarthy head-on in the early days of his administration—indeed, his failure ever to attack McCarthy directly. This probably underrates Eisenhower's realism and sense of tactics. According to a leading Eisenhower scholar, Professor Alfred Greenstein of Princeton, Eisenhower, "working most closely with Press Secretary Hagerty, conducted a virtual day-to-day campaign via the media and congressional allies to end McCarthy's effectiveness.

The overall strategy was to avoid *direct mention* of McCarthy in the president's public statements, lest McCarthy win sympathy as a spunky David battling against the presidential Goliath. Instead, Eisenhower systematically condemned the *types* of action in which McCarthy engaged."

From the beginning, Eisenhower saw that his problem with McCarthy was essentially a struggle over power, and he chose his terrain carefully. On May 17, 1954, in a letter to Secretary of Defense Charles Wilson, he stated a constitutional principle of immediate application to the McCarthy challenge: "Because it is essential to efficient and effective administration that employees of the Executive Branch be in a position to be completely candid in advising with each other on official matters, and because it is not in the public interest that any of their conversations or communications, or any documents or reproductions concerning such advice be disclosed, you will instruct employees of your Department that in all of their appearances before the Subcommittee of the Senate Committee on Government Operations regarding the inquiry now before it they are not to testify to any such conversations or communications or to produce any such documents or reproductions."

Knowing that he was in a struggle for power, Eisenhower had staked out the most favorable ground, the separation of powers, and implicitly was putting his immense prestige behind the attack. Six months earlier, on November 24, 1953, McCarthy had declared war on Eisenhower. In a nationwide TV broadcast, he shifted his denunciations from Truman's government to Eisenhower's State Department for keeping an alleged security-risk holdover, John Paton Davies, on the payroll. This speech was the opening shot in a war that McCarthy would lose.

It is important to recognize, as I have stressed, that Eisenhower versus McCarthy was a power struggle. They did not disagree over the issue of security risks in government. After his first year in office, the president made a list of his major accomplishments: peace in Korea, a revitalized, but economical defense policy, and third, that "the highest security standards are being insisted upon for those employed in government service," i.e., that the Civil Service Commission had fired 2,611 employees judged to be security risks, and that 4,314 other government employees had resigned when they found that they were under investigation.

Eisenhower assigned to Nixon the tough political work of

destroying Joseph McCarthy, and Nixon performed with efficient artistry. Eisenhower selected Nixon for this task, of course, because of Nixon's anti-Communist record and his high standing with the Republican Right. Nixon cleverly struck McCarthy not on his Communist charges but on his behavior with respect to his chief staffers, Roy Cohn and David Schine. Roy Cohn had been a precocious law student at Columbia and had been on the prosecution team against Julius and Ethel Rosenberg. He had brought to the McCarthy staff David Schine, heir to a hotel fortune, who had written a six-page pamphlet denouncing Communism which was left in all bedrooms of the Schine hotel chain. When Schine was drafted, McCarthy went beyond the limits of prudence. He tried to block Schine's induction. He tried to get him into the CIA. He got him special leaves. He tried to get him out of basic training. He demanded that Schine be assigned to West Point, to screen library books for subversive literature. Meanwhile, McCarthy had been investigating the radar and missile center at Fort Monmouth, New Jersey, announcing that he had uncovered thirty-three "espionage agents" at that facility.

In a speech on March 13, 1954, Nixon greased the skids for McCarthy. "It is true," he said, "that President Eisenhower does not engage in personal vituperation and vulgar name calling and promiscuous letter writing"—an oblique attack on Harry Truman—"in asserting his leadership, and I say, 'Thank God he doesn't.' " Without mentioning McCarthy by name, Nixon made it clear that the Eisenhower Administration had turned against him: "Men who in the past have done effective work exposing Communists in this country have, by reckless talk and questionable methods, made themselves the issue rather than the cause they believe in so deeply." The speech was effective, but the real damage was done by a report dealing with McCarthy's efforts on behalf of Private David Schine which had been drawn up by the Defense Department. At the instigation of the White House, Senator Charles Potter called Secretary of Defense Charles Wilson and asked for the report. It landed on his desk a half hour after he hung up the phone.

When the report was released to the press it caused a sensation. McCarthy had tried forty-four times to get extraordinary preferential treatment for Private Schine. Senator Ralph Flanders of Vermont introduced a formal resolution of censure. Vice President Nixon influenced the selection of the Senate committee that would consider the censure resolution. It would contain certified conservatives, but men committed to the proprieties of the Senate. McCarthy was finished.

Eisenhower has begun to get some retrospective accolades from liberals for his refusal to become involved in the Indochinese war, but his papers do not reveal anything like the dovish and even anti-American liberalism of the 1960s and 1970s. His reasons were about as liberal as the nose cone of a ballistic missile. He summed them up in a passage in his memoirs written in 1963: "The jungles of Indochina would have swallowed up division after division of United States troops, who, unaccustomed to this kind of warfare, would have sustained heavy casualties until they had learned to live in a new environment. Furthermore, the presence of ever more numbers of white men in uniform probably would have aggravated rather than assuaged Asian resentment."

At the time of the crisis over Dienbienphu, in which the beleaguered French were surrounded by the Vietminh and were sure to lose without relief, Eisenhower's sentiments were enough to freeze the blood of any dove. At a meeting of the National Security Council on April 29, 1953, when the discussion got around to the possibility of intervening with American ground forces, Ike had a brutal strategic reply: If the United States were to let its troops get into scattered conflicts around the world, the end result would be the undermining of all our defenses. Before he would decide to go into Indochina unilaterally, he said, he would first look at a direct attack on the Soviet Union. It would be better, he said, to hit the head of the snake than to play the enemy's game and all by ourselves fight Soviet satellites all over the world.

This last was not a mere theoretical option. In 1954, the United States possessed complete strategic superiority over the Soviet Union, and did so in 1960 as well, as President Kennedy demonstrated during the Cuban missile crisis.

Now, also, consider the affair of Patrice Lumumba. The exact circumstances at the time were murky, but the suspicion was widespread that the United States government had a hand in the downfall and 1961 death of the Congolese politician. A new book by Madeleine Kalb called *The Congo Cables: From Eisenhower to Kennedy*, sheds a good deal of light on this clandestine operation. Eisenhower emerges as tough and decisive. Based upon newly available material, most importantly, cable traffic, Madeleine

Kalb concludes that President Eisenhower probably ordered the murder, or at least political elimination, of Lumumba, but that the CIA failed to bring it off. She is probably correct.

What seems to have happened is this. With the hasty departure of the Belgians, the Congo descended into a chaos of contending political and tribal factions, a chaos further aggravated by the secession of the mineral-rich Katanga province under Moise Tshombe. Patrice Lumumba, a charismatic leader who was judged by Americans who met him to be mentally unstable, and who was almost certainly a Soviet agent, was operating what amounted to a private army complete with Soviet weapons and Soviet advisors. If Lumumba had succeeded in seizing power, it is likely he would have ordered the small U.N. force out of the country and turned the Congo into a client of the Soviets. A slaughter of remaining Europeans was a real possibility.

At a key meeting over the Congo emergency, President Eisenhower seems to have ordered that we get rid of Lumumba. The memories of the participants now differ, as might be expected. Some think the president meant "get rid of" Lumumba by political means. Others believe Eisenhower meant kill him. Almost certainly, both views are right. Eisenhower probaby meant "get rid of" Lumumba one way or another, but get him out of there.

The CIA swung into action with schemes involving exotic poisons and so forth, none of which came to anything. We got rid of Lumumba by another route. At U.S. prompting, President Joseph Kasavubu dismissed Lumumba as prime minister, and a U.S. protégé and army colonel named Joseph Mobutu took power. Lumumba tried to flee into the hinterland, where he had the capacity to cause a lot of trouble. Mobutu's troops seized him and threw him in jail, where he was physically abused and then murdered, evidently by his Katangan enemies.

What Eisenhower ordered was thus accomplished. Lumumba was gone, and Mobutu still runs the Congo, which became the Republic of Zaire in 1971. The operation was a little messy, as things in the Congo tend to be, but on the whole successful; and Eisenhower's decision seems fully justified.

But Madeleine Kalb doesn't think so, and she is campaigning hard against strengthening the CIA, as is Blanche Cook in her new book, *The Declassified Eisenhower,* which attacks Ike for the overthrow of the pro-Soviet Arbenz government in Guatemala and the Mossadegh regime in Iran. But none of this moralism addresses the real question. If you are not prepared to wage political warfare, as it has been waged throughout history, are you then prepared to give the Soviets a free ride? Eisenhower was not.

In retrospect, Eisenhower's economic record seems a kind of dream. After the mild recession of 1953–54, unemployment began to drop. Except for a few boom years in the 1920s, and the immediate aftermath of World War II, it reached the lowest peacetime percentage since 1907. All the production graphs pointed upward. In the third quarter of 1954, the GNP ran at $359 billion; then it took off, climbing through the successive quarters until it reached $420 billion in the fourth quarter of 1956. During the four years of Eisenhower's first term, personal income climbed 20 percent. No wonder people liked Ike. Increasingly, the members of America's growing middle class traveled abroad—and when they got there, they found that the dollar was golden. It was cheap to have fun in London, Paris, Madrid. At home, investment climbed.

In 1956, we launched the largest domestic program in the history of the country, the Interstate Highway System, linking all the major cities and providing a new world for the assembly lines of Detroit to conquer. It became the thing to do in the suburban middle class to call for your date in a car. The jet passenger plane, Salk vaccine, peaceful nuclear power, and the computer were coming out of the wings and onto center stage. Gabriel Hauge praised the Eisenhower economic approach: free markets, private initiative, plus ending controls, price-fixing, rationing, and preserving the integrity of the dollar, buffering the human costs through Social Security, public housing, collective bargaining. According to William Ewald, the economist Arthur Burns, "in an encompassing metaphor, would always recall the first time he saw Eisenhower: as Columbia's new president passed nearby in his 1948 inaugural procession, a flood of sunlight suddenly burst through the clouds." Burns called it "Eisenhower weather." By the time the campaign of 1956 rolled around, Republican orators could quote George Meany himself: "American labor has never had it so good." And: "Everything is booming but the guns."

Eisenhower's reputation is rising as the years go by, but it would be folly to endow him with a nostalgic perfection or to suppose that his presidency had no flaws. In his own time, he had his critics both on the left and on the right. Indeed, the conservative magazine *National Review* was founded in 1955 at least in part in response to what it perceived as the shortcomings of this Republican administration. When Eisenhower left office, the editor, William F. Buckley, Jr., summed up the case against Eisenhower in a major and controversial editorial: Eisenhower was a *naif*, who could not make the case for freedom against Marshal Zhukov, whom he stupidly called an "idealist." He next allowed himself to be politically rolled by the roughneck Khrushchev. He settled for strategic defeat in Korea, and a deteriorating situation in Laos. He sat on his hands during the smashing of Hungary.

According to William F. Buckley today, the most traumatic event of the Eisenhower period was the Hungarian uprising and its tragic aftermath, a crucifixion which seemed to alter very little the smooth course of Eisenhower's growing accommodation with Khrushchev. It seems to me that what Buckley is saying now, as well as in his 1956 editorial, is that Eisenhower was, in important ways, inadequate to a period of world revolution. He was *surprised* by Zhukov, and mislabeled what he heard as "idealism." He was a man of *power calculation* and *long-range design* and did not appreciate the moral cataclysm that Hungary represented.

Indeed, as the years lengthen between our time and his, Eisenhower does seem part of an older world. How strange, almost archaic, 1951 now seems. Eisenhower was the "liberal," Robert Taft the "conservative." As the "liberal," Eisenhower believed in military strength, universal military service, and the Atlantic Alliance. He was inclined against building the hydrogen bomb for a while, but only because we had the atomic bomb in mass production. Domestically, he favored lower taxes and hated the punitive aspect of the tax system. He considered the New Deal/Fair Deal bureaucracy a "national disgrace," though he did not wish to dismantle the major programs of the existing welfare state.

In 1951 and 1952, as we have seen, his quarrel with Robert Taft was over "internationalism," i.e., the Atlantic Alliance and NATO. This was then a passionate issue. But does anyone today, looking back, really believe that a President Taft would have abandoned Europe to chaos and Stalin, retreating to some kind of Fortress America? The whole issue seems archaic in any long view, rooted in Taft's Midwestern isolationist constituency.

As a supposed liberal, 1950s style, Eisenhower produced three of the five balanced budgets of the last thirty years. If the Communists should renew the war in Korea, he told a bipartisan group of Congressional leaders on January 5, 1954, we would "hit them," even their Manchurian factories, "with everything we've got." He considered the domino theory militarily and politically true. When he sent troops into Lebanon in 1958, he sent an overwhelming 14,000. "When you appeal to force," he said, "there's just one thing you must never do—lose. . . . Remember this: there's no such thing as a little force. You have to use it overwhelmingly."

In a now-forgotten sequence of events, Eisenhower tried to give birth to the "emerging Republican majority" beloved of later theorists. It came into existence briefly for Nixon in 1972, and it may now be crystallizing under President Reagan. But Eisenhower saw the obvious: if his minority party was to become a majority, it would have to attract plenty of Democrats. In the 1952 election, he had done so. He had brought large numbers of Irish Catholics and Italians to vote Republican, and he had cracked the Solid South. As the 1956 election approached, his top two vice-presidential choices were Robert Anderson, a Texas Democrat who had been Secretary of the Navy but had since returned to private life, and Frank Lausche, governor of Ohio, a conservative and a Catholic. Anderson was considered by Eisenhower to be the most intelligent man he had ever met; Anderson rejected the vice-presidential idea as politically impractical. Eisenhower saw the political possibilities of an Eisenhower-Lausche ticket, but in the end, though offered a top cabinet post, Richard Nixon dug in his heels and, having sufficient strength within the party, stayed on the ticket. He had beaten Eisenhower again, first on the Fund issue in 1952, and now in 1956.

The Eisenhower we meet in the mass of new material now available, and in recent works like Ewald's *Eisenhower, the President,* does not correspond at all to his popular image, of either then or now. He was, in reality, cold, intelligent, formidable. He was so reserved, said a close acquaintance, that if you tried to put your arm around him, he would remember it for sixty days. He was a master of, and heavily dependent upon, advisors and organization. His goals were everything, his subordinates strictly expendable. He made them and broke them, but at arm's length. His boa constrictor destruction of both Sherman Adams and Joseph

McCarthy was awesome. In the Adams case, particularly, the underlings did the dirty work, but destruction was inevitable.

Eisenhower also held permanent grudges. Ewald: "If Eisenhower did have a tragic flaw, it was sensitivity to personal attack. Emmett Hughes, a speechwriter who left to write a book attacking Eisenhower and then joined forces with Rockefeller, was not alone. Harry Truman of the 1952 campaign, Adlai Stevenson of the taunts and smears of 1952 and 1956, and Jack Kennedy of 1960—mention of these people's names would forever bring a tightening of the jaw and a reddening of the face." Ewald makes a strong case for the view that Eisenhower never forgave Nelson Rockefeller for hiring the political turncoat Emmett Hughes, and that Eisenhower's enmity helped destroy Rockefeller's presidential hopes.

Beloved by his people, Eisenhower was not especially lovable. There was something about his remoteness, his extreme sense of dignity, his formality. He was a distinctly premodern personality. For that reason, it was perhaps inevitable that he would make the greatest mistake of his presidency: underrate the political and psychological impact of Sputnik, the first vehicle to orbit the earth. Sputnik was worth less, in Eisenhower's hard-headed view, than a single good nuclear-tipped missile. *National Review* did see something important about him, though it did not put it quite that way. He was tone deaf to some of the major chords of a revolutionary era.

But, increasingly as the years pass, the inevitable human shortcomings of Eisenhower diminish in importance, and the overall impression of greatness grows more firm. America Liked Ike. It did so with good reason.

IN ANOTHER COUNTRY

Both Peter Martin and Ken Little had been graduated from Dartmouth in 1951.

Thirty years later, they were sitting at a banquet table at the Boston Sheraton. Dartmouth Night, Harvard football game the next day.

Peter Martin had played football at Dartmouth. He had been religion editor at *Time,* also a senior editor. He had written a novel. Amid the music, the cigar smoke and the official speeches, he reminisced.

"There was a great short story during the war," he said, "called 'Address Unknown.' It was about a collaborator in France. Some Free French in England were determined to get revenge. They sent him letters with things in them like 'three blues, one yellow, four green.' This meant nothing, of course, but it looked like code. They would send these letters. The collaborator in France wrote back, 'Stop sending these crazy letters. Don't you know they're being read?' They kept sending them. The last letter they sent was returned. It was stamped 'Address Unknown.'"

"You know," Peter Martin said, "I had a girl friend here. She was from Czechoslovakia. I really liked her. But she had to return to Czechoslovakia. This was after the Communist coup of 1948.

"I really liked this girl, and I knew things were pretty tough in Czechoslovakia. I wrote her a lot, but I also sent her CARE packages, food. Then, I got a letter from her saying, 'Please, don't send me any more packages. Don't write me.' So I didn't. But after graduation I went to Europe, and I tried to look her up. I went to Czechoslovakia, and I found her uncle. *He said he didn't know her.* She had totally disappeared. I found the house where I had last written her. *No one had ever heard of her.* At least they wouldn't admit it."

Ken Little was older than Peter Martin. Ken had been a young infantry lieutenant during the war. At college he had been an older student, a leader, he had worn infantry boots and an Eisenhower jacket, with the patches torn off. Now he was a successful businessman, and middle-aged.

"I will never forget the end of the war," he said. "We had all these German prisoners of war in France. Thousands of them. Hundreds of thousands of them. Now, you have to understand the system. In America, the system said that every drafted soldier had to be returned at government expense to the place of his induction. If he was drafted in Chicago, he had to be returned to Chicago.

"In Europe, we were ordered to treat these German draftees exactly the same way. The assumption seemed to be that Europe was like America.

"The first train back to Germany I was on had about 700 German draftees on it. They were in open cars, coal cars, cattle cars.

"When we went across France, there were Frenchmen on the overpasses trying to dump boulders down on the Germans. We shot at the French. Our orders were to deliver these men.

"When we got to the German border, we had to change locomotives. When our prisoners heard the bump of the German locomotive hooking up, they sent up a cheer. *God, they knew they were home.*

"The worst godawful thing happened when we got to the East German border. The prisoners were herded out onto the platform. A Russian officer appeared and took the list of names and carefully checked them off.

"Russian soldiers then marched the prisoners off into an assembly area. Then they were machine gunned."

"They were all killed?" people at the table asked Ken Little.

"They were all killed," he said. "Just like that."

"Didn't the Americans interfere?" he was asked.

"Yes," he said. "When we saw what was happening, we began to get ready to fight. We could have opened fire on the Russians with our automatic weapons. But our commanding officer drew his automatic pistol. 'Obey orders,' he said."

Peter Martin seemed to have a shock of recognition. His Czech girl.

"Did you take any more trains through?" Peter Martin asked.

"We took two more through," said Ken Little.

"Did the same thing happen?"

"They checked them off, and they machine gunned them every time," said Ken Little. "They never got back to their induction point."

"This is mind-distorting," said Peter Martin.

Then the glee club sang some Dartmouth songs, and the football coach made a rousing speech to the effect that Dartmouth would beat Harvard tomorrow.

CHAPTER FIVE

The Boys of Summer

The period from just before the war until 1957, the year both the Dodgers and the Giants departed for California, was a period of extraordinary intensity in the history of baseball, especially in New York City, where the Dodgers, the Giants and the Yankees had deep roots in local tradition, and possessed highly distinctive team personalities. Nothing like that period is likely to happen again.

Baseball is known as "the national pastime," and for good reason. In countless fascinating ways it is an expression of the American spirit, and it is rooted in an earlier America in which much of the American ethos was formed. It has symbolic qualities not possessed by any other American sport.

Consider walking off the street and into the ball park, as I once walked off Bedford Avenue in Brooklyn and into the old Ebbets Field. I began going to Dodger games in 1941, taking the subway into Brooklyn from our apartment in Queens. I would walk off the street and into the rotunda which served as a vestibule, and had a blue crossed-bat motif in its tiled floor. Then through the turnstile and up the ramps and stairs to the entrance to the stands, and through the entrance. The first, almost overwhelming visual impression was of greenness. Stepping through that gateway, you stepped from urban America, with its metallic rattling and banging subways, urban America with its concrete and asphalt and carbon monoxide and auto horns, into the pastoral green world of the baseball field, a manicured piece of the country, a piece of America's rural origins, existing magically in the midst of America's urban present. Even artificial turf, today, preserves the symbolism with its brilliant greenness.

Baseball is deliberately archaic, insisting on that relationship to the past. The uniforms, with their gaiters and long underwear, remind us of the 1890s. The contemporary Pittsburgh Pirates have managed to come up with uniforms that look more archaic still. The players, many of them, wear handlebar mustaches, like some old photograph on a barbershop wall. On the field, many players chew tobacco and spit out the juice—part of the act, as if the era of the old brass spittoon were still with us.

And, of course, the names of the baseball players. These, too, belong to that rural American past: "Dixie" Walker, Enos "Country" Slaughter, "Catfish" Hunter, Thurmon Munson, Pee Wee Reese, Ty Cobb, Bobo Newsome, Whitlow Wyatt. These names come right out of the rural world of Tom Sawyer and Huck Finn; and as a matter of fact, over the years, some sixty percent of all major league players have come from the rural South. Though its brains have moved to the cities, America's heart remains in those small towns out on the rolling plains and fields of the countryside, Norman Rockwell territory.

Then the game itself. Baseball is the only important team sport not involved with the clock, an amazing fact. It moves at a leisurely pace, a rural pace. It spreads what usually amounts to twenty minutes of action over a leisurely three hours. In some games, the outfielders could take naps if they wanted to. Then, there is the ritual seventh-inning stretch. Unlike the jazz rhythms of basketball, or the ferocious drive of football—the term "gridiron" sums it up—baseball is slow and pastoral, like a rural afternoon in the 1880s. It also has a nonurban sense of space. In football, basketball, boxing, the players are close together. They touch, hit, breathe, and sweat on one another. But the baseball player has his own territory, in the outfield hundreds of feet of it. Like an early rural American, he has neighbors, but they are "over there." Only under special circumstances, such as the catcher blocking the plate, do ball players make physical contact. The players are separate landowners, enclosed within an almost eighteenth-century decorum.

In many other ways, baseball is individualistic. A quarterback like Roger Staubach needs every player on his team to complete a pass play. Football is corporate, military. But the central characters in the baseball drama, pitcher and batter, face one another alone. The great batting feats—Ruth's 60 home runs in 1927, Joe DiMaggio's astonishing 1941 batting streak, in which he batted .576 and hit safely in 56 consecutive games—these were individual achievements.

Baseball is a "cool" sport. It belongs, as Michael Novak has argued, to the older spirit of the American enlightenment. It is the athletic equivalent of the "cool" temperament of the eighteenth-century men who designed the "balance" of our constitutional structure. The baseball diamond is geometrical, has clean lines. It is exactly 360 feet around the bases to home plate, and perhaps this geometrical figure can be seen as a metaphor for the 360 degrees of the circle and therefore an abstract representation of the world itself. Like a Yankee trader and his clipper ship, or like Lewis and Clark, the base runner launches forth. An adventurer, sometimes even a base-path privateer, he can reach home with the "score" if he is fortunate and skillful.

As in the Constitution, Novak points out, the sense of a balance of forces in baseball is exquisite. If you moved the mound three feet closer to the plate, there would be few hits. A little grease on the ball gives a pitcher an immense advantage. Unlike football, the opportunities to cheat in baseball are minimal.

Whether or not the decision was made in full aesthetic knowledge, the major leagues were right to reject the aluminum bat now commonplace in intercollegiate ball. Baseball, that rural archaic sport, needs the clean crack of that wooden bat on the leather ball. It is a clean rich sound, unlike the ping of the metal bat, and it cuts through urban ambiguities as the white ball flashes out across the green rural meadow of the field.

The Brooklyn Dodgers, who, under Larry MacPhail, emerged from futility and who prospered under Branch Rickey and Walter O'Malley, were a unique institution. During the 1930s, they had been clowns, stuck in the second division, notable for having fly balls drop on the skulls of outfielders, and for having three runners end up on third base. Attendance was down, the team in the hands of a bank, The Brooklyn Trust Company. Out in Cincinnati, MacPhail, always tempestuous, had been feuding with the owner, and in 1936 he took his departure. He was recommended to the Dodger ownership by St. Louis general manager Branch Rickey and Commissioner Ford Frick. MacPhail signed on as general manager of the Dodgers for the 1938 season, and, in Yeats' phrase, "all was changed, changed utterly." The unique atmosphere he created was made possible by the location and size of the Dodgers' home, Ebbets Field, in the Crown Heights section of a then tightly-knit residential borough of New York City.

Built in 1912–13, and first opening for the 1913 season, Ebbets Field was the smallest in the National League. Its double-deck structure accommodated 32,000 fans, sometimes swelled against the fire laws to almost 36,000, with people jamming the aisles and hanging from the rafters. The size of the place made for a special feeling of intimacy with the players. Fans in the front boxes were practically in the game, and from most seats you could see the changing expressions on a player's face, read his lips, judge his fatigue. As the team quickly became a serious pennant contender under MacPhail, it became a focus of intense local pride. By one estimate, about half the seats in Ebbets Field were filled by Brooklynites who had walked to the park from the surrounding neighborhood. These fans often knew one another, came all season to the old ball park. The team, even when a pennant winner, was known affectionately as "Dem Bums," an echo of an earlier year when Dodger incompetents really did play like "bums." According to Dodger legend, a vociferous fan during the 1930s would scream at his team, "Ya bum, youse bums, ya bums." Even when the Dodgers became the best team in the National League, and when baseballs were no longer striking them on the head, the name "Bums" stuck. Willard Mullin, the brilliant cartoonist for the old New York *Herald Tribune,* created a caricature "Bum" as a symbol of the Dodgers, with floppy hat, toes showing in his shoes, loose lips, ragged coat.

It was under the promotional talents of Leland Stanford Mac-Phail, a large, red-haired baseball genius who took over the team in 1938, that the Dodgers ceased to be bums. The Brooklyn Trust Company and the team's unhappy owners gave MacPhail unlimited funding, and the impresario never looked back. He had the old ball park repainted and redecorated. He installed lights for night baseball, a pioneering move. He hired Babe Ruth as a first base coach and took broadcaster Red Barber away from Cincinnati to provide New York City with its only continuous daily game broadcasting. Red Barber's Southern locutions would become part of New York's vocabulary: a quarrel on the field was a "rhubarb"; a pitcher who had a 2 and 0 count was "in the catbird seat." MacPhail, to the dismay of the bankers, paid Olympic star Jesse Owens $4,000 for a pregame sprinting exhibition. He hired Gladys Gooding to play a pipe organ he had installed behind first base. For the first night game in major league history, 38,748 fans—well over the legal limit—jammed Ebbets Field on June 15, 1938 to see Johnny Vandermeer of Cincinnati pitch his second successive no-hitter. People began to say that "Anything can happen at Ebbets Field."

Then there was a fan named Hilda Chester, a large woman who brought a cow bell to the games, plus a sign proclaiming "Hilda is Here." Tex Rickards ran the public address system and was famous for his malapropisms: "A little boy has been found lost." "Will the fans along the railing in left field please remove their clothes." A bunch of horn-blowers and drum-beaters impressed themselves on the national consciousness and entered history as the Dodger Sym-phoney. They were Italians from the Williamsburg section of Brooklyn, and at first they were pursued relentlessly through the stands by the private cops. They soon became so popular and famous that seats were reserved for them. When an umpire made a close call against the Dodgers, the Sym-phoney played "Three Blind Mice." When a rival player struck out, the musicians would play "The Worms Crawl In, The Worms Crawl Out," and they would musically follow him back to the dugout waiting for him to plant his posterior on the bench. At that point, the Sym-phonians would hit the big bass drum, BANG. The "enemy" ball players tried to sneak back to the bench, go to the water cooler, loaf on the dugout stairs. But when they sat down, the Sym-phoney caught them: BANG on the bass drum. The Sym-phoney band got to be so popular that the musicians' union got jealous and demanded that the Dodgers pay union rates for a standby band of professionals. They threatened to picket Ebbets Field. The Dodgers responded with a Music Appreciation Day. Anyone bringing a musical instrument was admitted to the park free. The fans brought bugles, harps, harmonicas, musical saws, drums, and washboards in the most successful strikebreaking operation in history.

MacPhail had more than a touch of Barnum, but he also knew baseball, and he quickly moved to create a pennant contender.

During his first season, 1938, the Dodgers finished seventh, but attendance nearly doubled. MacPhail hired Leo Durocher away from St. Louis and made him player-manager for 1939, acquiring one of the best shortstops and baseball tacticians in the game. MacPhail spent $50,000 to get home-run hitting first-baseman Dolph Camilli from the Phillies. Camilli would specialize in frozen-rope home runs in the small Brooklyn ball park. MacPhail spent $90,000 for star second baseman Billy Herman of the Cubs, and $100,000 for fast-balling pitcher Kirby Higbe of the Philadelphia Phillies. He bought heavy-hitting outfielder Dixie Walker from Detroit, and catcher Mickey Owen from St. Louis. He had two of the best, and fattest, relief pitchers in the major leagues, Hugh Casey and Freddy "Fat Freddy" Fitzimmons, a knuckleballer. In MacPhail's third year, 1941, the Dodgers won the National League pennant—but the Brooklyn Trust Company was furious. MacPhail had spent more than the pennant winners had earned.

But the atmosphere in the tiny old ball park amounted to a kind of continuous ecstasy, which reached an incendiary peak when the Dodgers played their arch rivals, the New York Giants. The bullpen for a visiting team was down in the left-field corner, and during a game, the souped-up Brooklyn fans would shower the "enemy" with tomatoes, hot dog rolls, rotten eggs, and other missiles. The Dodger third baseman was a wizard named "Cookie" Lavagetto, and one fan with a piercing scream would relentlessly yell "Cooookie, Coookie." He became known as the Cookie Monster.

The Brooklyn Dodger team Larry MacPhail built in the years just before World War II provided the basis for a baseball dynasty that would gradually dominate the National League, make history during the 1950s by integrating baseball with Jackie Robinson, outgrow Brooklyn and Ebbets Field—as demographic patterns changed—and, in 1957, move to Los Angeles and become an entirely different kind of team. But the MacPhail Dodgers had a pungent local identity.

If you arrived early for batting practice, as I always did, you would see the workout, and the players horsing around. Usually, before the game started, the players, in their white Dodger uniforms, would leave the park and walk a couple of blocks to a local saloon where they would down a few beers. Their cleats went clackety-clack on Bedford Avenue. I also ran into the Dodger team on off days at the beach. Long Island is a long piece of land sticking out into the Atlantic Ocean, and in those days the tip of the island nearest New York, the westernmost tip, was the site of a beach club known as the Breezy Point Beach Club, more irreverently as The Irish Riviera. For those days it was a pretty fancy place, with cabanas, waiters in white jackets bringing lunch and booze, and sun-tanned businessmen and politicos. The Dodgers had a membership, or maybe guest privileges, but, anyway, when they were not playing baseball they were on the beach at Breezy Point. It was startling to see these heroes joking around in bathing suits. The shortstop, Pee Wee Reese, who led the Fifties Dodgers as team captain, was a very white-skinned, skinny little fellow. Dolph Camilli, the first-baseman, was swarthy and friendly.

My personal god was an outfielder and switch-hitter named Pete Reiser, "Pistol Pete" Reiser, one of the great squandered talents in the history of the game. Reiser was a compact and powerful athlete with perfect coordination and—a tragic flaw—a ferocious competitive instinct that obliterated all caution. In his first full season with the Dodgers, 1941, he led the National League with a .343 batting average. He hit equally well as a left-hander or right-hander. He was an electrifying base runner who would score from second on a wild pitch. In 1941, Reiser seemed to be the superstar of the future, the heir of all the greats. Only he kept running into the concrete wall of the outfield, chasing fly balls. He did not seem to recognize that it was actually there. He broke numerous bones, and a great career was cut short. After he ruined himself, they put foam rubber on the wall. These were the Dodgers, most of them more or less college-age young men, who hung around the beach at Breezy Point, throwing baseballs, softballs, and footballs, in those summers before the war. In 1941, they won their first National League pennant in twenty years, but lost to the Yankees in the World Series, an encounter notable for Mickey Owen's dropped third strike.

The MacPhail Dodgers, coached by Leo "The Lip" Durocher, have classic status for me, my own first ball team, worshipped on the field, met down at the beach. I can still remember the Dodger lineup from the last MacPhail year, a team that had something, no, a lot of everything. At first base was Dolph Camilli, the slugger. At second base Billy Herman, a superb fielder and solid hitter. Pee Wee Reese, the "Little Colonel," had replaced Leo Durocher at shortstop, and people fought over whether Reese was better than Phil "Scooter" Rizzuto of the Yankees up in the Bronx. Third base belonged to Harry "Cooookie!" Lavegetto. In the outfield, they had Fred "Dixie" Walker, of the effortless line drives, and electric Pistol Pete Reiser and Joe "Ducky" Medwick, whose nickname derived from his gait, and who ritually stepped on second base every time he came from the outfield to the dugout. Whitlow Wyatt and Hugh Casey and Fat Freddie Fitzimmons and fast-balling Kirby Higbe provided pitching. In the pennant drive against the St. Louis Cardinals, Higbe pitched in pain, said to be from a hernia, but rumored to be gonorrhea. The Cardinals had Stan "The Man" Musial, with his clothesline home runs, and the great Cooper Brothers combination—Mort, the pitcher, and Walker, the catcher—and Big Johnny Mize, in whose hands the bat looked like a toothpick. Somehow, my father knew the Coopers, and we sometimes had dinner in New York with them. I especially remember Mort, the twenty-game winner, a giant of a country boy who gave me an autographed baseball. These were the boys of summer, the summer before the war.

After Pearl Harbor, Larry MacPhail, over fifty, immediately enlisted in the United States Army and received the rank of major. His place with the Dodgers was taken by Branch Rickey, known as "The Brain" and "The Mahatma," an especially shrewd baseball organizer. With the St. Louis Cardinals, Rickey had invented the farm club system in 1919, providing a steady flow of talent that carried the Cardinals to six National League championships and four world championships. He brought his extraordinary talents to Brooklyn in 1942. Rickey built the great Dodger teams of the 1950s. He had a long-range strategic sense. He liked to assemble a talented crew of players of approximately the same age and plan for a decade or more of service from them. Jackie Robinson, Gil Hodges, and Duke Snider joined the Dodgers in 1947. The next year came Roy Campanella and ace pitcher Carl Erskine. Don Newcombe was added to the roster in 1949, Billy Loes and Clem Labine in 1950. During the war years, most major league teams cut back on their recruiting and training activities. Not Branch Rickey. By the end of the war, the Dodger system had twenty-five farm clubs stocked with premilitary-age talent. In 1946, the Newport News club had fifteen players who were 17 years old. One of them was "Duke" Snider. As a Dodger he would hold the team record for home runs (389), extra base hits (814), and runs batted in

(1,271). The "Dook of Flatbush" made it into the Hall of Fame in 1980. It was players like these who brought the Fifties Dodgers what Branch Rickey publicly promised in 1946: "Pennants, pennants, pennants."

April 15, 1947, opening day of the season: Jackie Robinson started at first base for the Dodgers. It is because of baseball's deep American symbolism that this was so important, an historic moment. Baseball had always moved with the pulse of the country. Before World War I, baseball was a low-scoring game, featuring tight defense and effective pitching. Ty Cobb, a tough singles hitter and clever base-runner, was the ideal prewar ball player. But after the war, the temper of America shifted drastically, with nineteenth-century form giving way to twentieth-century energy. This was reflected in the culture generally, in the arts, and in sports. Americans began to drive cars, listen to radios, dance to the new jazz rhythms. The great names in the arts were those of innovators. In sports, defense gave way to attack, the demand for speed and scoring. The shape of the football changed, making the forward pass a major weapon. Bill Tilden developed the all-court attack, and Jack Dempsey, with his knockout punch, drew the first million-dollar gate. In baseball, Ty Cobb gave way to Babe Ruth, the "Sultan of Swat," whose popularity built Yankee Stadium, and who hit 60 home runs in 1927, the same year Lindbergh flew alone across the Atlantic. Ruth and the home run expressed the spirit of the age. On that April afternoon in 1947 when Jackie Robinson took the field as a Dodger, it meant the beginning of the end for segregation, not only in major league baseball but for the country itself. In 1952, Ralph Ellison's award-winning novel, *The Invisible Man*, expressed the plight of the "unseen" black man in American culture. The idea had some validity in 1952, but Jackie Robinson had already made it somewhat anachronistic. Since 1947, the ebony-skinned athlete had become the most visible baseball player since Babe Ruth.

Robinson, a native of Los Angeles, had been a star athlete at UCLA, an Army officer in the war, and a star shortstop for the Kansas City Monarchs in the Negro Leagues. For some time, Branch Rickey had been giving serious thought to the color line in baseball, and he had sent his Dodger scouts out across the country and to Cuba to identify the most promising black players. He decided to make his move with Jackie Robinson. The two men met on August 28, 1945 at the Dodger headquarters, 215 Montague Street in Brooklyn Heights. Rickey tested Robinson's self-control by deliberately taunting him, cursing at him. Both he and Robinson were fully aware that Robinson faced difficult days ahead in the southern-flavored big leagues. Robinson, always a proud man, reluctantly agreed to endure abuse in silence, and he signed a Dodger contract to play for the Montreal Royals for the season of 1946.

The Royals opened the season against the Jersey City Giants across the river in Jersey City, and thousands of New Yorkers journeyed through the tubes to see Robinson play. He was spectacular. He hit three singles and a three-run home run, stole two bases, and flim-flammed the Giant pitchers into committing two balks. With Robinson the dominating figure on the field, Montreal rolled over Jersey City 14-1 and went on to win the International League pennant. The next year, Robinson came up to the Dodgers.

Bill "Bojangles" Robinson, the famous black dancer, called Jackie Robinson "Ty Cobb in Technicolor." He had an astonishing rookie season, playing in 150 games—more than any other Dodger—and batting .297. His base-stealing exploits became legendary. Robinson possessed explosive speed, and he was restlessly active once on base. He took long leads, feet always moving, taunting the pitcher, creating a mounting tension. His first year in the big leagues, he led the National League in stolen bases and easily won the Rookie of the Year award. Black fans began to turn out in unprecedented numbers to see the new star. Robinson was integrating the stands as well as the field.

In the beginning, abuse was often savage. Reserve catcher Bobby Bragan refused to play on the same team with a black man, and was sent to the minor leagues. Abuse was constant from the stands. Black cats would appear insultingly in rival dugouts. On the road, Robinson often could not eat with his teammates or stay at the same hotel. "It was a sensitive, even delicate situation," recalls Red Barber. It "was not something you were suddenly confronted with one day and then didn't have to worry about any more. It had to be handled inning by inning, game by game, month by month. It was there all the time, because when Robinson came, he came to stay."

He not only stayed, not only succeeded as a Dodger, he became a superstar on a Fifties Dodger team that was loaded with superstars. In 1949, the "Technicolor Ty Cobb" batted .342 and led the league. This was the first of his six consecutive seasons of over .300 hitting. He was averaging better than 100 runs and around 70 bases on balls per season. Jackie Robinson earned universal respect as an athlete and gradually gained the same respect as a human being, preparing the way for the other black players who followed him into the big leagues, players like Roy Campanella and Joe Black and Don Newcombe of the Dodgers, Hank Thompson, Monte Irvin and the great Willie Mays of the New York Giants. Mays played for twenty-two seasons, led the league in batting five times, in home runs four, and played the outfield with extraordinary natural grace. By 1953, Branch Rickey and Jackie Robinson had won their battle. Seven teams in the major leagues had black players, twenty-three of them. Racial prejudice was on the way out, both inside and outside baseball. The long-range social process that had been accelerated during the war years had been carried another large step forward by the courage and patience of Rickey and Robinson.

The Rickey Dodgers of the Fifties were far more formidable than the team built by MacPhail in the Forties. The extensive farm club system established by Rickey produced a steady flow of high-grade talent, and the tiny old ball park at Ebbets Field housed the most powerful offensive baseball team since the New York Yankees of DiMaggio and Gehrig. In those sunset years of the Brooklyn franchise, the Dodgers were a team of stars: Jackie Robinson, Pee Wee Reese, Sandy Amoros, Carl Furillo—"Furiller" in Brooklynese—who had the best throw in baseball from the outfield, Gil Hodges, the huge first baseman, a home-run slugger, Duke Snider, Roy Campanella. Campanella, the catcher, was only 5'9" but he weighed 200 pounds and all of it was muscle. He led the league in fielding four times and the same number of times hit more than thirty home runs. In three seasons, he batted in more than a hundred runs and hit at over .300.

There was also Billy Cox, the skinny, sad-looking third baseman who used a glove that looked like a child's purchased at Woolworth's. But Cox could handle any kind of batted ball and quickly established possession of the left side of the infield.

The offensive power of this 1950s Dodger team was awesome. On August 31, 1952, the Dodgers scored 15 runs against the Cincinnati Reds in the first inning. On June 25, 1953, the Dodgers hit five home runs in a 12-3 rout of the same Reds. On July 10, Roy Campanella hit the twenty-fourth consecutive Dodger home run in a game against Sal Maglie—"Sal, the Barber"—of the New York Giants. Ten days later, they shelled the St. Louis Cardinals 20-4. On June 16, 1956, Duke Snider hit four home runs as the Dodgers won their sixth straight.

The only flaw in the Dodger operation was the pitching. They had great pitchers, but not quite enough of them: Ralph Branca, Don Newcombe, Preacher Roe with his impossible spitball, Clem Labine, Carl Erskine, Joe Black, Johnny Podres. Nevertheless, pennant followed pennant, though not World Series victories. It was after the move to Los Angeles in 1957 that a weaker team, led by ace pitcher Sandy Koufax, achieved the consistency that always seemed just to elude the Dodgers in their last Brooklyn years.

Part of the Dodger magic depended on their relationship to the two other and also distinctive New York City teams, the Giants and the Yankees. The Dodgers were rowdy, uproarious, unpredictable in their seething Ebbets Field ball park. The Giants and the Yankees were entirely different.

Back in the 1880s, the Giants had played just north of Central Park in Manhattan on a field also used by New York's upper crust for playing polo. When they moved uptown in 1889 to a new stadium on Eighth Avenue and 155th Street, it was therefore natural that the place was called The Polo Grounds, the largest field in the National League. Over in Brooklyn, the Dodger crowds were composed of local Brooklyn people plus a lot of vivid "characters." The Giant scene was much more respectable. Businessmen from midtown, Wall Streeters, celebrities made the regular trip to The Polo Grounds during the Thirties and Forties. The Giants had a large number of season ticket holders, and there was a sense of dynasty about the club: John McGraw, Carl Hubbell, Bill Terry, Mel Ott. Mel Ott, a powerful right-handed batter who kicked his left foot out as he swung, was also the epitome of the Giants, a perfect gentleman.

During the war years of the Forties, the Giants regularly finished in the vicinity of the cellar, and in 1947 the management decided to make a radical change. Horace Stoneham, the owner, did the unthinkable. He replaced manager Mel Ott with none other than the epitome of Dodgerness, Leo "The Lip" Durocher, who, when not fighting with umpires and getting thrown out of games and fined and banned, was a Broadway character who wore expensive suits and had an actress, Laraine Day, for a wife.

Leo "The Lip" did not like what he saw on the Giant roster. He was the Billy Martin of his era, a mercurial baseball genius who favored speed, surprise and shrewd tactics, but the 1948 Giant squad he took over was based on several slow-moving home run sluggers. Among them, the outfield of Bobby Thompson, Sid Gordon and Willard Marshall hit seventy-eight home runs. The huge first baseman and former Cardinal, Johnny Mize, hit fifty-one home runs that year, and catcher Walker Cooper, another alumnus of the St. Louis Gas House Gang, hit thirty-five. But Mize was slow, and Durocher dealt him away to the Yankees. Walker Cooper went to Cincinnati. The Giants bought Hank Thompson and Monte Irvin, their first two blacks. Willard Marshall, Sid Gordon, and Buddy Kerr were traded away, but the Giants picked up shortstop Alvin Dark and second baseman Eddie Stanky, and then, in 1950, Sal "The Barber" Maglie. In 1951, Willie Mays came aboard and the Giants were ready for their "miracle run" at the pennant. Durocher had created a team in his own image, a team of speed, mobility, and surprise. Both the Dodgers and the Yankees had more talent, but the Giants had verve and players precisely matched to team need, and they had Durocher to infuse his own combative energy into the entire mechanism. All through the 1951 season, the Giants pursued the Dodgers, finally forcing them into a playoff, which they won in the final game—"The Miracle of Coogan's Bluff"—when Bobby Thompson cracked a game-winning, two-out, ninth-inning home run off Dodger ace Ralph Branca.

The New York Yankees, for as long as anyone could remember, that is, at least since they purchased Babe Ruth from the Boston Red Sox in 1920, had been something entirely special in American baseball. The phrase "New York Yankees" had the same sort of aura as words like "The Bank of England," "General Motors" or "Rockefeller." Back in the 1920s, the team had been the property of the beer millionaire, Jacob Rupert. He purchased a tract of farmland across the river from The Polo Grounds and contracted for a rival New York stadium to be built there. He was betting on the enormous crowd attraction provided by Babe Ruth to fill it. The Yankee Stadium opened for business on April 18, 1923, with the National Anthem played by John Philip Sousa's band. Ruth hit a home run. After all, it was known as "The House That Ruth Built."

Though a man once died of a heart attack in the excitement of watching the Babe hit a home run, the atmosphere at Yankee Stadium was not one of hysteria, nothing like Ebbets Field. The Yankees were rich, and they could afford excellence. Yankee fans expected excellence. It was appreciated, but it did not come as a surprise. The monuments to Yankee greats out there in center field, 450 feet from home plate said it all, plaques honoring Miller Huggins, Ed Barrow, Babe Ruth, and Lou Gehrig. The Yankee legends. When another team played the Yankees, they not only went up against the pin-striped players visible on the field, a formidable enough assignment, they also had to fight the legend behind the Yankees. Any clash between the Dodgers and the Yankees was like a war between two entirely different cultures.

The first great Yankee manager of modern times was the redoubtable Miller Huggins, who presided over the fortunes of the team during the roaring Twenties. They rolled over the opposition to six consecutive American League pennants and two Series victories. Then Joe McCarthy took over—"Marse Joe," a laconic baseball perfectionist—and Yankee dominance continued, as McCarthy, DiMaggio and Company scored six World Series triumphs: 1932, 1936, 1937, 1938, 1939, and 1941. In 1942, they lost to the St. Louis Cardinals in the series, but returned the next year to beat them.

Going up to Yankee Stadium in the Bronx was an entirely different experience from seeing the Dodgers play in Ebbets Field. The Stadium was so big it looked as if it could hold three Ebbets Fields. The Yankee fans were more reserved, and looked better off—a lot of businessmen and professional people from Manhattan and the nearby suburbs in Long Island and New Jersey. Such Dodger items as "Hilda" or "The Cookie Monster" or the "Symphoney" would have been unthinkable in this dignified atmosphere.

The player everyone watched most closely was Joe DiMaggio, both in the outfield and at the plate. DiMaggio was very fast, but didn't look it. He moved over the grass with long, easy strides and made impossible catches look routine. He played with his famous emotional reserve, practically expressionless. When he entered the batter's circle, anticipation mounted, and when he was at the plate the stands usually fell silent. He possessed a perfect swing, a long, smooth swing that produced explosive power. He did not look as if he were swinging hard, like Stan Musial; but his timing must have been perfect because he could hit any sort of pitch to any field and often hit extra base hits and home runs.

On May 15, 1941, DiMaggio commenced one of the extraordinary performances in baseball history—statistically "impossible," according to computer expert and former President of Dartmouth College, John G. Kemeny. On May 15, DiMaggio hit one single in four times at bat against the Chicago White Sox. That single launched what became a national obsession during the next two months. Day after day, in game after game, DiMaggio continued to hit, getting hotter and hotter at the plate. In July, he broke Willie Keeler's 1897 major league record of 44 consecutive games. From games 47 through 56, he came to bat 40 times and hit safely 23 times for a streak average of .575. By the time he finally went hitless, on July 17 in a night game in Cleveland, he had hit safely in 56 consecutive games. The hit tune of that summer—you heard it over and over on the radio—was a song called "Joltin' Joe DiMaggio."

Of course, DiMaggio had around him a superb team. Lou Gehrig played his last game, his career succumbing to fatal illness, on May 2, 1939. But the Yankees were formidable all through the lineup. In the outfield: Tommy Henrich, Charlie "King Kong" Keller, and Joe DiMaggio. Bill Dickey, the great catcher, was a premier slugger, too, with a lifetime average of .313 before he stepped aside in favor of Yogi Berra. Red Rolfe at third base was not a power hitter, but he hit .362 in 1936 and was always in the vicinity of .300—and he played flawlessly on defense. Phil Rizzuto at short and Joe Gordon at second were a great double-play combination.

Joe DiMaggio lost three years to military service and then returned to lead the Yankees into the postwar era before retiring because of injuries in 1951. It epitomizes the Yankee operation that to replace DiMaggio they came up with a nineteen-year-old slugger named Mickey Mantle, from the Joplin, Missouri Class C club. Thus the succession: Babe Ruth, Joe DiMaggio, Mickey Mantle. The Yankee system really delivered the goods.

Despite DiMaggio's stoical reserve, he was not the perfect machine he sometimes appeared. He was a perfectionist who would brood silently in the clubhouse after what he considered a poor performance. He sometimes snapped in frustrated anger. He never showed more class than during his comeback season of 1949. During 1947 and 1948, his magnificent six-two, two-hundred-pound body began breaking down. In that year, he hit .315 and committed only one error in the field, earning the remarkable average of .997. He was the league's most valuable player. He was the principal force in powering the Yankees to the American League Championship and into the Series against the Dodgers. That Series was notable for a spectacular play during the sixth game by Dodger outfielder Al Gionfriddo, who made an acrobatic catch of a DiMaggio blast, robbing him of a three-run home run and forcing the Series into a seventh and final game—which the Yankees won.

But DiMaggio's career was coming to its close. In 1948, he played in pain with calcium deposits in his right heel. Running became excruciating, and he committed thirteen outfield errors. For a perfectionist like DiMaggio, this must have been an equally excruciating humiliation. With DiMaggio below par, the Yankees finished third, and in November the heel was operated on. He had also developed ulcers and gone through a divorce.

The foot healed slowly. The Yankee season opened without him. He finally broke back into the lineup on June 27 in an exhibition game against the Giants. He had missed half of the season. For the rest of the season, he played with an orthopedic shoe with no spikes and a raised heel. In his first regular game, up in Boston against the Red Sox, he singled in his first at-bat and then hit a two-run homer that provided the Yankee margin of victory. In the next game of the series, with the Yankees losing 7-1, he hit a three-run homer to help tie the score, and then, in the eighth inning, a two-run homer to win the game. Then he won the third game with a three-run blast. Even the Boston fans gave him a standing ovation.

During that 1948 season, DiMaggio played in seventy-six games. He hit fourteen home runs, had seventy-six RBIs, and ended with a .346 average. Two years later he would retire, two years after that marry Marilyn Monroe, and then, in 1955, he was elected to the Hall of Fame.

In 1951, the succession passed to Mickey Mantle, and a new version of Yankee perfection dominated the new decade. Mickey Mantle had been born in 1931 in Commerce, Oklahoma, and he was more heavily muscled than DiMaggio. Mantle's home runs had a spectacular feature. The ball did not rise and sink into the stands in a parabola. It went straight and hit the seats rising. The sports writers dubbed them "tape measure homers." That first year with the Yankees, he hit .267—he was young and green—but the next year it was .311, and Mantle was on his way. In 1956, his .353 won the batting title, and he led the league with 52 home runs and in runs batted in (130). The Yankees won the title in 1950, 1951, 1952, 1953, 1955, 1956, and 1957. Yankee excellence was practically overpowering. In the outfield they had, in addition to Mantle, Hank Bauer and Gene Woodling. Infielders Joe Collins, Gil McDougald, Phil Rizzuto, and Billy Martin provided first-rate defense. Yogi Berra, a great catcher and slugger, provided colorful quotations for the press, as did manager Casey Stengel, who talked in his peculiar fractured English, called "Stengelese." On the mound, they had Vic Raschi, Ed Lopat, Whitey Ford, Allie Reynolds, Don Larsen, Tom Sturdivant. If it seemed that there was no end to the talent available to the Yankees, that's because there wasn't. And old Casey Stengel himself provided an almost impossible expression of baseball tradition. On that cloudy day of April 9, 1913, when Ebbets Field in Brooklyn first opened its doors, the Dodgers dropped a 2-1 game to the Phillies. One of the Dodger outfielders was . . . Casey Stengel.

The relationship and the rivalry between these three New York teams became something special. Their contrasting styles and personalities enriched the game and made every encounter between two of them an occasion of more than usual excitement. The two National League clubs, the Dodgers and the Giants, seemed to hate one another, as did their fans. When the Giants visited Ebbets Field, their bullpen was exposed to insults and missiles—hotdog rolls, half-filled paper cups—thrown from the stands. The Giants expressed Manhattan, and solidity and tradition. They were respectable. The Dodgers were scrappy, colorful, democratic, local. The distant Yankees, waiting like executioners at the end of the season in the World Series, were Olympian. They were like Joe Louis in boxing, FDR in politics, *The New York Times* in journalism, the British Fleet in World War I.

In the year 1957, all this came to an end. The whole equation, the whole relationship, was destroyed. The personalities of the teams changed. Two of them left for the riches of California. The Empire City would never see a Brooklyn-New York "subway series" again. The Los Angeles Dodgers proved, often, to be a very fine team—but they were just another team after 1957.

No doubt the West Coast move was inevitable. In long-range perspective, it can be understood as a response to vast demographic changes in the United States which are still profoundly shaping our national life, and not least our politics. The economic and demographic center of gravity after World War II was shifting sharply South and West. Money and population were moving to what soon became known as the Sun Belt. Nevertheless, the decision of the Dodgers and Giants to move to California was a wound in the heart to their ardent constituencies and represented the destruction of something that can probably never be replaced.

The old Boston Braves had relocated in Milwaukee in 1953, and despite the fact that the Dodgers won the National League championship in 1955 and 1956, the Milwaukee club far outdrew them in home attendance. Ebbets Field was too small for the Dodgers of the mid-Fifties, and the surrounding apartment buildings made enlarging it impossible. The prosperity of the Fifties and the new highway construction meant that Americans became accustomed to driving, not riding on subways and buses, and Ebbets Field had next to no parking facilities. The old residential patterns of Brooklyn were also changing, and the specter of street violence haunted Ebbets Field, especially for night games. By this time, in a management power struggle, Branch Rickey had been replaced as general manager by Walter O'Malley, "The O'Malley," a hard-driving businessman, who commenced serious talks with California political figures who were eager for a big league franchise. Lengthy talks with New York City and State officials produced nothing concrete. On September 24, 1957, the Dodgers played their last game at Ebbets Field after forty-four seasons.

When the game was over, Gladys Gooding played "May the Good Lord Bless You and Keep You" on the organ and then "Auld Lang Syne." Pee Wee Reese waved farewell, and the fans tore the place apart for souvenirs. In February 1960, a two-ton wrecking ball leveled Ebbets Field and made way for a housing project.

With the departure of the Dodgers, the flight of the Giants to California was inevitable. For Horace Stoneham, the Giant owner, the Dodger-Giant rivalry was essential, part of the Giants' assets. Giant attendance in the Polo Grounds had dropped sharply. In July 1957, Stoneham announced that "I will recommend to the board of directors of the New York Giants that we leave and go to San Francisco after this season."

It is an extraordinary symbol of the new age of air travel that the Dodgers and Giants who had been historic rivals when separated by a half-hour subway ride in the same city now proposed to continue that rivalry when located in Los Angeles and San Francisco, over 400 miles apart. But, of course, it would never be the same again.

HIROSHIMA

Today, Paul Fussell is a professor at Rutgers University. He has written three of the important books of our time and will write others. In August 1945, however, he was a 21-year-old second lieutenant leading a rifle platoon.

He has recalled the actuality.

"On Okinawa, only weeks before Hiroshima, 123,000 Japanese and Americans had *killed* each other. 'Just awful,' was the comment not of some pacifist but of MacArthur. One million American casualties was his estimate of the cost of the forthcoming invasion. And that invasion was not just a hypothetical threat, as some theorists have argued. It was genuinely in train, as I know because I was to be in it. When the bomb ended the war I was in the 45th Infantry Division, which had been through the European war to the degree that it had needed to be reconstituted two or three times. We were in a staging area near Reims, ready to be shipped across the United States for final preparation in the Philippines. My division was to take part in the invasion of Hon Shu in March 1946. (The earlier invasion of Kyushu was to be carried out by 700,000 infantry already in the Pacific.) I was a 21-year-old second lieutenant leading a rifle platoon. Although still officially in one piece, in the German war I had already been wounded in the leg and back severely enough to be adjudged, after the war, 40 percent disabled. But even if my legs buckled whenever I jumped out of the back of the truck, my condition was held to be satisfactory for whatever lay ahead. When the bombs dropped and the news began to circulate that 'Operation Olympic' would not, after all, take place, that we would not be obliged to run up the beaches near Tokyo assault-firing while being mortared and shelled, for all the fake manliness of our facades, we cried with relief and joy. We were going to live. We were going to grow to adulthood after all. When the *Enola Gay* dropped its package, 'There were cheers,' says John Toland, 'over the intercom; it meant the end of the war.' "

Fussell is literary. Most of the men who would have had to run up the beach on Kyushu and Honshu were not.

James Jones, on the other hand, was an army man. About Hiroshima, he reflected on "What it must have been like to some old-timer buck sergeant or staff sergeant who had been through Guadalcanal or Bougainville or the Philippines, to stand on some beach and watch this huge war machine beginning to stir around him and know that he very likely had survived this far only to fall dead on the dirt of Japan's home islands, hardly bears thinking about."

William Manchester, a writer who was a Marine, recalls: "After Biak the enemy withdrew to deep caverns. Rooting them out became a bloody business which reached its ultimate horror in the last months of the war. You think of the lives which could have been lost in an invasion of Japan's home islands—a staggering number of Americans but millions more of Japanese."

John Kenneth Galbraith was in the Office of Price Administration in Washington. He thinks the dropping of the two bombs was unjustified.

"Experience whispers," writes Fussell, "that the pity is not that we used the bomb to end the Japanese war but that it wasn't ready earlier to end the German one. If only it could have been rushed into production and dropped at the right moment on the Reich chancellery or Berchtesgaden or Hitler's military headquarters in East Prussia or—Wagnerian *coup de theatre*—at Rommel's phony state funeral, most of the Nazi hierarchy could have been pulverized immediately, saving not just the embarrassment of the Nuremberg trials but the lives of about four million Jews, Poles, Slavs, gypsies, and other 'sub-humans,' not to mention the lives and limbs of millions of Allied and Axis soldiers. If the bomb could have been ready even as late as July 1944, it could have reinforced the Von Stauffenberg plot and ended the war then and there. If the bomb had only been ready in time, the men of my infantry platoon would not have been killed and maimed."

The bomb was part of the Fifties, too, and its shadow lay over that splendid decade, even as it does our own.

CHAPTER SIX

White Flannels, Grass Courts

The period between the end of World War II and the emergence of big-money professional tennis under Jack Kramer and Pancho Gonzales in the late 1950s represented a kind of Silver Age of the amateur game. With the advent of the big money, everything changed. We have far greater numbers of first-rate players today than in the late Forties and early Fifties, but the entire style of the operation is totally different. The grass is mostly gone now, as is the white clothes requirement. No one throws a point to an opponent to offset a bad call anymore. During its Silver Age, after the war, tennis still had something of the aristocratic flavor of an earlier era.

This is going to be a Valentine card to an old girl, the game of tennis as I knew it most intensely, a declaration of love for an activity to which I totally committed myself during my most impressionable years, and which sometimes, at certain moments, still gives me as much pleasure as almost anything else.

All sports have a metaphorical quality. We have touched on some of the metaphors at the heart of the game of baseball. For me, tennis was also a powerful metaphor.

When I first hit a tennis ball—it must have been in 1944, against the cement handball wall of a public school in Queens, Long Island—I would not have known what the word "metaphor" meant. Nevertheless I knew, I was made vividly aware by my peers, that tennis was in fact . . . *hated*.

Tennis in those pre-affluent years was considered elitist, possibly decadent. Slugging the ball against that humble concrete wall, I heard from my peers flat declarations that I was undoubtedly a snob and probably a sexual deviant. Later, when I was going to Stuyvesant High School in Manhattan and carrying my tennis rackets through the New York subways, I had to endure the "queer" charge daily.

It is possible that the snob charge was correct. Inside my puny frame I was an intense romantic. I knew that tennis had always been an elite sport, and that in the 1940s it still was. I knew nothing about the great public tennis programs in Los Angeles. And I freely confess that as a twelve-year-old, this elite flavoring meant a great deal to me. I read eagerly about the marvelous tennis matches of the 1920s and 1930s at Wimbledon, Cannes, Nice. I had not yet even stepped onto an actual tennis court. I was merely hitting the ball against the cement wall in a school yard, but my heart belonged to grass courts, striped awnings, and clear blue Riviera skies—under which, I knew, people like the Doherty brothers had played, and Tilden, and R. N. Williams, and Vinnie Richards. "Hart Wins at Monte Carlo." The notion was breath-taking.

In retrospect, the period in which I played, or tried to play, serious tennis represents the sunset of the elite period of the game, what I have called a "Silver Age." The American championships are no longer played on the grass courts in Forest Hills, in the concrete stadium built to accommodate the unprecedented tennis crowds that wanted to see Bill Tilden play during the 1920s. Moreover, I know now, as I did not know then as a child player, that much about the amateur game was rotten, hypocritical, and corrupt. Had I been an important adult player in 1945, knowing what I know now about big-time sports, I certainly would have been a rebel against the tennis establishment.

But what my naive eyes saw was also true, and even now I cannot judge that it was less important. For a dozen years after World War II, the Eastern grass court circuit was a thing of great elegance and beauty. Between Wimbledon early in the summer, and Forest Hills around Labor Day, wonderful tournaments were held at places like Seabright, New Jersey; Southampton, Long Island; Newport, Rhode Island; Short Hills, New Jersey; and the Longwood Cricket Club in Chestnut Hill, Massachusetts.

Somewhat paradoxically, in view of my attitude toward this perceived elegance, my own attitude toward competition was relentlessly Calvinistic. Beneath my off-white, monogrammed polo shirts and cable-stitch sweaters, there beat the fierce heart of a Cromwellian. As a tournament player, I correctly regarded any unforced error or other mistake as a moral lapse: perhaps I had lazily let my attention flag, perhaps I had lazily reached for a shot instead of taking an extra half step. There is no reason short of an atomic attack why a technically competent and attentive player should ever make an unforced error. Every set, game, stroke thus became a moral test. Bunyan's Pilgrim in *Pilgrim's Progress*? Bah. Compared with a fanatical athlete, he was squishy soft. The experience of ease in athletics comes through total mastery of technique—as it does in music, or anything else.

Every morning during the tournament season I would show up at the West Side Tennis Club in Forest Hills around 8:30. I would place tennis ball cartons in the four corners of the service courts, and then hit fifty serves into each of them. You can develop a pretty decent serve that way, even if you are not especially powerful physically.

From those adolescent days some absolutely exquisite matches remain indelibly in my mind. Two of them, as it happens, involved William F. Talbert, one of the finest stylists in the history of the game.

The first of them, it must have been in the summer of 1947, was the grass-court final at Seabright, New Jersey, Talbert against Frank Parker, the national champion. From the wooden stands you could look over the grass courts to the club house, and beyond the club house you could see the Atlantic Ocean.

Parker was a remarkable player, scientific, a sort of American René Lacoste. He enhanced the scientific aura by wearing tinted sunglasses, which, every few points, he would remove and polish. Parker was remarkably steady, but he was not, contrary to lay opinion, defensive. No purely defensive player can get very far in big time tennis. I have never understood how a backhand hit with slight underspin could be hit as hard as Parker hit his and still stay in the court. Talbert in this match was the rapier, a stylist and abrupt shot-maker. For two hours they dueled. Talbert did not have the power to overwhelm Parker. He therefore had to play "against the percentage," and bring off shots that were very risky.

Talbert hung in against Parker, trusted to brilliance, and won aesthetically but lost the Seabright Bowl.

The second exquisite match, later that season, took place at the Meadow Club in Southampton, Long Island. Pancho Gonzales, age 18, had come East from Los Angeles, knife scar on his cheek, legendary serve, and panther grace. Throughout the summer he had been raising hell on the Eastern circuit with the established players. Spectacularly, he had made it to the Southampton finals against Talbert, and I drove out there with my cronies for the match.

When we got there, I saw immediately why Gonzales had reached the finals, upsetting the seed. He had a heavy serve, like a Dempsey punch. It had rained off and on all week. You could see the water spin off the ball as it left the grass, and Gonzales' serve must have weighed fifty pounds on Talbert's racket. I sat on the porch of the Meadow Club and watched Talbert play supremely great tennis. He held his own serve, he waited, he waited, and then he won.

My finest hour in tennis. I was sitting on the porch at the West Side Club drinking a Coke, and Frank Parker walked up. "Want to hit some?" he asked. I nearly fell out of my chair. "I'm not happy with my backhand," Parker went on. A two-time national champion, he probably had the best backhand in the world. "Okay," I said, and we went out onto one of the composition courts near the clubhouse.

Parker wanted to fine-tune his backhand. We began hitting them cross-court at each other. At the outset, Parker's backhands were landing perhaps two feet from the baseline. Gradually, inch by inch, they got deeper, like a creeping artillery barrage. We would hit dozens of shots back and forth before an error, inevitably by me. In due course, Parker's backhand was hitting two or three inches from the baseline with relentless regularity. Despite this, I managed to return most of them hard and deep. Parker seemed to get curious. "Nice backhand," he said. "Where did you learn that?" "From Bill Talbert," I said, "in a junior clinic." Talbert had stressed the importance of getting your weight on the forward foot at the moment of impact. "He knows the stroke," Parker said; then: "Let's play a set." By that time, a fair-sized crowd was watching from the porch and from behind the fence.

Play a set we did, and Parker let me win two games. A couple of days later, in one of the finest matches of his career, he carried Jack Kramer to five sets in the Stadium.

Jack Kramer, of course, was the dominant tennis player of the Fifties. A rangy Californian from Montebello, he was very powerfully built and in those days wore his blond hair in a crew cut. Before the war interrupted his career, he had once reached the finals against Joe Hunt, but then came Pearl Harbor, and most of the players disappeared into the armed services, Kramer into the Coast Guard. When the war was over, they all come back—Kramer, Ted Schroeder, Don McNeill and the others—and Kramer began to clean up on the circuit. Despite the war, his game had matured. He was an exponent of "controlled power," and you sensed the seriousness of both of those words when you watched him or hit with him. He had an awesome serve, or, rather, several of them—a very hard first serve, usually hit with some slice; and, usually, an American twist second serve that bounced high and to your left, buzzing like a swarm of bees. Bobby Riggs once told me that it was Kramer's second serve that gave him the most trouble, leaping high and wide to Riggs' backhand. Riggs said he even hoped that Kramer would get the first hard one in when they played—at least you could deal with it. Invariably, Kramer followed his serve to the net, where, at over six feet, he was almost impossible to pass. My own opinion, for what it is worth, is that Kramer would beat Bjorn Borg on any surface but clay, and maybe there, too.

In those more relaxed days, the big players would spend the morning at the Club, playing one another for bet money, playing, often, with us junior players. Hitting out on the grass courts with Kramer—we called him "Jake"—was an extraordinary experience. What he liked to do was hit from the baseline, gradually increasing the power of his shots. He hit a very "heavy" ball, forehand and backhand, crunch, crunch, crunch. He and Riggs and Pancho Segura were friendly and generous with the junior tournament players. They would give us pointers about strokes, strategy, everything. Riggs had one peculiarity. He always had to bet, even if it was only a Coke. He would spot a junior three points and bet a soft drink on the game. Even watching a match, Riggs had to bet. "One Coke says the next serve is a fault." "Okay, you're on."

At the end of the day, we would sit on the clubhouse porch as the sprinkler system watered the thirty or so grass courts and the setting sun made rainbow effects in the arching streams of water and spray.

Tennis. Everything comes flowing back, everything.

I must have been a very young child at the time, but I remember a neighborhood squabble at the time over the great Davis Cup match between Don Budge and the German ace, Baron von Cramm. It was a tennis version of the Louis-Schmeling fight. Budge came from behind in the fifth and deciding set to win for the United States.

My family lived in a depression-wracked middle-class neighborhood in Queens. My father had gone to Dartmouth, and his father had been a wealthy and successful businessman, but the Thirties had wrecked his fortunes. We were, however, uncomplicated patriots. We didn't hate the Germans in that prewar year, but we wanted the *American,* Budge, to win. Astonishingly enough, I found that all of our depression-era middle-class neighbors were rooting for . . . Von Cramm and against the local boy from Los Angeles. I think I understood this at the time as pure snobbery. It was fancy to be for the foreigner, fancy to be for him, especially since he was a real baron. It was one of my first glimpses of one of the dynamics of liberalism, the snob motive. It is normal and ordinary to be for the American player . . . what a bore. We will be for the foreigner. Of course, we really aren't *for* him. We are using him to make a statement about ourselves.

Later on, as a mature player, I saw a lot of Don Budge, especially around the West Side Tennis Club. He talked straightforwardly about the Von Cramm match. It was the great moment of his career. In his charming and California way, he referred to the Baron as "Cramm."

It is possible that Don Budge hit an even heavier ball than Jack Kramer, especially off his explosive backhand. It is well-known that Budge used one of the heaviest rackets in the history of the game, and that his right arm was as muscular as the average athlete's thigh. One day around 1951, I stopped off in the pro shop at the West Side Club, and there was Budge with his huge bat held in a vise. He was taping strips of lead to the head of his racket. "What are you doing, Don?" I asked. "It puts more punch in my volley," he replied. I imagine it did.

In one of the greatest tennis spectacles I have ever seen, Budge played Jack Kramer in one of the early professional tournaments in the Stadium at Forest Hills. Kramer was at his peak and had totally dominated the amateur game. Budge was over the hill. But Budge won the first two sets. His astonishing backhand return of service—he was tall enough, and he hit over the ball—made it impossible for Kramer to follow the American twist, high-bouncing serve to net. Budge would just blast the ball. From the baseline, he could hold his own with Kramer. After two sets, Budge ran out of gas, and the world champion swept through the next three sets.

No doubt the greatest, most glamorous figure in the history of tennis was Big Bill Tilden. I knew little about him during the period after the war, but he was highly visible in and around the tennis scene, and my own life touched his very briefly.

For me and my 13- and 14-year-old tennis cronies who were competing in boys' tennis tournaments around Long Island and in New Jersey, Tilden was a sort of god. He hung around a lot at the Club in Forest Hills.

I happened to be taking lessons from two different pros at the time—they were confusing me with rival theories about the forehand—but they both, mysteriously, hated Tilden. One kept remarking that Tilden was "a pathetic fellow." The other said that Tilden was "a horse's ass." After that, he always dropped the subject.

This sort of thing meant nothing to me and my friends. We assumed they were jealous of Tilden. We knew that Tilden was over fifty years old, practically dead, but earlier that year he had blasted the current men's champion, Frank Parker, off the court, and earlier had done the same thing to a previous champion and current leading contender, Ted Schroeder. We assumed that if Tilden could do that when he was practically ready to crawl into the grave that he must have been uncontainable when he was at his peak. We were right.

Tilden struck me as extremely flamboyant and theatrical, traits I attributed to his having often played in such, to me, mythical locales as Paris, London, the Riviera, and California.

I remember playing set after set one morning at the Club with a young protégé Tilden had brought East with him from the Coast. As we struggled, Tilden himself sat above us on the clubhouse porch loudly coaching his young protégé: "Lob! Lob! Lob! Play his backhand. The backhand! Now! Go to the net! Attack, attack!"

To me, it all seemed overdone and even ridiculous—as did the tennis shirts Tilden favored, with large black and white vertical stripes, rather like the colors of a football referee. In the days of mandatory white clothes on the court, those shirts went over big with tennis officials. But, Tilden was Tilden.

However, Tilden did not care what they thought. He mostly ignored other adults. He preferred the company of junior boy players, and he was full of eye-widening tennis stories for us younger players. He explained, for example, how he had lost a Davis Cup match in Paris to the French team. Under the rules, the host country controls all the facilities, and the French froze the tennis balls. This was their answer to Tilden's serve. They kept the balls in a refrigerator under the stands, and brought them out every seven games. Tilden could not have served an ace with a howitzer. The competitive hearts of my friends and me went out to Big Bill. Imagine! The greatest player in the world, trapped on those damned clay courts in Paris and trying to play with frozen tennis balls.

One piece of advice Tilden gave me that summer seemed startling and even heroic. In July, trained to the hilt and enormously eager about my junior tournaments, I pulled an arm muscle— very painful. "Play right through it," Tilden said. "Dominate it." He indicated that nothing as laughably trivial as a mere muscle pain could possibly stand in *his* way. I now understand that Tilden could virtually ignore physical pain. Against all the advice of my coaches, I played right through it, and the arm healed.

In those days, I knew nothing about Tilden but what I saw on a daily basis or what I had read in the record books and in histories of tennis. A recent book by Frank Deford called *Big Bill Tilden*, however, throws an eerie and tragic light on this glamorous sports figure. Tilden's athletic greatness turns out to have been bound up inextricably with his peculiar psyche. Emotionally a cripple in most ways, he was able to focus his volcanic emotions—chief among them the desire to dominate—entirely on tennis. It seems to me doubtful that in the entire history of sports so much intelligence and so much passion has been focused so narrowly and so intensely.

Tilden's boyhood home in then-fashionable Germantown, Pennsylvania, was a chamber of psychological horrors. Nine years before Tilden was born, three earlier Tilden children, two girls and a boy, died of diphtheria. Three years before Tilden was born, his mother gave birth to another son, Herbert. Then she deeply desired a girl to replace the two she had lost.

When Tilden himself arrived, he was therefore a big disappointment.

The mother made the best of her bad luck by raising him as if he were a girl. Named William T. Tilden, Junior, he was actually called "June" throughout his childhood. He was kept out of school and tutored at home. The mother maintained the pretense that he was frail, and if not in fact ill, at least about to be ill. She would not let him die, as his sisters had died. On his 21st birthday, astonishingly enough, Tilden was actually given a debutante-style coming-out party.

Tilden's mother died in 1911, his father in 1915, and then, at the age of 22, apparently released psychologically by these deaths, the strange and isolated young man underwent a spectacular metamorphosis, one of the oddest stories in the history of sports, or indeed of the human psyche. He was reborn, as symbolized by his insistence on a name change. Henceforth, he was no longer "Junior," much less "June." He was William T. Tilden II.

So far in his life he had shown no promise and had accomplished nothing. As a tennis player, he had not even been good enough to make his college varsity team at Penn. Beginning in 1915, however, this newly invented being, William T. Tilden II, gave his life totally to tennis. "He suddenly was compelled to be supreme in the game of lawn tennis," recalls one acquaintance. "Nobody ever worked so hard at anything as he did at tennis." The word "compelled" there is precisely accurate. Some tremendous psychological force drove Tilden to the pinnacle of this sport.

The next year, 1916, when Tilden was 23—getting a bit long in the tooth in athletic terms—he ranked an insignificant 70th in the United States and lost in the first round at Forest Hills. Four years later, through total application, he had perfected the game that would make him the champion of the world and the best tennis player of all time. For nine consecutive years, he would be ranked first in the U.S. Largely because of the interest generated by Tilden's spectacular emergence and dominance, a new concrete stadium was built at the West Side Club in Forest Hills. In the year 1920, a second act of self-invention seems to have occurred, a new persona strode forth and the name changed again: "Big Bill Tilden." He had become a flamboyant world figure. He had made himself not only into a total player, possessing every shot plus numerous variations on every shot, but also into a total student of the game. In the following sentences which he later wrote, the word "love" should be understood as utterly central. Tilden expressed his powerful, but thwarted and impossible erotic feelings through tennis. "The great majority of players are not students of the game. It is the love of tennis that had led me to the point where I never hit a shot without conscious application of twist or the deliberate attempt to use none."

In view of the jail terms and scandals of Tilden's last years, what everyone knows about him is that he was a homosexual. As he aged, indeed, his manners grew more conspicuously effeminate. But all the evidence suggests that he was a practicing homosexual in only the most limited sense. Throughout his adult career he was extraordinarily narcissistic. It is doubtful that he ever had sexual relations, homosexual or otherwise, with anyone. The following contemporary account of his 1924 Davis Cup victory over Gerald Patterson of Australia is highly suggestive of his temperament: "Throughout the match, Tilden looked as if he were merely practicing strokes or experimenting with them. He paid comparatively little attention to Patterson's shots. If they were good, as they not infrequently were, he let them go, or, if he could reach them, he would return them with interest. But it was his own shots he was thinking of most of the time, studying them as if he were in a laboratory and they were specimens." Not at all surprisingly, when his tennis finally faded, he was drawn backward emotionally toward adolescence and searched among a series of boy players and other boys for some earlier version of himself.

He served time in jail toward the end of his life for homosexual behavior with young boys in California. On the evidence, the boys themselves were the aggressors and had picked Tilden up. And, on the evidence, very little happened. Tilden was entirely narcissistic and onanistic.

Today, there are no monuments to the game's greatest player, no Tilden trophies at the West Side Tennis Club, none at the new Louis Armstrong National Tennis Center in Flushing Meadow. His trophies from nine national championships, from the doubles championships, from Wimbledon and the Davis Cup matches, are in a warehouse in Los Angeles. He died old and broke and in disgrace.

A few days before his death through heart failure in 1953, at age 60, Tilden and a friend played doubles against a couple of Canadians who were on the U.C.L.A. team. Big Bill began the proceedings by announcing that this was a Davis Cup match, Canada versus the United States. "He was exhilarated," recalls one of the Canadians. "He conducted a draw," and, as they played, "He said things like 'Advantage, United States,' and 'Canada leads, four games to three, first set . . .' We were just playing to get some practice, but he was like a real tiger, and he agonized when they lost. It was all very real to him."

That was a flashback, to a career that peaked in the twenties and ended sadly in the Fifties. Now for a flash forward. Alice Marble had the most powerful all court game in the history of women's tennis. In the year 1950, when I was playing varsity tennis for Columbia, she taught me a lesson about women's equality. Marble, a tall Californian with exceptionally wide shoulders, was glamorous in a blond and weather-beaten way, but she was not especially feminine. She practically never played with other women. They did not hit the ball hard enough. One afternoon, another college player and I were playing doubles against Marble and another fellow out on the grass at West Side. Marble served her American twist and ran to the net. I had the settled opinion that women could not hit serious overhead smashes, so I threw the ball up to her and moved forward, expecting to volley her female smash. *Crack.* The thing went past me like a stone. It probably dug up the court.

I must record here one of the most astonishing phenomena in the history of the game. It is not clear to me why it is not better remembered. The phenomenon is Tom Brown, Jr.

The year was 1946, just after the war. It seemed to be, and in a sense it was, the rebirth of tennis. But, in retrospect, it was the beginning of the last act of the amateur phase of the game. What everyone was wondering was whether any of the players returning from the war could beat two-time national champion Frank Parker, the tennis machine. My own coach flatly predicted that Parker would win a third national championship, because his consistent stroke production would show up the—as we now know mythical—flaws in Kramer's game. A lot of players were coming back, Kramer, Schroeder, Don McNeill. McNeill was in especially good form, a former national champion with overspin drives off both sides. But then, all of a sudden, there was Tom Brown, Jr. of San Francisco, practically unknown. Earlier that year, unseeded, he had created a stir at Wimbledon with several upsets. Something unexpected seemed to be brewing. But his extraordinary week came during the National Championships at Forest Hills.

Tom Brown, Jr. was a rangy, loping player with short curly brown hair and muscles like hawsers. During the war he had been a fighting soldier, not a tennis-playing soldier entertaining the troops like most of the others. He had fought his way across Europe as a trench-mortar sergeant. That week, during the national championships at Forest Hills, Brown experienced a tremendous release of energy.

Brown's strokes on both sides were unorthodox. He was what the orthodox stigmatized as a "lift shot" artist, which meant that his stroke started low and ended high, imparting severe top-spin to the ball. A Tom Brown forehand or backhand would end with his racket pointing toward the sky. This type of shot is difficult to control, but control began to set in for Brown that week in Forest Hills. The sportswriters were writing that Brown was hitting the ball as hard off the ground as Ellsworth Vines had hit his famous forehand—but, of course, Brown was doing it with his backhand, too. He was hitting untouchable placements around the court from the baseline. Early in the tournament, Brown played the French champion, a giant named Evon Petra, who was given a fair chance to win the tournament. Brown simply blotted him out, and began to gather momentum. In addition to his unorthodox ground strokes, Brown had an unorthodox serve, hit facing the net with a sort of delayed motion. There was no way an opponent could tell which way this thing was going. Brown could swing it off court, spinning out of reach. Or, with the same peculiar undecipherable motion, he could scorch you with an ace down the center. I do not think I have ever seen a greater expenditure of athletic energy than Brown showed that week.

Brown had one glaring weakness. He could not really play the net. But that week he did not have to. In the quarter finals, he did the impossible. He defied science, statistics, all experience. He blasted Frank Parker off the court from the baseline. Those hissing whip-crack placements down the line and cross-court flowed from his racket. Parker could not believe what was happening. He kept taking off his tinted glasses and cleaning them. Unable to live with Brown from the baseline, Parker charged the net. Nothing availed. Parker was out of the tournament, and there would be no Parker-Kramer final. That day, against Frank Parker, Tom Brown, Jr.

hit more low-percentage winners than I—and I suspect anyone else—had ever seen in a match.

But Brown, unbelievably, got better.

In the semifinals, he played Gardner Mulloy, a superb craftsman. Mulloy had a relaxed grace and could trade shots with anyone. With Talbert, he had been national doubles champion numerous times. He could return serve, volley, do anything. But he had watched the evolution of Brown's game, and he knew he was in deep trouble. Before the match, back in the clubhouse at West Side, Mulloy was naturally puzzled about how he should deal with the Brown problem now confronting him. "You've got to go to net," the other players told him. "You just can't stand there and hit with this guy. He'll kill you. Go to net, and cut it off."

That was good and sane advice. Gardner Mulloy had fine stroke production. But it was obvious that he could not stand back and trade shots with Tom Brown, Jr. On the other hand, Mulloy was a great net player, as a repeated doubles champion would have to be. Mulloy decided to attack Brown from the net.

The trouble was that on that hot August afternoon in the Stadium at Forest Hills, Tom Brown, Jr. was hitting the ball so hard off the ground that it could not be cut off at the net. Mulloy, one of the quickest and best volleyers in tennis, found that he was dealing with rockets. The damned things could not be volleyed. Mulloy would hit a reasonable approach shot, run to the net, and an unorthodox screecher would come off Brown's racket. Several times, the force of Brown's shots blew the racket out of Mulloy's hand. Brown's shots were not at this point entirely under control. He was like a fast ball pitcher. A couple of times, when Mulloy hit a good approach shot and ran to the net, Brown's incredible bullets hit him in the chest, in the shoulder. Nothing worked for Mulloy. Tom Brown, Jr. that day was simply unplayable. Brown, beating Mulloy in straight sets, advanced to the finals against . . . Kramer.

"Jake," the greatest player of the post-war period and the dominant tennis figure of the 1950s, knew he had a real problem on his hands. In a jammed stadium, under a broiling Labor Day weekend sun, he took the court against Tom Brown, Jr. Watching the two players walk into the Stadium and begin warming up, I sensed that Kramer was nervous. He possessed all the tennis weapons that anyone would ever need, and he clearly stood in the line of succession to the great players of the past: Tilden, Vines, Budge, and Riggs. But he was not playing a known quantity, like

Mulloy or Frank Parker. He was playing Tom Brown, Jr., who seemed to have a couple of extra quarts of adrenaline in his system and was doing strange things with the tennis ball.

For the only time in his life, Kramer played conservatively. By no means did he want to trade shots with Brown. He clearly had calculated that he could keep winning his big serve, and he put all of his energy into doing so. He served a couple of untouchable serves in each of his service games, and otherwise ran to the net behind his leaping and buzzing American twist. But all through the first set Kramer failed to solve the Tom Brown problem. Brown was holding his crazy unorthodox serve, too. The damned thing was aceing Kramer. You could not tell where it was going to go. Nor did Brown feel the need to go to the net. He was content to stand on the baseline and hit outright winners past Kramer. Kramer! It is possible that Brown, on that day, could have won baseline exchanges with anyone in the history of tennis, even Tilden. Possibly a tennis ball has never been hit that hard off the ground. But Kramer held serve, held serve, and finally Brown made a couple of mistakes, and the set was over, and then the match was over.

(Incidentally, in 1968, I saw Tom Brown again. He is a San Francisco lawyer and a weekend player, and he was playing in a Sacramento tournament against Bob Lutz, an international class player half his age. Brown can still play. He took the first set from Lutz, before youth prevailed.)

Looking back, I think that the Tom Brown phenomenon was a symbolic moment, a turning point in the history of tennis. Brown, a soldier and a lawyer, was the Last Great Amateur. During the decade of the Fifties, tennis began to change rapidly. With the spread of affluence and leisure, millions of people began to take up the game. Tennis clubs sprang up in all of the new suburbs, coast to coast. The older aristocratic aura evaporated. The big money entered the picture, first with the one-on-one professional tours, then with the organized professional tournament circuit. Players not yet twenty, pimply adolescents and little girls, would become millionaires.

As might well be imagined, I have some mixed feelings about tennis as it has recently developed.

Of course there are more first-rate players now than there were in the Forties and Fifties. A couple of hundred of them are making honest livings in the pro ranks. I approve of all that. And Borg,

Connors, McEnroe, Jaeger, Austin, Shriver are enormously exciting players. For a couple of years I think I was in love with Chris Evert.

We do not now necessarily have greater players than in the now passed era. In my judgment, none of the top men stars today could have beaten Kramer or Budge, let alone Tilden. And, of course, the ethos is gone. Neither Caesar's Palace in Las Vegas nor the fine new Louis Armstrong Tennis Center in Flushing Meadow reminds me of Seabright or Longwood, and The Boston Lobsters do not carry overtones of Southhampton. Tennis is now entertainment. "Now that thing is gone," Scott Fitzgerald once wrote in a famous story, "That thing will come no more."

Reading over what I have written here about baseball and tennis, I see that it is pervaded by an elegaic tone, by a consciousness of endings. The late Forties and the Fifties were a beautiful era in sports. But eras come to an end and things change; even when they change for the better, and often they do not, something is inevitably lost. Sports make this especially vivid. We see a decade in baseball or tennis more clearly than in politics or in the general culture, because the field of vision is so well defined and because the stars observed are relatively few. But there is another sense, indeed more than one sense, in which sports press upon us the knowledge of endings. Here the experience of playing or watching sports differs from most other activities, and yet dramatizes something true about our lives.

Intellectuals, and academic intellectuals especially, customarily condescend to athletes and athletics. This is as true at Dartmouth, where I am an English professor, as it is elsewhere. But the experience of athletics is different in valuable ways from most academic experience. They key point is that athletic contests *come to an end*. The clock runs out, or the ninth inning ends, or you win or lose the last point. And it is over. Part of the experience of athletics resides in dealing with that finality—often a kind of death. This is not true of a seminar discussion or even a lecture; there is always more to be said. It is not true even of reading a book; you can always read the book again. That feature of the athletic experience, plus the experience of pursuing excellence, plus the requirements of courage and personal discipline, make athletics—as Homer, Plato and Aristotle knew, as Thomas Arnold of Rugby knew—vital to a liberal education.

And there is another feature of our relationship to athletes. In their athletic careers they enact the destiny to which we are all subject. The athlete undergoes an early death—the death of his talent, usually around age thirty. He still looks fine, but he is a step slower, his eye less keen, and he knows that the hungry generations are preparing to tread him down. The last competitive days of Babe Ruth, of Joe Louis, of Joe DiMaggio or Muhammad Ali, are almost unendurably painful emotionally, both for the player and for those who loved his athletic genius. They rise higher and therefore fall farther than the rest of us, and for this reason they prepare the rest of us for what we too will finally one day have to undergo. The beauty of the world is always passing, passing.

ESTES KEFAUVER

Richard Nixon sat in the paneled study on the ground floor of his Manhattan town house on East Sixty-fifth Street. He had mixed the drinks in the bar in the alcove off the study. "You have the most expensive bartender in Manhattan," he said. Now he relaxed in his leather chair and sipped his martini.

"That Kefauver," he went on, continuing a string of political anecdotes, "he was a real character. The coon-skin cap. He made a name in those crime investigations on television, and then he beat Truman in the 1952 New Hampshire primary. That was enough to end Truman. If he couldn't beat Estes in New Hampshire, he certainly couldn't beat Eisenhower or Taft in November. Truman had to get out.

"But the Democratic establishment certainly didn't want Estes at the top of the ticket. Something had to be done. Kefauver had to be beaten in the Florida primary. But who would do it? They decided that Senator Richard Russell was the man. Now Dick Russell was a great gentleman, a southern constitutionalist. He hated the idea of a rough and tumble fight with Kefauver in Florida. Dick Russell always won easily and decorously in Georgia. But they prevailed upon him, and Russell went down to Florida to stop Kefauver.

"One day, in the midst of the Florida campaign, Russell had

to come back to Washington for the Senate. We asked him
how the Florida campaign was going.

"Now you have to remember that Estes was a great man
with the women, a real swordsman.

"Well, Dick Russell said the Florida campaign was the
worst experience of his life. He hated every minute of it. 'That
Kefauver,' he said, 'He's going all over the state, with a Bible
in one hand and his cock in the other.' "

Nixon sipped his martini.

"Did you know," asked Nixon, "that I once actually saved
Drew Pearson's life?"

He sipped the martini again.

"I was having dinner at the Sulgrave Club in Washington,
and when I went down to the coatroom I saw Joe McCarthy in
there with his hands around Pearson's throat. He was stran-
gling him, also trying to knee him in the groin. McCarthy was
a big bear of a man—he'd been a boxer—and Pearson was beginning to turn grey. When McCarthy saw me, he gave Pearson a terrific slap in the face with one hand. 'That's one for
you, Dick,' he said. I grabbed him by the arm, and tried to
pull him off Pearson. 'You shouldn't be doing this,' I said. I
said something about letting a Quaker make peace here.

" 'He's an evil sonofabitch,' Joe said.

"While we were discussing Pearson's character, he scurried
out of the coatroom and got away."

Nixon sipped his martini. "It was pretty close," he said.

CHAPTER SEVEN

I Write the Songs

The sound of music. It surrounded me when I was a boy. Those were grim depression years, and we lived in a thirty-five-dollar-a-month apartment in Queens, but my mother had had minor dancing and singing parts in some of the great musicals of the Twenties. She rode on a swing in one of the *Ziegfeld Follies* before the bright lights of the New Amsterdam Theater. She knew Irving Berlin, W. C. Fields, and Eddie Cantor. She told me that Fields could not function on the stage without a few shots of whiskey. Without them, he wasn't funny at all. Mother's brother Walter was a songwriter, a cripple in a wheelchair who had published songs you could hear on the radio in the Thirties.

For several years, she played in *The Music Box Review,* in the Music Box Theater, a new theater built on 45th Street for a million dollars by Irving Berlin and Sam Harris. The new theater was known for its elegance, scenery, tableaux, its spare-no-expense productions. In 1921, *The Music Box Review,* with a top price of five dollars a ticket—the highest on Broadway at the time—ran for 441 performances and made half a million dollars. For the successive *Reviews,* Irving Berlin wrote most of the music, hits like "Say It With Music," "Everybody Step," and "Lady of the Evening." One of the stars, Billy Gaxton, was a good friend of Mother's. She played in *Poppy* and *Showboat,* one of the landmarks of American theater, with book and lyrics by Oscar Hammerstein and music by

Jerome Kern: "Ol' Man River," "Bill," "Can't Help Lovin' Dat Man," "Why Do I Love You?" I've dropped in a couple of times at Mother's old dressing room at the Music Box. Most recently it has been occupied by Marian Seldes, the intelligent and beautiful star of the murder-thriller *Death Trap*. I've always been struck by the penury of these accommodations, even in the big time, with their cheap furniture and exposed backstage steam pipes, all somehow the glamor.

It was music and the memory of the theater that sustained my mother through the grim years of depression and war. She hated the whole idea of war. As a young actress, she and the company from the musicals had entertained in the veterans' hospitals and seen the men brought back from Belleau Wood and the Argonne, people with no arms, no legs, faces shot to pieces, lungs destroyed by mustard and chlorine gas. In 1940, she voted for Wilkie—"One-man rule leads down the road to *warrr*," Wilkie shouted hoarsely over the radio, while Franklin Roosevelt proclaimed that he had said "again and again" that American boys would not fight in foreign wars. Mother was an expert pianist, and our little apartment in Queens was alive with the show tunes of the Twenties and Thirties. I remember that she even had a marvelous red silk dress with pennies sewn into it, a design based on the depression-era Bing Crosby hit song, "Pennies From Heaven."

With the end of World War II, my family, like many others, had more money to spend, and mother could go to the theater more often, weekly even, sometimes taking me along to a matinee.

No one thought of it that way at the time, but in retrospect, the ten years following the war were the climactic years, the triumphant years, of a great phase in American popular music. It was the golden era of a period that had begun before the First World War with the emergence of a surprising number of talented popular songwriters and composers, most of them Jewish. They were the men of "Tin Pan Alley": Irving Berlin, Jerome Kern, George Gershwin, Richard Rodgers, Lorenz Hart, Oscar Hammerstein, Stephen Sondheim and—from the Midwest, Yale and gentile private wealth—Cole Porter. These men perfected a tradition, which produced an extraordinary popular music between 1945 and 1955, and then suddenly gave way before the creative explosion of Rock and Roll, which drew on black and regional sources. In the popular music of America, you can trace the ethnic, regional, political and emotional life of the nation.

I am not going to attempt to write a history of the popular music of the Fifties here. That would take a large volume, so rich, various, and energetic is the period. What I would like to do is outline the larger shapes of Fifties music, and recall some of the major and representative figures. In the Fifties, we see an older tradition reach perfection, then be displaced by an unforeseeable development, a revolution in musical form energized by black, country, and foreign traditions. We see the musical focus of America move away from Manhattan and off to the Sunbelt and to rural and religious America. These developments clearly coincide with profound changes in the life of America in the Fifties.

The American show tune of the first half of the twentieth century conformed to a formula as rigid as any sonnet or sestina, but these composers and songwriters learned to enrich the formula by lifting tunes and musical devices from the classical music of the nineteenth century. Within the formula, they exercised an extraordinary inventiveness, and the songs they wrote for the great musicals, and for movies and records, will always be sung. The song formula resembled a romantic opera in miniature. It set forth the dramatic situation in a couple of very short stanzas, three or four lines each. Then you got the lyrical and romantic "chorus," which most listeners regarded as the "song."

Time and again I've longed for adventure,
    Something to make my heart beat the faster.
What did I long for? I never really knew.

Finding your love I've found my adventure,
    Touching your hand, my heart beats the faster,
All that I want in all of this world is you.

You are the promised kiss of springtime
That makes the lonely winter seem long.
You are the breathless hush of evening
That trembles on the brink of a lovely song.
You are the angel glow that lights a star,
The dearest things I know are what you are.
Some day my happy arms will hold you,
And some day I'll know that moment divine,
When all the things you are, are mine.

"All the Things You Are" (1939),
    Jerome Kern and Oscar Hammerstein II

It was powerful and romantic stuff. It was verbally unimpressive, awful poetry, but with its musical back-up, it worked. We danced to it then, and it dominated popular culture until the middle Fifties, providing the basis for the great musicals of the postwar period. These writers took over from classical music the technique of creating forward momentum by arranging chords in a pattern which led to a musical climax, and through melodic sequence, that is patterns of melody repeated at different pitch levels. They created an entirely different effect from previous American popular music. They also drew on the rhythmic patterns of ragtime and the Harlem jazz bands of the Twenties.

One of the great musicals of all time opened on April 7, 1949, at the Majestic Theater. Popular jokes and comic routines quickly developed about the strategems and humiliations people would go through to get tickets to it. *South Pacific* was adapted by Rodgers and Hammerstein from James Michener's *Tales of the South Pacific,* and it starred Mary Martin and the opera singer Ezio Pinza, who now appeared for the first time on the popular stage. "It is a thrilling and exultant musical play," said Ward Morehouse in the *Sun*. Brooks Atkinson wrote that it was "a tenderly beautiful idyll of genuine people" in *The New York Times*. "Pearls, pure pearly . . . rare enchantment," reported Harold Barnes in the *Herald Tribune*. Richard Watts in the *Post* called it "an utterly captivating work of theatrical art." They were right.

Against the exotic background of a French-run Pacific island captured from the Japanese during the war, the plot revolves around a romance between an American nurse, Ensign Nellie Forbush, and a wealthy middle-aged plantation owner named Emile deBecque. *South Pacific* was unique among musicals in the relationship that existed between the songs and the characters who sang them. Rodgers said: "I tried to weave his [deBecque's] personality into his songs—romantic, rather powerful, but not too involved." Thus Ezio Pinza's "Some Enchanted Evening" and "This Nearly Was Mine." Rodgers went on: "Nellie Forbush is a Navy nurse out of Arkansas, a kid whose musical background had probably been limited to the movies, radio, and maybe a touring musical comedy. It gave me a chance for a change of pace, and the music I composed for her is light, contemporary, and rhythmic." Mary Martin sang "I'm Gonna Wash That Man Right Outa My Hair" and "A Wonderful Guy." The Tonganese Bloody Mary sings the wonderful "Bali Ha'i," and the young naval man,

Lieutenant Cable, has "Younger Than Springtime." South Pacific ran for 1,925 performances on Broadway and set a new box office record of $2.5 million, in its first year. Before it closed, it was seen by three and a half million people who paid more than nine million dollars at the box office. It won every available award, including the Pulitzer Prize for Drama.

Astonishingly enough, while *South Pacific* was still playing to packed houses at the Majestic Theater, Rodgers and Hammerstein came forward with another incandescent musical, *The King and I,* starring Yul Brynner and the great Gertrude Lawrence. It opened on March 29, 1951, at the St. James Theater and was based on a novel by Margaret Landon, *Anna and the King of Siam,* about a widowed school teacher who is brought to Siam by the king to teach English to his large brood of children. Rodgers brilliantly solved the problem of creating an oriental atmosphere by means of small and subtle changes in melodic and harmonic structure. Jerome Robbins' choreography included a ballet, and the production was full of great songs, such as "Hello, Young Lovers" and "Getting to Know You."

The extraordinary sequence of Rodgers and Hammerstein musicals during the Fifties—*Me and Juliet* (1953), *Pipe Dream* (1955), *The Flower Drum Song* (1958)—concluded with *The Sound of Music* in 1959, a kind of operetta combined with a musical play, about the famous Trapp family of Austrian singers. Rodgers captured the spirit of Austrian folk song with "Edelweiss," and the production included such brilliant numbers as "Do-Re-Mi," in which Mary Martin, playing Maria, teaches the children to sing.

Merely to list the most popular of the many songs written by Richard Rodgers is to suggest the magnitude of an achievement flowing forward from the mid-1920s into the Fifties. His first big hit was "The Blue Room" (1926), followed by "My Heart Stood Still" (1927), "With a Song in My Heart" (1929), "Blue Moon" (1934), and "It's Easy to Remember" (1935). When "Your Hit Parade" came on the air in April, 1935, its first number one song was Rodgers' "Soon" from the movie *Mississippi*. He followed with "This Can't Be Love" (1938) and "People Will Say We're in Love" (1943, from *Oklahoma*) which was broadcast for thirty straight weeks; then "Oh, What a Beautiful Morning" (1943), "If I Loved You" (1945), "It Might as Well Be Spring" (1945, from the movie *State Fair*), "Some Enchanted Evening" (1949, among songs from *South Pacific*), "Bali Ha'i" (1949) and "No Other Love" (1953). Rodgers tied Irving Berlin for first place in *Variety*'s list of the "Golden Hundred" songs of the Broadway era.

Harold Arlen is less well known to the general public than Richard Rodgers, but he ranks just behind Berlin and Rodgers in the Golden Hundred, with seven songs. Arlen's "Blues in the Night" (1941) was a big hit in the movie of the same name. Pearl Bailey's first major role came in *St. Louis Woman* (1944), with music by Harold Arlen. His "It's Only a Paper Moon" (1933) has retained its popularity through every vicissitude of taste. Judy Garland sang his "Over the Rainbow" in *The Wizard of Oz* (1939). He wrote "That Old Black Magic" (1942), and "Come Rain or Come Shine" (1946). The list of successful song writers could be greatly extended, through Vincent Youmans, Jimmy McHugh, Walter Donaldson, Hoagy Carmichael, Duke Ellington and others.

The great songs of the Broadway era were designed for an eastern, sophisticated, mostly middle-class and white audience. While these songs fanned out across the country on the airwaves, they were not part of a rural, western or southern culture at the grass roots level. When the Rock and Country revolution hit in the mid-Fifties, it represented an eruption of popular strains of music and culture that had been obscured by the predominance of the Broadway hit tune. The advent of the "big band" in the 1930s, and then the "big singer" in the 1940s, did not change the kind of song that achieved wide popularity. The big Broadway song had not changed in form for fifty years, but as the Broadway era drew to a close during the Forties and early Fifties, evidence existed that audiences wished for more variety, in form, but also in regional and cultural flavor. "Come on-a My House" (1951) exhibited new rhythms. A taste for Western themes was expressed in such hits as "Mule Train" (1949), "On the Atchison, Topeka, and the Santa Fe" (1945), and "Ghost Riders in the Sky" (1949). These were premonitory tremors. As the twentieth century passed its midpoint and moved into the Fifties, the Broadway style had been dominant since the turn of the century. Manhattan was the capital of the music business, and Broadway was the place where the great musicals appeared.

The tremendous box-office success of *The Jolson Story* (1946) and *Jolson Sings Again* (1949) persuaded Hollywood that a major audience existed for the musical movie, and the Fifties saw major popular songs written for the screen. *Three Little Words* (1950), with Fred Astaire and Debbie Reynolds, had "I Wanna Be Loved by You," and 1951 brought *I'll See You in My Dreams,* with Danny Thomas and Doris Day. In 1952, Susan Hayward played Jane Froman, the singer who had been seriously injured during the war, in a movie called *With a Song in My Heart,* which included the title song by Rodgers and Hart, plus "Embraceable You," by the Gershwin brothers, "Blue Moon" (Rodgers and Hart), "That Old Feeling" (Les Brown and Sammy Fain) and many others. The songs were there for these and countless other musical films during the Forties and Fifties because of the eastern and urban tradition that had been born early in the century in Tin Pan Alley, as Broadway was affectionately known. Thus the theme song from the movie *Moulin Rouge* (1952), starring Jose Ferrer as Toulouse Lautrec, climbed to the top of the charts and rivaled the great hits from the Broadway stage.

Popular songs also created an audience for star singers, and the period after the war could also be called the era of the Big Singer, who quickly eclipsed the Big Band of the late Thirties and Forties. Bing Crosby of course is legendary, but there was also Frank Sinatra, who became the biggest male erotic sensation since Rudolph Valentino. Dick Haymes, who had sung with the Harry James and Benny Goodman bands, became a soloist in 1943 and had major successes with "It Can't Be Wrong" and "You'll Never Know." Dinah Shore left the Xavier Cugat band for a solo career and scored her first big success with the marvelous "I'll Walk Alone" in 1944. And among the Big Singers of the late Forties and early Fifties, we also had Perry Como, Mel Torme, Sammy Kaye, Jo Stafford, Patti Page, the Andrews Sisters, and Nat "King" Cole. Eddie Fisher was all set to become the new Bing Crosby/Frank Sinatra when the Rock Revolution rolled over him and over the "formula" songs he sang, which had dominated the first half of the century.

In black slang, the phrase "rock and roll" means sex, and it appears to have first been put in general circulation and attached to a particular kind of music by Alan Freed, a Cleveland disc jockey, in 1951. Freed had been told by a record dealer that teenagers were buying recordings of black rhythm and blues groups in staggering quantities, and Freed decided to put some of that music on the air. The response was overwhelming. Freed had stumbled on the fact that there existed out there a new and hitherto unidentified audience that was going berserk about a kind of music generally considered marginal. Freed was deluged with requests for rhythm and blues music, so many that he responded by starting a new radio show which he called "Moon Dog's Rock and Roll Party"—he had found the word "rock and roll" in a rhythm and blues number. On the air, Freed often shouted in rhythm with the music, yelling "go man, go," and "yeah, yeah, yeah." He pounded the table with his fist. His audience wanted the insistent, hypnotic beat, and they liked the implicit and explicit sexuality of the songs. The insistent rhythm itself has a sexual character, bong, bong, bong. In his commentary between discs, Freed egged his young audience on in their rebellion against their parents and against the official mores of the society.

In 1951, white song writers and groups began to experiment with this kind of music. Bill Haley recorded "Rocket 88" in Philadelphia and then wrote "Rock a-Beaten Boogie," which began with the line "rock, rock, rock everybody, roll, roll, roll everybody." This was *The Kinsey Report* set to music. In 1952, a white group called The Ravens recorded "Rock Me All Night Long." The effect was explosive. This music was no "Some Enchanted Evening." This music was about *doing it!* It was a music of rebellion, certainly, but the protest it voiced was not directed at any great public political issue. It had nothing to do with the rights of blacks or anything of the sort. It had everything to do with what went on in the back seat of a car or down at the beach on a summer night. In 1953, a rock jamboree organized by Alan Freed drew eighty thousand people to Cleveland Stadium—which held only ten thousand. The resulting melee forced the cancellation of the show. When Freed appeared at the Paramount Theater in Brooklyn, he broke box-office records that had been established by Frank Sinatra in the Forties.

In 1954, Freed widened his audience by moving to station WINS in New York. "I'll never forget the first time I heard the Freed show," wrote Clark Whelton in *The New York Times*. "I couldn't believe sounds like that were coming out of a radio. In 1954 radio was Gruen Watch commercials, soap operas, and Snooky Lanson Hit Parade music . . . Alan Freed jumped into radio like a stripper into Swan Lake. He was a teenager's mind funneled into 50,000 watts." Imitators of Freed quickly spread the Rock Revolution to every city in the country.

The first big rock hit was "Rock Around the Clock," written 1953 by Max Freedman and Jimmy DeKnight. It went unnoticed until Bill Haley and the Comets recorded it for Decca, in 1955 and also played it for the sound track of the movie *Blackboard Jungle*. "To say that 'Rock Around the Clock' was a sensation," wrote Lillian Roxon, "is a rare understatement. It was the 'Marseillaise' of the teenage revolution . . . It became the first song to have a special secret defiant meaning for teenagers only. It was the first inkling teenagers had that they might be a force to be reckoned with, in numbers alone." "Rock Around the Clock" meant sexual utopia. This recording by Haley and The Comets went to the top of the charts and became one of the largest selling singles ever made.

Bill Haley claimed, with some reason, to be the founder of rock and roll. He contributed some of its distinguishing features in its early phase—the insistent, heavy beat with guitars and drums dominating the melody, the shouted rather than sung lyrics, the repetitious phrasing, the ear-splitting electronic amplification that contributed to the atmosphere of feverish excitement, the use of the Fuzz Box, which blurred sounds, and the Wahwah Pedal, which produced nasal twangs.

But if Haley was in on the beginnings of rock, he could not be its hero. Small and plump, with his hair plastered in a curl in the middle of his forehead, he was hardly a figure to embody a kind of music in which sexuality was so central and sometimes brutally explicit: "Baby, Let Me Bang Your Box," and "Drill, Daddy, Drill." The world of rock found its hero in Elvis Presley. "Before Elvis," Nick Cohen wrote in *Rock,* "rock had been a gesture of vague rebellion. Once he'd happened, it immediately became solid, self-contained . . . it spawned its own style in clothes and language and sex, a total independence in almost everything . . . he became one of the people who radically affected the way other people think and live." He was the incarnation of the rock meaning.

Presley hit the big time in 1955 with television appearances on the Milton Berle and the Steve Allen shows and three appearances on Ed Sullivan's "Toast of the Town."

A country singer named Bob Luman describes, in *Nashville Sound,* a characteristic Presley concert performance: "This cat came out in red pants and a green coat and a pink shirt and socks, and he had this sneer on his face and he stood behind the mike for five minutes, I'll bet, before he made a move. Then he hit his guitar a lick, and he broke two strings. I'd been playing ten years, and I hadn't broken a *total* of two strings. So there he was, these two strings dangling, and he hadn't done anything yet, and these high school girls were screaming and fainting and running up to the stage, and then he started to move his hips real slow like he had a thing for his guitar."

Presley had been discovered by Sam Phillips, who ran Sun Records in Memphis and had an insight that turned out to be spectacularly correct. "Over and over," recalls Marion Keisker, Phillips' secretary, "I remember Sam saying, 'If I could find a white man who had the black sound and the black feel, I could make a billion dollars." Sam Phillips found him in Presley. If you closed your eyes when Presley was singing, you could imagine that you were listening to a southern black. He had grown up in the midst of black musical culture. His religious roots in evangelical Christianity were similar. He expressed a direct sexuality that seemed more black than white, though it was part of the new rock culture, and he was a master of the exuberant rock beat that was flowing out of black music into white culture. Powerful emotions were involved.

Consciously or by accident, Presley also brought together visual elements that had been prepared by the Fifties, but which he combined with a new intensity. Tony Curtis had had the ducktail. Brando, in *The Wild One,* had the truculent expression. Robert Mitchum had the sneer. Presley's synthesis of these things expressed a kind of derision, a derision directed at adult "normal" culture. His physical being provided a visual metaphor for what amounted to a revolutionary attack.

At the end of 1955, Victor Records released two of the songs Presley had recorded for Sun, "I Forgot to Remember to Forget" and "Mystery Trail." In 1956 came his first recordings for Victor, "Heartbreak Hotel" and "I Was the One." It sold over two million and won a gold disc. The rest is musical history. In 1956, his records were at the top of the charts for twenty-five weeks: "I Want You, I Need You, I Love You," "Hound Dog," "Love Me Tender," "Any Way You Want Me," and other hits. His records sold ten million, and in his first five years as a superstar he accumulated thirty-eight gold discs, unprecedented, with gross sales of $150 million.

By 1958, though no one guessed it at the time, he had made his contribution as an artist. He entered the army in 1958, and rock fans eagerly anticipated his release in 1960. There were other rock stars, but none seemed capable of moving further in the vein of early rock. When Presley returned from the army, he made some good recordings and some tumultuous personal appearances, but it was largely repetition, and sometimes had an element of self-parody.

The rock musician who might have deepened and sophisticated the rock tradition, Buddy Holly, out of Lubbock, Texas, died in a plane crash in 1959, at the age of twenty-two. In the famous phrase of Don McLean in "American Pie," this was "the day the music died." McLean wrote the great eulogy for the passing of the early phase of American rock. Holly, with his horn-rimmed glasses and cleancut looks, expressed none of Presley's sexual menace. His songs often had a light-hearted bounce and a joking quality, a wink, as one critic said, rather than Presley's snarl. He was a thorough student of the American tradition of popular music and had the capacity to draw on multiple styles. As Malcolm Jones put it in an English rock magazine, Holly "scored with a dazzling series of firsts in an era when everyone followed the flock. He was one of the first white rock stars to rely almost exclusively on his own material. The Crickets were probably the first white group to feature the lead/rhythm/bass/drums lineup. He was the first rock singer to double-track his voice and guitar. He was the first to use strings on a rock and roll record. In addition, he popularized the Fender Stratocaster and was probably the only rock star to wear glasses on stage."

Holly was a master technician, and he was unusual in the rock tradition in that his music had minimal sexual/rebellious expression, and he himself liked to observe that his music did not drive a wedge between young and old. In the fall of 1957, "That'll Be the Day" by Holly and The Crickets was a tremendous success both here and in England, reaching number one in both countries. Other hits followed for both The Crickets and Holly in 1958, "Oh, Boy," "Maybe Baby," and "Think It Over." "Peggy Sue" was the first big hit for Holly alone. He toured the country and appeared on the Ed Sullivan show. At the age of twenty-two, his ability and accomplishment made his future seem unlimited. On February 3, 1959, he was killed when he crashed in a four-seater chartered plane in Clear Lake, Iowa.

The American rock and roll tradition had been thoroughly absorbed by some young men in Liverpool, England. They knew the work of Haley, Presley, Holly. In 1956, John Lennon, then fifteen, and Paul McCartney, then thirteen, began playing as the Quarrymen. They were joined in 1958 by George Harrison, a fifteen-year-old guitar player. Known successively as the Moondogs, then the Silver Beatles, they acquired an astute manager in Brian Epstein, who ran a record business, and a drummer in Ringo Starr. Finally known as The Beatles, they brought the American tradition of rock and roll back across the Atlantic in the Sixties, rejuvenated it and complicated it and made possible the major new musical developments of the Sixties.

The richness of the American musical culture of the Fifties is suggested by the mention of other groups who stood somewhat outside the main line of rock and roll. The Everly Brothers, Phil and Don, created a special fusion of white country music with rock.

The Kingston Trio will always be associated by many people who heard them at the time with the last years of the Fifties. Though two of the trio had been born in Hawaii and one in California, they had an Ivy League look about them, with short hair and collegiate shirts. They all sang and played the guitar, and Dave Guard also played the banjo. They were scholars of the American folk tradition, and "Tom Dooley," their first great success, was an adaptation of an 1868 folk song from the Blue Ridge Mountains about a man named Tom Dooley who was hanged for murdering his girl friend. In 1959, they scored again with "Tijuana Jail" and "Worried Man," the latter adapted from another American folk song. The Kingston Trio favored small clubs, like "The Hungry i" in San Francisco. Between songs, they could be iconoclastic and humorous, but often Dave Guard would explain the background of the upcoming song, initiating the audience into some knowledge of the folk and other traditions, extending the audience's range of cultural reference, appealing to an audience better educated, perhaps, than most popular groups.

The Kingston Trio, which is still active today, always struck me as the aristocrats of popular groups, and they are memorable for such songs as "Lemon Tree," "Scotch and Soda," "Jane, Jane, Jane," "This Land is Your Land," "En El Agua," and "They Call the Wind Maria." The ballad "Where Have All the Flowers Gone?" is now perhaps best known as a Joan Baez song of protest against the Vietnam war, but the Kingston Trio had introduced it several years earlier without the political overtone. It was a traditional Russian folk ballad in the vein of "Where are the snows of yesteryear?," a nonpolitical song of loss and regret. Later on these songs, like "This Land is Your Land," introduced by Pete Seeger, became leftist hymns. But the Kingston Trio somehow depoliticized their music, let the folk traditions exist in their own beauty, and without insistent "relevance."

In the Sixties and early Seventies, rock music reached its technical apogee. It became subtler, absorbed the idioms of serious modern music and the electrified instruments of avant-garde composers. It brought in other exotic instruments, and, as its young audience followed these developments, it created a mass audience of surprising musical sophistication. It had all begun with the LP musical revolution of the early Fifties, which created a mass audience for good music. For the most part, nevertheless, the adult population remained fiercely hostile to rock and its influence. Local governments removed rock from jukeboxes. Many communities banned rock concerts because of the extravagant behavior associated with the August 1969 Woodstock Rock Festival, which attracted 300,000 people to a six-hundred acre area in New York State. Though it was supposed to be a festival of "peace and love," the property damage and personal injury was extensive. In December of that year, the Rolling Stones gave a free concert at the Altamont Speedway near San Francisco. A gang of Hell's Angels had been hired to sit on the stage and act as bouncers and bodyguards. They were paid in beer, with which they washed down pills. In the mounting tension produced by a long delay, a scuffle ensued, motorcycles were tipped over, a black youth was stabbed to death, and there were plenty of other injuries.

By the late Seventies, the whole extraordinary development had come to an end. A new generation had to be content with the banality of disco. The music really had died. But it all began back in the Fifties, with Alan Freed, Bill Haley, and "Rock Around the Clock."

WILLIAM F. BUCKLEY, JR.

The year was 1956, and something new and strange was in the air. A large Harvard crowd had turned out to hear William F. Buckley, Jr. debate the liberal editor of *The New York Post,* James Wechsler.

Buckley had entered public consciousness when, a year out of Yale, he had published *God and Man at Yale*. This book had caused a furor by stating publicly what everyone knew was fact—that the Ivy League establishment was liberal. It was committed neither to the economic views nor the religious and moral views of most alumni, or, at least, the views they publicly proclaimed. The big establishment guns of the book-reviewing world had been rolled out to repel Buckley's attack.

At Yale, it was well known, Buckley had been the editor of the student newspaper, *The Yale News,* from which podium he had roasted the liberal faculty. At Yale, he had been a formidable debater. After a couple of public encounters, the faculty declined to debate with him. After *God and Man at Yale,* Buckley had started a new conservative magazine, *National Review,* bright and sassy.

That night, in the spring of 1956, Harvard's Sanders Theater was packed. The crowd did not know what to expect, but it knew that something was going to happen. Buckley had a legendary reputation as a debater, but Wechsler was no slouch either.

Buckley, his wife, Pat, Wechsler, and a student moderator entered from the rear and walked down the center aisle. The Buckleys were flamboyant. Pat, who is around six feet tall, wore an enormous round leopard-skin hat and carried a large leopard-skin handbag. Buckley grinned and waved. This was no tacky, defensive, lower-middle-class conservatism, this was not Westbrook Pegler or George Sokolsky or Henry J. Taylor. This was something entirely new.

Buckley, Wechsler, and the student made their way to the platform. Wechsler was perky and confident and wore a polka-dot bow tie. After introductions, he led off with his opening remarks.

What Wechsler said was orthodox enough, and he spoke with conviction. Liberalism was not dead, he maintained. In fact, liberalism was central to the American tradition. Liberalism had compassion. Wechsler cited the poor and the black. He looked back to the New Deal, which had saved American capitalism. But above all, he said, liberalism was pragmatic and flexible. It could change with changing problems. Whatever it was that was new in Buckley's conservatism, he concluded, was certainly unsound—and what was not new we had seen under Coolidge and Hoover.

Wechsler, a Columbia graduate, gazed down over his bow tie and met the approving gaze of Harvard historian Arthur Schlesinger, Jr., who was sitting in the fourth row, and also wearing a bow tie. Schlesinger had written a book about liberalism called *The Vital Center*. Liberalism was the center, between the extremes of Robert Taft and the Marxist Left. That night at Harvard, Wechsler had delivered Schlesinger's position to the audience. Schlesinger beamed and applauded. The whole Harvard crowd applauded.

William F. Buckley, Jr. got up and moved to the podium. When he spoke, his manner was ironic, droll, elegant. He affected weariness at having to state the obvious. He had noticed Arthur Schlesinger, Jr. there in the fourth row.

"I am glad to see present here," Buckley said, "Professor . . . Arthur . . . Schlesinger . . . Junior. Of course," Buckley went on, "the accumulated works of . . . Professor Schlesinger . . . would be dangerous . . . if they weren't so boring."

The crowd in Sanders Theater, after an initial intake of breath, loved it. They had been used to regarding Schlesinger as an academic god. Buckley was outrageous, iconoclastic, entertaining. Even Schlesinger was roaring with laughter. Buckley's languidly delivered barbs made him seem not quite American. He was something out of the 1890s, the era of Whistler, Beardsley, Wilde. The Ivy League was supposed to be aristocratic. Well, Buckley *was* aristocratic. The Ivy League was supposed to have style. Buckley *had* style. You would not have been surprised to see him leading a lobster on a leash.

"Mister . . . Wechsler," Buckley said, "is . . . so perfect a liberal . . . that he should be placed permanently in the Smithsonian."

The idea was irresistible, and the crowd roared. Wechsler, bow tie and all, the Complete Liberal, would be stuffed and placed on permanent exhibition, like Jeremy Bentham at London University, where you can still see the eighteenth-century philosopher in a glass case.

"The academic world," Buckley was saying, "contains the biggest collection of cranks and extremists this side of the nut house. As a matter of fact, I would rather be governed by the first three hundred names in the Boston telephone book than by the faculty of Harvard University."

The audience in Sanders Theater ate it up. One thought of the Oxford theologian, who was famous for the tutorials he conducted while rolled up and invisible inside a rug, and the Harvard biblical scholar who, winter and summer, wore a long black overcoat and galoshes. Buckley was at the same time outrageous and sound. A Nobel Prize in microbiology is not a guarantee of political common sense.

"It is a curious fact," Buckley observed, "that alumni are held in great disesteem by students, which is strange indeed considering that only flunking out, taking the academic veil, or dying, will rescue them from the inevitable fate of alumnihood. That contempt is shared by—indeed, it originates with—the faculty and administration. Herman Hickman used to say, when he coached football at Yale, 'I believe in keeping the alumni sullen, but not mutinous.' The colleges today have gone way beyond that. Alumni bodies get pushed around far more than Herman Hickman's unsuccessful teams ever did—

only they never fight back any more. They are rapidly earning the contempt the students hold for them."

Buckley did not spare the Republicans. He said that "The most analytical statement made by Thomas E. Dewey during the 1948 campaign had been, 'Ladies and gentlemen, the future lies before us.' "

"Mr. Eisenhower," he observed, "has always had difficulty in describing the Eisenhower program. It is a difficulty traceable to something more subtle than the difficulty he has in formulating a phrase. . . ."

He spotted John Kenneth Galbraith in the audience. "Professor Galbraith," he said, "is horrified by the number of Americans who have bought cars with tail fins on them. I . . . am horrified by the number of Americans who take seriously the proposals of Mr. Galbraith."

Wechsler was articulate but predictable. Harvard agreed with his liberalism but, aesthetically, was tired of it. The year was 1956, and something new was stirring in American politics.

CHAPTER EIGHT

Lucy, Jack, and Ed

Beginning about 1949, a powerful new force entered American life. It not only changed marketing, politics, behavior, style, it changed *consciousness*. It altered the harmony, rhythm, perhaps even altered metabolism. During the 1920s, millions of homes acquired radios for the first time. America became alive with sound, music from open windows on summer nights. Radio also created a stronger national consciousness, a transcontinental consciousness. New Yorkers tuned in shows from Los Angeles. The entire country listened to Roosevelt's fireside chats from the White House. For the first time in history, news became instantaneous on a mass basis. Radio was powerful, but it also permitted the listener a degree of physical freedom. The housewife could do the dishes while listening to an afternoon soap opera. You could wash the car while listening to the ball game. Television changed all that.

Beginning in 1949, millions of Americans became stationary in front of the Tube. Television, thus, is much more imperial in its claims on the consciousness than radio. You cannot easily perform other activities. And because television is visual as well as aural, it created a more comprehensive reality than radio was able to achieve. It gathered to itself more of the senses, invited you to live in its alternative reality.

Rick Mitz was a young boy during the early years of television, the birth of the medium during the Fifties. He is doubtless an extreme case, but millions of Americans participated to one degree or another in his experience, which he describes in his zany but wonderful *The Great TV Sitcom Book*:

> I am a child of the tube. I was born on a Wednesday, ten minutes past "The Honeymooners." I was born on the cusp between Bilko and the Beaver. Lucy is my rising star. My sign is Panasonic. . . .
>
> Sitcoms were my babysitters, my guardians, a mini-community within a television chassis, full of magic tricks. Miss Brooks and Mr. Peepers were the teachers. Mr. Ed brought wildlife to the television environs and moved right next door to our country cousins, the Beverly Hillbillies. Susie McNamara, that publicly private secretary, showed us what the world of business was all about. Amos 'n' Andy integrated the television neighborhood and moved in next door to Molly Goldberg who dispensed chicken soup right through the TV screen. . . .
>
> But sitcoms aren't an end to themselves. I have tried to integrate them into the rest of my life. From them I have learned a fractured sense of American ethics. I have learned how to behave; that good conversation is witty and chatty; that funny lines come once every twenty-eight seconds; that I get two minutes off every thirteen minutes for a commercial break. . . .
>
> While my parents were across the hall yelling at each other, I hid away in my room, watching my portable black-and-white, playing voyeur to a neighborhood of television families that got along better than we did. When Paul Petersen had a problem, his mother, Donna Reed, and his father, Carl Betz, dealt with him respectfully and lovingly. Donna Reed didn't scream at her kids to clean up their room. On the other hand, Donna's kids never gave her the problems I gave my mother. I screamed and ranted and rebelled. "Aw shucks," was about all the lip Donna got from her kids. . . .
>
> TV brothers and sisters, although they often fought and scrapped, always came through for one another when the music got mellow at the end of the show. So where was that mellow music? And why weren't our neighbors wacky and fun-loving like Fred and Ethel? Why did we drive an old car when everyone on the sitcom block always had a new car (except of course, "The Beverly Hillbillies" and "My Mother the Car")? How come nobody ever sweated on sitcoms? Real life (everything that went on between sitcoms) was so complicated; my sitcoms were so . . . so innocent.

Today it's different. Today I have conversations with nine-year-olds about Maude's abortion, Walter's vasectomy, Mary Tyler Moore's affairs, Archie Bunker's sex hang-ups. . . .

But one thing for sure: Any minute now, sitcoms are going to become Art. That's right—just like they've done to old Bob Hope movies and other bits of elevated nostalgia, some guy who works for a film society somewhere will come across a faded print of "Mr. Ed" and discover that—yes, yes—the sitcom is the Art Form of Today. "Laverne and Shirley" an Art Form? "My Three Sons"? "The Beverly Hillbillies"? Art Forms?

Sure, but we knew that all along.

The new medium almost immediately flowed into every corner of existence, blurring distinctions between fact and fiction. Nixon's 1952 Checkers speech was a situation comedy, or perhaps a situation drama, live on prime time—the Dick and Pat show, with Pat right there on the screen with Dick in a studio made to look like a living room. Nixon's script was carefully structured to build, change pace, include some jokes, and come to a climax. It differed in one respect from the usual sitcom, since the only commercial came at the end, when Nixon asked everyone to write to the Republican National Committee, a commercial that came as a rude jolt to Eisenhower. The Checkers speech belongs to the sitcom subcategory of couplecom—"I Love Lucy," "Pete and Gladys," "Burns and Allen." Nor is it entirely easy to say that these shows were fiction, the Checkers speech reality. George Burns and Desi Arnaz were just as real as Nixon, and the whole "fund" charge was a kind of fiction, created by media hype. The fund was perfectly legal. Adlai Stevenson himself had one.

Estes Kefauver catapulted himself into national attention and a presidential candidacy that was at least partially plausible with his televised Senate inquiries into organized crime, a sitcom that ran day after day and kept millions glued to the tube, with Kefauver grilling Frank Costello and other mobsters in the manner of a Perry Mason. In the televised Army-McCarthy hearings, Joseph Welch rose to stardom in an established sitcom role, the Lovable and Wise Elder. Sam Ervin re-created the part during the Watergate sitcom, but added a charming regional twist, the Southern Lovable and Wise Elder, the simple country boy who is really much shrewder than those city fellers, an aged Huck Finn. We will probably never know, but it seems likely that when he shot Lee

Harvey Oswald in Dallas, Jack Ruby was fantasizing himself as a character in a TV drama, and he in fact made it onto every screen in the country. John Hinckley, who was obsessed by a movie actress and tried to kill President Reagan, and Mark Chapman, who did kill John Lennon, appear to have had only the most tenuous hold upon reality, and also, perhaps, to have imagined themselves acting out some television scenario. The Tet offensive in Vietnam was a military disaster on the ground for the Communist forces, but they won the battle and the war on American television screens. The war protesters of the 1960s and 1970s had grown up in a television environment, amid all those sitcoms, with their mellow music building to the happy ending and the list of credits. Did this have anything to do with the young protesters' failure to understand the tough choices in Vietnam, and the potentiality for disaster? There was no mellow music when Saigon fell and people were clinging to the outside of the last helicopter off the roof of the American embassy. There were no credits listed following that scene, although a list of names could easily be supplied. It might be an unusual aesthetic experience to play that scene with the accompaniment of some canned laughter from the old sitcoms.

The first really big, long-running sitcom hit, "I Love Lucy," went on the air at 9 P.M. on Monday, October 15, 1951. It had begun almost accidentally, a desperate effort by Lucille Ball to save her marriage to Desi Arnaz, a Cuban conga-player with a thick Latin accent. Ball's movie career had not been flourishing, and she had been doing a radio show called "My Favorite Husband" with Richard Denning, a couplecom sitcom. CBS-TV wanted the show on television, but Ball was adamant that Desi Arnaz play her husband on television. She had been working on radio, he had been touring the country with the band, and their divergent careers were putting intolerable pressure on the marriage. She hoped that working together would save it.

CBS did not think much of the idea. Would an American audience go for the notion of this Latino with a thick Cuban accent married to a regular American wife with red hair? The whole thing seemed pretty unlikely. Oscar Hammerstein II, a friend of the couple, came up with the idea of a dramatic situation involving a couple that was nice but a bit wacky, along the lines of radio's "Fibber McGee and Molly." Ball would supply the dizzy stuff, Arnaz would be mostly a straight man. Thus you got a nice trade-off. The exotic-seeming Cuban was really normal. The regular American housewife was the zany who precipitated the comic situations. The advertising agency that handled Philip Morris went for the idea. Thus was born Lucy and Ricky Ricardo, married, living in an apartment at 623 East 68th Street in Manhattan. He worked as a musician at the Tropicana. Lucy was a housewife who longed for a career in show biz. They populated the sitcom with a cast of characters who became more vivid than reality for millions of Americans: the Mertzes, who were the landlords; Mrs. Trumbull from upstairs, the baby sitter; Little Ricky. They decided against doing the show live from Los Angeles since viewers in the East would get an inferior image; instead, they would film the show like a movie and distribute the film. No one had filmed a half-hour TV show before. They hired Karl Freund, who had won an Oscar in 1937 for *The Good Earth,* and worked out the technical details. The show would be put on like a play in front of a live audience and be filmed by four cameras to provide a variety of angles. They rented a seven-acre lot in Hollywood, which they called the Desilu Playhouse.

The first show, in October, 1951, established the formula from which the show never deviated. It was called "The Girls Want to Go to a Nightclub." Two husbands, Fred and Ricky, plot to go to the boxing matches despite the fact that their wives have made plans to go to a nightclub for the Mertzes' anniversary. Lucy and Ethel refuse to go to the fights. Fred and Ricky arrange for a couple of blind dates, but Ethel and Lucy disguise themselves as hillbillies and substitute for the dates. This first show drew raves from the television critics and was an instant success with the television audience. Lucille Ball's groan of "E-u-u-u-u," whenever she—frequently—got into trouble became as familiar as "Yes, we have no bananas" had once been.

A couple of times, real life intermixed with the fictional show. Toward the end of the first season, it was announced that Lucille Ball was pregnant. They decided to use the fact of the pregnancy as part of the show. CBS thought this might be a terrible mistake. Rick Mitz quotes a CBS official: "When Lucille Ball announced that she was going to have a baby, all we could think of at first was complete disaster. As it turned out it was the best thing that ever happened to 'I Love Lucy.' It gave the show a change of pace, a change of perspective." There was a lot of nervousness about the whole thing at the time. Pregnancy had never been televised before. Philip Morris insisted that a priest and a rabbi review all scripts dealing with the subject, possibly afraid that people might associate their cigarettes with the idea of pregnancy. CBS would not allow the word pregnant to be used. It had to be "expectancy." Life and art fused at the baby's birth. The day Lucille Ball had her real child, by caesarean section, the fictional Lucy had one on the show, as 44 million people watched "Lucy Goes to the Hospital." Less than half that number watched the Eisenhower inauguration the following day.

The real world intruded on another occasion in 1953—this time much less pleasantly—on "I Love Lucy." Walter Winchell announced that "America's top comedienne has been confronted with her membership in the Communist Party." The headlines blared, "LUCILLE BALL NAMED RED." The year before Ball had told HUAC that she had registered as a Communist in 1936 "to please my grandfather," and the committee had cleared her. The sponsor supported her, but there was a lot of anxiety about the public reaction.

At the Desilu Playhouse that week, before the show started, Desi Arnaz went out on the stage and said to the audience: "Lucille Ball is no Communist. Lucy has never been a Communist, not now and never will be. I was kicked out of Cuba because of Communism. We both despise the Communists for everything they stand for. Lucille is one hundred percent American. She's as American as Barney Baruch and Ike Eisenhower. Please, ladies and gentlemen, don't believe every piece of bunk you read in today's papers." Arnaz got a standing, cheering ovation as Lucille Ball stood in the wings and sobbed. Then he called her out on the stage and said: "And now I want you to meet my favorite wife—my favorite redhead—in fact, that's the only thing red about her, and even *that's* not legitimate." Despite Arnaz's fractured English, it was a moving moment. There was a sign on the door of his dressing room that read "English Broken Here." Ball and Arnaz were divorced in 1960.

"I Love Lucy" was the great breakthrough for the Fifties sitcom, and others quickly followed, a central feature of national life during the decade: "Mr. Peepers," "The Adventures of Ozzie and Harriet," "The Life of Riley," "Our Miss Brooks," "Private Secretary," "The Danny Thomas Show," "Father Knows Best," "The Phil Silvers Show," "You'll Never Get Rich," "Leave It to Beaver," "The Real McCoys," "The Donna Reed Show," "How to Marry a Millionaire," "The Many Loves of Dobie Gillis." The sitcoms came and went, but those were the days when everybody loved Lucy.

Jack Benny was one of the few major stars of radio comedy to negotiate the difficult transition to the new medium at the beginning of the Fifties. He moved slowly, feeling his way, solving problems for which there were no precedents to draw upon. He did two shows during 1950, the first one a forty-five-minute program, over CBS, on October 21, 1950. Benny felt that a half-hour show would be too short, but an hour show too long to hold the audience's attention. So he split the difference. The next year he did four TV shows and raised it to six or eight during the next few years. By the 1956–57 season, he was broadcasting every other week. In 1960, he began a weekly show.

One of his main writers was Milt Josefsberg, an extremely able writer who had been with the Benny radio show. Josefsberg invented Benny's most famous joke, in which the holdup man says "Your money or your life." Long silence. "Well, what are you going to do?" says the holdup man. Benny: "I'm thinking." Josefsberg remembers the problems they had to solve in the transition to television in the early Fifties:

Jack's radio programs were still outdrawing the most popular television shows in the early 1950s, but we knew that we would have to switch sometime soon, and we tried to prepare for that inevitable day. As we did so, the debates and discussions between Jack and his writers were simultaneously serious and ridiculous—but with good reason. We had all written his radio show for years, and we had heard his programs for many more years prior to joining his staff. I frequently quote a famous Fred Allen line comparing radio and television because it ably described our dilemma. Allen felt that radio was a far better medium than TV because it left more to the imagination. Fred said, "Television is much too blunt. Radio is more subtle and lets each listener enjoy it on his own intellectual level."

That was part of our problem. We all had different mental pictures of Benny's home, his den, his living room, Rochester's quarters, the vault, and other familiar locales for which sets would have to be built in television. In radio, if we heard a doorbell ring Jack would say "I'll answer it" or "Rochester, please get the door." Then we'd have the sound effects of footsteps and a door opening. It was that simple. But for television each of us had a different concept of how an unimportant brief scene like this should be done. One thought that there should be an entrance hall. Another said, "No, the door should open right into Jack's den." The third writer thought that there should be six locks and bolts on the door, while the fourth wanted to know if we were discussing the front, side, or rear door.

Jack himself visualized his television home as almost an exact replica of his actual one. We all fought Jack on this point, saying that a character as parsimonious as he was would not live in so luxurious a mansion. Jack defended himself by emphatically stating, "Fellows, I've lived in that house on my radio program for twenty years." It then turned out that Jack and each of the writers subconsciously had integrated characteristics of his own home into Jack's imaginary radio residence, and then each had drawn his own individual conception in his mind of what the rest of the house would look like.

In radio we would use a simple line, such as Jack saying, "I'm going upstairs to bed," and we'd hear the sound of footsteps ascending the stairs. No member of the writing staff ever questioned a line like this on radio. However, on television just the question of where to locate the staircase took hours to decide. Some people pictured it in the entrance hall, while others, including the writer who visualized the house as having no hall, said that it would be next to the den or the living room. There were more days of debate about the kitchen. Did he have a large or small refrigerator? Was there a lock on it? On some radio programs, when Jack or Rochester would say he wanted orange juice or milk, we'd hear the refrigerator door open and close. However, on one show, we had Mary, during a visit to Jack's house, say that she was thirsty and was going to the refrigerator for a cold drink. A few seconds later she returned and Jack asked, "Did you get your drink?" Mary answered, "No, I couldn't open the refrigerator; you changed the combination on the lock again."

This sounds like a hair-splitting triviality, but in radio we knew that one week we could say the refrigerator had a lock on it and forget about it the next week. On television we felt that once the audience *saw* a lock on the refrigerator, the impact would be so strong that the audience would remember it, and we would have to keep the lock on permanently. . . .

As we prepared for television, we were aware of all these aspects of the new medium, and we tried to keep abreast of changes and innovations in TV which were occurring with remarkable frequency. Words like "coaxial cable," "kinescope," and "chroma-key" were used daily then, but are almost forgotten now. We had to change our thinking. We had to write for the eye as well as the ear.

On radio a member of the cast could come into Jack's house and say, "Oh, I see that you've had your whole house repainted." And Jack could answer, "Yes, I did it all in blue to match my eyes." Our listeners would take our word for it, and the moment they heard it said that the house was painted blue, they accepted it. In television, and particularly later on with the advent of color television, to change the color of a room took lots of labor, material, and money. In fact, even the color of the rooms in Jack's home caused controversy. We initially wanted the walls of his den done in blue to match his eyes. Then someone said that the room should be painted in Jack's favorite color, "Dollar Bill Green." However, all our talk on this point went for naught, because the set designer and cameraman eventually decided what color would photograph best. I don't know their name for it, but we called it "Kinescope Gray" . . .

Any idea or suggestion was given consideration in those trial-and-error days, and was discarded only when the majority of us thought that it was silly or impractical. One that interested us, if only temporarily, was the possibility of broadcasting our radio shows as television shows. The millions of outside listeners and the few hundred people seated in our studio audience each week had loved and remained loyal to the program through the entire history of radio. Maybe, we thought, if we just televised the cast reading their scripts into a microphone and showed the sound effects men making their necessary noises, we could still retain our huge army of fans.

With the tremendous technical improvements that have come along in a short quarter of a century, these ideas seem idiotic now, but it is possible that in those early days they may have worked for several seasons. After all, during those first years when the roofs of the nation's houses seemed to be sprouting an ever-increasing forest of TV antennas, Jack's radio programs continued to be fully sponsored for over seven more years. It was only when we felt that we couldn't postpone the day any longer that we took the big jump.

Jack's first television appearance on his own show, the forty-five minute one, saw him supported by several regular cast members—Don Wilson, Rochester, The Sportsmen Quartet, "Mr. Kitzle," and Mel Blanc. Dennis Day didn't appear on the program because he had a prior commitment and had to stay in Los Angeles. Phil Harris was no longer with us at the time, and Mary Livingstone had asked not to be written into the show. She had never been too crazy about appearing on radio, and she liked television even less. Her appearances on the small screen were quite limited. The guests on that premiere program were Dinah Shore and comedian Ken Murray.

The critics were kind, but not overly so, to Jack's debut. For the most part the show got good reviews, but few real raves. On the other hand, while some of the reviews were not too favorable, there were no real slams either.

One columnist made a valid point when he accused the program of using too many "radio lines," and those two words became anathema to all of us. For example, on radio, if Jack were going out, he'd say, "I'll get my coat and go out." On TV there was no need to do this. The audience didn't have to hear Jack say "I think I'll put on my hat."

The second show, the usual thirty minutes in length this time, turned out a bit better than the first. One of the high spots was the purely physical, visual humor involving Jack and guest star Ben Hogan. We had their scene start with Hogan coming into the locker room of Jack's golf club where he was going to play a practice round. He was immediately greeted by one or two extras who said something along the lines of "Nice to have you here, Mr. Hogan" or "Hope you like our course, Ben." Then Hogan was informed that if he wished to take a few practice swings, they had an area inside the locker room where he could do so. Hogan walked over to this spot and, using a driver, demonstrated his perfect swing twice. At this point Jack entered the locker room and saw this stranger with his back to him practicing. Every time Hogan swung, Jack would shake his head pityingly like the greatest professional in the world watching the ineffectual efforts of the worst hacker in golfdom.

Finally, like a Good Samaritan helping a hopeless case, Jack said, "Excuse me, Mister, but you're doing it all wrong," and he then proceeded to give Ben Hogan a golf lesson, not knowing who his pupil was. He changed Hogan's stance, bent his knees way in, bent his elbows way out, pushed his head down until he had his chin on his chest, and then made him crouch as though he were sitting in an invisible chair.

All of these moves got excellent laughs from the audience, and the biggest one came when Jack made Hogan swing from the contorted position in which he had placed him. Hogan swung, got his arms and legs twisted around each other, and looked like a human pretzel, getting another big laugh. Then Jack looked at Hogan, who was now acting as though he couldn't straighten himself out, patted him on the shoulder, and said, "Now you've got it."

This show opened with Jack getting a violin lesson from his teacher, Professor LeBlanc. On the wall of the room where the lesson was taking place were pictures of Mischa Elman and Jascha Heifetz whom, via dialogue, we identified as two of the world's greatest violinists. When Jack played his first note, both pictures fell off the wall and smashed on the floor.

Later in the program, at the start of the locker room scene, before Jack entered, we had Hogan look at some pictures on the wall there. These were pictures of Gene Sarazen and Bobby Jones, and through dialogue we identified them as two of golf's greatest immortals. After Jack showed Hogan how to swing, we did one of the show's trademarks—the running gag or the playback. Jack told Hogan that he could learn more by watching how *he* swung. Then he took a practice swing with a gold club, and the pictures of Jones and Sarazan fell off the wall and smashed on the floor.

Hogan gave an excellent performance, proving that he was as good an actor as he was a golfer, while Jack proved that he was as good a golfer as he was a violinist. Of course, in the script Jack didn't find out whom he was instructing until several minutes later, and then his embarrassment received the expected excellent audience reaction.

Ed Sullivan was the least likely individual to rise to the heights of television success in the Fifties. He always looked awkward and uncomfortable on the screen. He spoke with a harsh New York accent, and his voice had an erratic pitch. When he walked stiffly out to the center of the stage his eyes were often fixed on the ceiling, as if hoping for divine assistance to make up for his doubtful talents. He would throw credibility to the winds by referring to the forthcoming performers as his "very good friends," as if his circle of friends included everyone in show business, here and abroad. One critic remarked that if you did not know who Sullivan was and simply tuned into "Toast of the Town" Sunday evening at 8 P.M., you might plausibly conclude that the real star had suddenly taken ill and that the producers in desperation had pressed a security guard into a Dunhill suit, shoved him out onto the stage, and hoped for the best.

Sullivan was himself an anachronism of sorts, and he succeeded in rising to television eminence by reshaping another anachronism. It was a truism that the movies had killed vaudeville, but vaudeville rose from the dead on "Toast of the Town" under the aegis of the glum Irishman.

Sullivan's vaudeville consisted of a variety of elements. As a former newsman, he had a shrewd sense of the week's headlines. If a heroic fireman had made news by rescuing someone or talking a would-be suicide out of it, he might get a walk-on and introduction on the Sullivan show. If someone had made athletic news, he might come on for a brief exchange with the emcee. Sullivan had clowns, comics, plate spinners, and dog acts, but he also did more than anyone else in television to introduce high culture to middle America.

Sullivan is sometimes thought to have discovered new talent, but what he really did was identify talent on the upward swing and confirm it, propelling it still further upward. He also modified the vaudeville formula in the direction of artistic "class." On "Toast of the Town," you saw Rudolf Nureyev, Margot Fonteyn, the Moisiev Ballet, Roberta Peters, and Maria Callas. You saw excerpts from Broadway shows, Charles Laughton reading the Bible. Sullivan was eclectic, an ambassador of the new once it had begun to be recognized as a comer. Elvis Presley had been on several TV shows, but he really took off after his "Toast of the Town" appearance in 1955. The Beatles made their first major American impact in 1960 on the Sullivan show.

Like many things in the early days of television, the whole thing could not have been foreseen. In 1947, Sullivan was known as a professional emcee at things like the Harvest Moon Ball, and he was also a gossip columnist for the New York *Daily News,* but gossip columns were a waning feature, and Sullivan's career was going nowhere.

In the spring of 1948, a man named Worthington "Tony" Miner became manager of program development for CBS. He had instructions to create a major dramatic show and also a major musical variety show. The dramatic show would be the highly esteemed "Studio One." The competition for the variety show looked formidable. NBC was about to launch "Texaco Star Theater" with Milton Berle. Tony Miner decided that he would not get someone who could compete with Berle as a performer and comic. The show would have to depend on the quality of its acts. The host would present talent, not necessarily be a talent himself.

As it happened, CBS was televising, live from Madison Square Garden, the annual Harvest Moon Ball, with Ed Sullivan as emcee. Sullivan afterward claimed that he did not realize he was on TV, that he thought the cameras were movie cameras, newsreel cameras. Tony Miner saw the broadcast, and had an inspiration. Sullivan was calm and polished, he thought, but not a performer, not a star. He would not be compared unfavorably with Berle.

Miner finally convinced his skeptical superiors that a fading Broadway columnist could be reissued as a variety show host. Having no alternative suggestions to make, they agreed.

"I was playing the Roxy Theater with the Harvest Moon winners," Sullivan recalls, "when Marlo Lewis charged through the dressing room door. 'Do you want to do a TV show for CBS?' he gasped. 'I hope you do, Ed, because I brought Tony Miner with me.'"

Miner joined Sullivan as a subordinate co-producer, and they scurried around for talent for the opening show. "Toast of the Town" went on the air for the first time on June 20, 1948. On the recommendation of his daughter, Sullivan had a young Italian-American romantic singer named Dean Martin, who had recently teamed up with a borsht-belt comic named Jerry Lewis. He had the concert pianist Eugene List. Rodgers and Hammerstein came on for free. He added the boxing referee, Ruby Goldstein, fresh from the Joe Louis-Jersey Joe Walcott fight.

The audience for "Toast of the Town" grew rapidly, but the pros in CBS management were appalled by Sullivan's own amateurishness. The TV critic John Crosby roasted Sullivan in the *New York Herald Tribune*: "One of the small but vexing questions confronting anyone in this area with a television set is: 'Why is Ed Sullivan on it every Sunday night?' If the set owner has been properly conditioned by soap opera, he is likely to add 'Why? Why? Why?' It's in all respects a darn hard question, almost a jackpot question, and it seems to baffle Mr. Sullivan as much as anyone else."

None of this mattered. Tony Miner's instincts had been sure. Sullivan had a good sense of the "mixture" on the show and an unsuspected sense of theater. He also listened to people in the entertainment field, in the media. He was quick to identify rising talent and sometimes ruthless in getting it on his show. By 1952, thirty-seven of the 108 television stations then broadcasting carried "Toast of the Town" to 13,600,000 viewers every week. Sullivan blew his Sunday night competition on the other networks out of the water. Sullivan was the king of Sunday evening during the Fifties.

Given the extraordinary power developed by television during the Fifties, it is not at all surprising that the political figure who first mastered that medium should now be the president of the United States. In 1954, Ronald Reagan's movie career had come

154 WHEN THE GOING WAS GOOD!

to an end. He had done some work in night clubs, in Las Vegas and elsewhere, but did not much like that line of work. As it happened, in 1954 the General Electric Corporation was looking for a host to handle its new half-hour television series, someone who could act, appeal to a wide audience, enhance the corporation's public image, and visit its plants around the country to help employee relations. The man in charge of the Music Corporation of America's Revenue Productions, Taft Schreiber, recalls that he could think of only one man, Ronald Reagan. Schreiber and Reagan negotiated a $125,000-a-year contract which was later raised to $150,000. Reagan took over as host of "General Electric Theater," which turned out to be a highly successful show. Reagan brought in as guest stars the great names of Hollywood. Charles Laughton made his television debut on Reagan's show. Fred Astaire appeared, Tony Curtis played a bullfighter, Jimmy Stewart starred in a Western version of Dickens' *Christmas Carol*. The "General Electric Theater" introduced more big name movie stars to television than any other series, and it also gave Reagan the opportunity over an eight-year period to perfect his television skills.

Reagan burst on the national political scene in 1964 with The Speech, a set speech about free enterprise and patriotism which he had been delivering, with slight variations, for several years. It was one of the few bright spots in the Goldwater campaign, and it led directly to Reagan's race for the governorship in 1966, in which his television skills contributed importantly to his million-vote landslide over Pat Brown.

On television, Reagan has a superb sense of pace and timing, he knows when to use a joke, his famous one-liners, and how to build to a climax. He never reads from a script, believing that doing so puts a barrier between him and the audience. He speaks from file cards on which he writes words and phrases that function as "mental triggers," each of the cards good for several minutes of the speech. Reagan knows how to be emotional on the tube, but in McLuhan's sense, he is "cool"—he does not shout at you in your own living room, and he comes across as serious but natural. Reagan is to television politics what William Jennings Bryan was to the outdoor stump speech, or Franklin Roosevelt to the radio speech—a complete master. He clinched the 1980 presidential election in his TV debate with President Carter, at a key moment projecting a relaxed condescension—"There you go again. . . ."

—and when he went on television to promote his tax cut bill in Congress, old fashioned politicians like Tip O'Neill never knew what hit them. A whole new era in politics opened up in the Fifties with the advent of television, and Reagan was the first national figure to master the new situation.

YOU CAN STEAL THE PRESIDENCY

Robert Finch sat next to the pool at the Newporter Inn in Newport Beach, California, his gin and tonic on the table beside him. Finch, an ex-marine, had been close to Richard Nixon for years. He was now Secretary of Health, Education and Welfare. Along with Len Hall, he had been co-manager of the losing 1960 presidential campaign against Kennedy. The two-headed structure was a horror, he reflected. Finch was tanned, physically powerful, Californian. Women were walking around in bikinis, and in those see-through plastic knee-pants that required colorful underwear. A hundred yards away, helicopters were landing and taking off on the regular passenger service between the Inn and the L.A. airport. Nixon was down the beach at San Clemente, surviving some crisis in the Middle East, and I was doing research on the 1960 presidential election.

"Without Illinois and Texas," Finch said, "Kennedy would have been down the tubes. He needed Missouri, too, which was very close, but we didn't think he stole that."

"Stole?"

"Well, you can read all about it in Earl Mazo. Kennedy carried Illinois by less than 9,000 votes, out of a total of nearly 5 million. Mayor Daley's vacant lot and tombstone votes, plus the votes of the mafia-dominated wards, made the difference. Nixon really *won* Illinois. After the voting, they threw the machines in the river.

"The Lyndon Johnson crowd was in total control of the Texas voting. They had control at every level, from county clerk up to the state Board of Canvassers, which had the final say. Ballot-box stuffing was commonplace. Some precincts reported more votes for Kennedy-Johnson than they had total population. In one district, 86 people voted. Kennedy-Johnson got 148 votes, Nixon-Lodge 24.

"Earl Mazo, who was national political correspondent for the *New York Herald Tribune,* went to Texas, and he was appalled by the extent of the ballot fraud. Paper ballots—half the vote in Texas in 1960—were thrown out in huge numbers on technicalities. There were always more technical violations in Nixon districts. Mazo did some simple arithmetic. It indicated that 100,000 Kennedy-Johnson votes simply did not exist. But they carried the state by 46,000 votes, and that was the ball game.

"I'll tell you, one of our big priorities in 1968 was our volunteer pollwatchers operation. We had our people all over the place in Cook County, and also in other key areas. We decided we wouldn't be burned twice.

"Now Mazo wrote a series of articles on all this for the *Herald Tribune.* It was supposed to be a series of twelve articles, but only four were printed. After the fourth one appeared, the Vice President invited Mazo to his office for a chat. When Mazo shook hands with him, Nixon said, 'Earl, those are interesting articles you are writing—but no one steals the presidency of the United States.'

"Mazo thought Nixon was kidding, but he wasn't.

"Nixon talked about various upcoming crisis points around the world, continent by continent. He said that an electoral crisis had to be avoided. It was in the national interest.

"Anyway, it would have taken at least a year to get any kind of a recount in Chicago. And there was no recount procedure in Texas."

The Secretary of Health, Education and Welfare ordered another gin and tonic. "Nixon is a tiger," he said, "an unusual person. This could be a great presidency."

CHAPTER NINE

Ike, Dick, and Ron

The taste of defeat for Dwight Eisenhower must have been a kind of death. It was at least a derailment of the freight train of greatness. The commander of "Overlord," the conqueror of Europe, was outmaneuvered by a thirty-nine-year-old U.S. Senator from California.

On September 18, 1952, a Thursday in the midst of the presidential campaign, the story of Nixon's $16,000 political fund hit the front pages. Eisenhower had been barreling along with a highly moralistic campaign against "corruption in Washington." The Nixon item in terms of the Eisenhower campaign was poison, nemesis. The weight of opinion among Eisenhower's top campaign advisors was that Nixon had to get off the ticket. Tom Dewey phoned Nixon and told him so. *The New York Herald Tribune,* the *El Aram* of Eastern Republicanism, called editorially for Nixon's resignation. Nixon, on the other hand, knew that a Price, Waterhouse audit was in the works and that it would clear him of any wrongdoing. He demanded support from the general. Eisenhower refused to say yes or no. He would await the public reaction to Nixon's Sunday evening television address to the nation. Then he would decide. But Nixon wrenched the power of decision out of Eisenhower's hands and beat him.

The general was scheduled to give a speech in Cleveland as

soon as Nixon went off the air, and he had a TV set installed in an office backstage at the auditorium. As he watched the tense, pale figure on the screen reveal everything about his meager personal assets, the general was watchfully calm. He had a yellow legal pad on the arm of his chair, and he tapped on it with a pencil. Some of the other people in the room were moved by Nixon's presentation. A few could not hold back tears. Not Eisenhower. He had no interest in the motionless Pat Nixon, sitting there on the screen and gazing at Nixon with adoring eyes. When Nixon stood up and came forward to set up the climax of his speech, the general did not change expression.

Nixon was landing the first wounding blow on him. He knew it instantly and jabbed the point of the pencil into the yellow pad. Nixon was cloaking menace in a virtuous proposal. He was making a virtue out of financial disclosure, demanding that *other* candidates do as he had just done. "I would suggest that under the circumstances both Mr. Sparkman and Mr. Stevenson should come before the American people as I have, and make a complete statement as to their financial history." Nixon omitted the name of Eisenhower. The effect may have been to call attention to the omission. Eisenhower had no desire to make his records public. He had a special tax deal on *Crusade in Europe*. His charitable contributions were meager. Jab went the pencil into the yellow pad. Eisenhower had imposed this painful broadcast on Nixon. Now he was receiving counter-battery fire.

From Eisenhower's standpoint, still worse followed. There was Nixon on the screen saying, "I am submitting to the Republican National Committee tonight, through this broadcast, the decision it is theirs to make. . . . Wire and write the Republican National Committee whether you think I should stay or whether I should get off; and whatever their decision is I will abide by it."

The general jabbed the pencil into the yellow pad with such force that the point broke. He knew at once what had happened to him. Nixon had wrenched the power of decision from his hands and transferred it to the television screen, and, in a rubber stamp way to the friendly Republican National Committee. In an instant, Eisenhower and his top professionals found that they were no longer entirely in control of the Eisenhower campaign.

Nixon himself knew very well that he was in a *war*. Throughout his published writings, he is entirely respectful about Eisenhower. There exist several amazing photographs of the two of them on the golf course, Nixon glowing with pleasure to be there with Ike. Nixon took up golf late, but learned to beat Ike at it.

In private conversation, he maintains that their relationship was excellent. But the metaphors in his description of the fund crisis reveal the reality. Nixon saw his situation in military terms, as a battle with Eisenhower. A battle with Eisenhower! "A new tension was building up," he wrote in *Six Crises,* "the tension that precedes battle when all the plans have been drawn and one stands poised for action. This speech was to be the most important part of my life. I felt now that it was my battle alone. I had been deserted by so many I had thought were friends but who had panicked in battle when the first shots were fired."

Nixon's Checkers speech has come to be synonymous with political snake oil, but it was one of the most effective television addresses in political history, right up there with Reagan's 1981 appeal for tax cuts. Nixon demonstrated for the first time the enormous political potential of TV. He evoked a remarkable audience response. He also probably developed the illusion, which led him into his TV debates with Kennedy in 1960, that he was a first-rate television performer. Today, the Checkers speech, with its studied gestures, with Pat looking like a mannequin, with its emotionalism and sheer corn, strikes a modern audience as embarrassing; but Nixon went into battle against Eisenhower, and won.

Eisenhower's attitude toward Nixon is impossible to fathom. The scholars who have worked on Eisenhower's career simply throw up their hands on this one. Today, Nixon speaks of Eisenhower with a good deal of warmth and respect which might even be sincere, and his daughter Julie seems to be happily married to Eisenhower's grandson David. The fact is, though, that Eisenhower never socialized with the Nixons beyond the formalities. He wanted to replace Nixon on the ticket in both the 1952 and 1956 campaigns. In the 1960 election, his combative energies seemed to be evoked more by the Kennedy attacks on his own record than by any fervor for Nixon. Eisenhower's *Diaries* record Nixon's comings and goings, but express no interest in the man. The Eisenhower emotional world was a chilly one. Beyond a small circle that included his brother, Milton Eisenhower, Bob Anderson, and a few others, he seems to have had little use for friendship. The *Diaries* are full of cold analysis and intellectual disdain. In the case of Senator William Knowland, the Republican majority leader, writes Eisenhower, "there seems to be no final answer to the question 'How stupid can you get?'"

Nixon once revealed to me in conversation an interesting piece of tactical advice Eisenhower had given him. When you are asked a question in public, in a press conference, Eisenhower told Nixon, don't answer it too quickly. Even if you *know the answer,* hesitate. Back and fill. It makes you look thoughtful. It brings you closer to the *people,* who have only dimly begun to think about the issue at all.

Where his relationship with Nixon is concerned, my own guess is that Eisenhower was completely cold-blooded. To suppose, as some historians have done, that Eisenhower disliked Nixon or looked down on him socially strikes me as sentimental. Such feelings were useless to Eisenhower, and he would not bother with them. He probably regarded Nixon as a useful piece of equipment. Nixon had been effective against McCarthy. Nixon had a constituency. But Nixon, under certain circumstances, could be discarded like a piece of Kleenex, or like Sherman Adams. Ironically, in his own final political crisis of Watergate, Nixon fell chiefly because he lacked the coldness to sacrifice John Mitchell and send him to jail. Eisenhower would hardly have given such a move a second thought.

In 1956, Eisenhower made it pretty clear that he wanted Nixon off the ticket, offering him a cabinet post as, allegedly, better training for leadership. Bryce Harlow much later told John Osborne of *The New Republic* that Nixon then went through a period of "absolutely indescribable anguish." Eisenhower also delegated Leonard Hall to tell Nixon bluntly that he would have to get off the ticket. Eisenhower wanted Governor Frank Lausche of Ohio, a conservative Catholic Democrat, or Robert Anderson, a conservative Texas Democrat, a lean and scholarly man who had been his Secretary of the Navy and whom he would elevate in his second term to Secretary of the Treasury. As he had done in 1960 over the fund crisis, Nixon dug in his heels. His supporters organized a successful write-in campaign for the New Hampshire primary. Of the 56,464 voters who supported Eisenhower, 22,936 wrote in the name of Nixon. The Nixon operation did it again in Oregon. Republican professionals were heavily for Nixon, and once again Nixon thwarted Eisenhower politically. As he wrote in his memoirs, Nixon "felt as if the clock had been turned back to the fund crisis."

Nixon also seems to have perceived as social slights what Eisenhower undoubtedly considered routine behavior toward a subordinate. Pat and Dick Nixon had never been invited to dinner in the residential quarters of the White House. When the Nixons were at the Gettysburg farm for party functions, they were not invited into the house itself.

Eisenhower failed to dump Nixon in 1952 and failed again in 1956. The Checkers speech was the first collision between two of the major political figures of the Fifties, and Eisenhower lost it. Then he lost again to Nixon in 1956.

Eisenhower's reconciliation with Nixon at Wheeling, West Virginia in 1952 had a sardonic edge to it. The general put his arm around the young but battered senator. "You're my boy," he said. The true hierarchy was thus reasserted, Nixon reminded of who was boss. And, of course, the election was won. From the perspective of hardball politics, it is difficult to understand what had been passing through the brains of political professionals like Dewey and Brownell when they urged that Nixon be dumped. That might have *lost* the election. It would have underlined Eisenhower's only political vulnerability, his amateur standing as a politician. The 1972 dumping of Tom Eagleton became an insuperable metaphor for George McGovern's ineptness and absurdity. With his Checkers speech, Nixon may well have saved the Eisenhower presidency. At the same time, I believe it is possible that Nixon's eight years with Eisenhower, that icy tactician, added damage to Nixon's earlier wounds in ways that even Nixon does not understand. No one ever opposed Eisenhower and finally won out. His career is littered with shattered opponents. With that Checkers speech, Nixon swam into dangerous waters.

An understanding of the politics of the Fifties requires that we put them within a time frame of what came before and what went after. For American politics, let us now assess what came after Eisenhower, and what it meant. Late in the year 1967, Bill Buckley was having dinner with his friend Ronald Reagan at Reagan's place in Pacific Palisades. In 1964, Reagan had gained national attention with a stirring speech on behalf of Barry Goldwater, and then, in 1966, using various adaptations of The Speech, he had swept into the California governorship with a million-vote victory over Pat Brown. As Buckley and Reagan chatted over white wine, it became clear to Buckley that Reagan was thinking of trying for the 1968 Republican presidential nomination.

Of course, he had been governor for little more than a year. That was his liability. Inexperience. An actor. But, over dinner in late 1967, Reagan's competition did not seem unbeatable. Nixon and Rockefeller were running, of course, but both had serious liabilities. Nixon had lost narrowly to Kennedy in 1960, but, worse, he had lost pretty badly to the same Pat Brown in 1962. Nixon had not won an election on his own since 1950, seventeen years earlier. And, of course, there was that amazing "last press conference" happening in 1962, where Nixon seemed to have lost all control, had talked about the press giving him "the shaft," and said that "You won't have Nixon to kick around anymore, because, gentlemen, this is my last press conference. . . ." That Nixon actually had any political mileage left in him was open to question in 1967. As for Nelson Rockefeller, he had shown that he could win in New York state, but not anywhere else. Barry Goldwater had beaten him, one on one, in California in 1964. Rockefeller also represented a Northeastern Republicanism that was in historical decline. Yes, it was a long shot, of course, but Ronald Reagan was going to try for the White House in 1968.

"Ron, if you're going to run for president," said Buckley, "you need a Sorensen."

By that, Buckley meant someone who would give an aura of erudition to the candidate's orations by weaving into them quotations from people like Heraclitus and Hobbes. Ted Sorensen had done this for Jack Kennedy in 1960, ushering in a new era in political rhetoric. Sorensen's Kennedy stuff had reflected the growing importance of the intellectuals and the verbalists in American life since World War II. Kennedy had never read Heraclitus, Hobbes, or even Madison, but Sorensen provided him with an important component of his image. By 1967, education was the most important item in the California state budget. The California university system was a major battleground politically, with riots at Berkeley, Sacramento State, Santa Barbara. For Reagan's Sorensen, Buckley suggested me.

I took leave from Dartmouth for the spring term of 1968 and flew out to Sacramento, where I was installed in an unused Spanish-style building near the state capitol, with its golden dome and its gardens. Except for the color of its dome, this state capitol looked suggestively like the Capitol in Washington. An unavowed

and semi-secret Reagan presidential campaign was well underway, and I gradually began to understand, during that hectic
summer, what long-term forces were operating in American politics and within the Republican party. Not immediately, by any
means, but gradually the whole pattern became apparent. It included the 1948 Dewey campaign, the defeat of Taft and the role of
Eisenhower, the career of Nixon—a career of historic importance
unfolding through the entire postwar period—and, as I now see,
the emergence of Reagan as president.

When I got to Sacramento in March of 1968, the assumption in
the Reagan presidential campaign was that Nixon would "stumble." The two men had met at the Bohemian Grove, a spa near San
Francisco, and though they differ in their interpretation of what
was said and agreed to, Reagan in general agreed to let Nixon have
an unchallenged try for the nomination. If Nixon "stumbled,"
Reagan would go public as a presidential candidate.

Reagan's chief of staff in Sacramento when I arrived was an
enormously sympathetic young lawyer named Bill Clark, who was
later to become National Security Advisor in the Reagan Administration. He struck me as relaxed, "western," with cowboy boots
and silver belt buckle in his paneled office. He had been a moder-
ate Republican in California politics, but a conservative Catholic.
He had stepped in during the early days of Reagan's governorship,
when the governor's office had been rocked by a homosexual
scandal, and Clark's unruffled equanimity had been a major factor
in pulling the whole operation back together.

Bill Clark's assistant was Mike Deaver, now in the White
House. Deaver was a talented musician who had knocked around
the country a lot during the Sixties, and he had a good sense of
perspective on whatever surprises came down the road. Ed Meese,
a gentle bear, was Reagan's top adviser on legal matters, and an
able student of the crime problem. He later established an institute
to study law enforcement and taught a criminology program in San
Diego. He, too, is now a top aide in the White House. Lyn
Nofziger, a hard-nosed operator and former journalist, handled
Reagan's political chores. Caspar "Cap" Weinberger, who had,
like Clark, come to Reagan from the liberal-moderate wing of
California Republicanism, was the authority on the state budget, a
key function since the budget was the focus of Reagan's struggles
with the Democratic-controlled legislature. Weinberger had a

tough, no-nonsense mind and a clear grasp of fact and option. He is now Secretary of Defense, no news.

The week I arrived in Sacramento, two noisy demonstrations were taking place outside the capital. One was the usual anti-Vietnam picketing, signs saying "Make Love, Not War." The other demonstration had to do with a more local issue. Reagan was trying to reform the California mental health system over the strenuous objections of the mental health establishment. Reagan understood that useful advances had been made in drug therapy and that many kinds of mental illness could be controlled chemically and through other kinds of therapy. He therefore wanted to move such patients out of the big state mental hospitals, where they were essentially being warehoused—many of them just rotting—and have them treated on an outpatient basis in their local communities. It was a humane, cost-effective, and modern idea, and it eventually worked, but it was resisted tooth and nail by the mental health workers, the nurses, attendants, and bureaucracy, all of whom were adept at generating scare headlines and projecting all sorts of horrors. Outside Reagan's office, they were picketing and carrying coffins representing the "death" of mental health care in California. It was absurd, but typical of a bureaucracy on the defensive against reform.

Reagan's regular press conferences in an auditorium in the capitol were a kind of good–natured sporting event. Reagan is articulate and funny, and although the reporters enjoyed him, they also had a kind of sporting interest in seeing whether they could trip him up or somehow best him. They seldom could. One time, trying to get him to say something newsworthy about the Vietnam war, a reporter asked him whether he had noticed the demonstration outside. "You mean the one with the signs that say 'Make love, not war?' " asked Reagan.

"Yes," the reporter said.

"I saw them," Reagan said, "and they didn't look to me like they could do much of either."

I found Reagan to be an odd mixture of relaxation and precision. At a staff meeting, he did not put pressure on anyone, and there was a great sense that any idea could be discussed openly. But he wanted his options clarified, and when he made a decision, everyone was supposed to work for it without reservation. He would not tolerate halfhearted compliance once the direction was set, and he also made it clear that he disliked personal rivalries and self-promotion on the staff. A failure to perceive this nearly wrecked the career of Alexander Haig as Secretary of State during the first months of Reagan's presidency.

In Sacramento, I learned to write a political speech. It is a peculiar genre. I read through a collection of addresses by past presidents, and through a collection of Kennedy speeches. I saw that the function of a political speech is not to convey information, but to establish communion. What the political speech must succeed in saying, by whatever means—and there are many—is that the man giving it understands the situation of his listeners. He may not be like them, but he knows where they are. Of course the style and content of a political speech, one of the means of getting its real message across, are determined by the nature of the audience with which the candidate desires to establish those bonds of communion. I examined Nelson Rockefeller's recent speeches. He had high-priced talent on his staff, but they did not seem to have analyzed the problem. Rockefeller's speeches sounded like *essays,* pieces in *The New York Times.* Maybe he was trying to establish communion with the Sulzbergers. All a Rockefeller speech really *said* was that he had the information. Who gave a damn. You could pick up the phone and get the information. The main number at Columbia is (212) 280-1754.

I loved Sacramento. The park around the state capitol is stocked with examples of California trees and shrubbery, often exotic, identified with plaques. There were pools of fish to feed. The city has an old section, dating from the nineteenth-century, which was in the process of being restored. Parts of it looked like a Western movie. Not far outside of town was a nineteenth-century wooden village, populated entirely by Chinese, and living in a very Chinese way. They were the descendants of people who had been brought over to build the railroad and work on the farms in the great, fertile central valley. American history was all around you, a different history than I was used to back East.

The weekend following the assassination of Martin Luther King, and with reports flowing in of spreading black riots in the major cities, I had, nevertheless, one of the most glamorous couple of days in my experience. Reagan and some of his staff went up to Heavenly Valley, the ski area overlooking Lake Tahoe, for the final races of the 1968 World Cup. Heavenly Valley is a huge snow bowl up in the Sierra Nevadas. You look down on the cold blue water of the lake, and on the gambling casinos. It was spring skiing, bright sun, skiing in sweaters and sunglasses. Jean Claude Killy had already won the World Cup with his European performances, and he skied the race as a sort of exhibition, making those distinctive, almost double-jointed moves that no other skier has ever matched. The crowd cheered as Killy came down the course. Killy won the World Cup, presented to him in a ceremony by Reagan, but Spider Sabich, a local boy, won the race and received the Governor's Cup. I spent the day skiing with some Australian test pilots who were over here to fly American jets of a type that had been crashing in West Germany. These Australian boys were very tough. The planes' record of fatalities did not bother them a bit. "Fucking krauts can't fly, mate," they said.

One of the managers of the ski resort told me an extraordinary story. Bobby Kennedy had been all over California, campaigning for the Democratic nomination. I had never seen anything like his campaign, and neither had anyone else. It was more like an Elvis Presley appearance than a political campaign. Women were tearing out his cuff links, screaming, fighting with his bodyguards. Kennedy was denouncing the war, promising the Israelis all the jets they wanted, but it was more a "happening" than a political campaign. The weekend before the World Cup race, Kennedy and his large retinue had come up to Heavenly Valley to ski, the manager said. They demanded free lift tickets. Worse, on a crowded weekend, with long lift lines, they demanded to go right to the head of the line. The crowd of waiting skiers got furious. They did not care whether it was Bobby Kennedy or Bobby God. They pelted Kennedy with paper cups, hot dogs, empty Coke cans. Bobby made obscene gestures. Fights started. The manager had to ask the Kennedy crowd to leave the area. A few weeks later, right after winning the California primary over Gene McCarthy, Kennedy was murdered by Sirhan Sirhan in Los Angeles. It was that kind of a year.

Nixon did not stumble. His streak of primary victories in 1968 represented a carefully analyzed and professional political operation. Even before the voting, George Romney, understood to be a Rockefeller surrogate, withdrew from the New Hampshire primary. He was low in the polls. He had made himself ludicrous with his remark that he had been "brainwashed" by the American military in Vietnam, a remark that made people suddenly aware that they did not think he had much of a brain in the first place. The

Nixon people had also solved most of Nixon's image problem by an ingenious use of television. In private, with his men friends and close aides, Nixon is excellent company. He can be earthy. He loves political anecdotes. His analyses of political tactics can be brilliant. But at some point along the line he invented another personality for public appearances, the plastic man, the talking head that "makes one thing very clear." During the primaries that year, Nixon's TV people had him spend long, informal sessions chatting with local citizens about anything and everything, and these sessions were videotaped. In these groups, Nixon relaxed a bit. The tapes were then studied and edited, and those sections in which he seemed relatively human were used for TV spots over the air. They were extraordinarily effective. Once again, people thought they discerned a New Nixon.

As Nixon marched through the primaries, we saw that Reagan's chances were vanishing, and Reagan made a major decision. F. Clifton White, Goldwater's magical delegate hunter, now working for Reagan, told him that he simply could not round up delegates for an undeclared candidate. Okay, Reagan would virtually declare. He went on nationwide TV with a major address on law and order, a superb performance. But the Nixon delegate count continued to mount. Reagan flew to the Miami convention, announced his candidacy openly for the first time—earning Nixon's professional contempt, an attitude that lasted until 1980. Reagan struggled desperately to crack Nixon's southern support, but failed.

During the week before the convention, Nixon, correctly believing that he had the nomination sewed up, secluded himself at Montauk Point and composed his acceptance speech. It was one of his best. It was based in part, oddly enough, on the rhythm and mood of Martin Luther King's "I have a dream" speech in Washington, but it also evoked in a powerful and lyrical way Nixon's own struggle upward from poverty. In a dreadful year, it reaffirmed the American Dream. I much admired it both politically and professionally:

> I see another child tonight.
> He hears a train go by at night and he dreams of faraway places where he'd like to go.
> It seems like an impossible dream.

But he is helped on his journey through life.

A father who had to go to work before he finished the sixth grade, sacrificed everything he had so that his sons could go to college.

A gentle, Quaker mother, with a passionate concern for peace, quietly wept when he went to war but she understood why he had to go.

A great teacher, a remarkable football coach, an inspirational minister encouraged him on his way.

A courageous wife and loyal children stood by him in victory and also defeat.

And in his chosen profession of politics, first there were scores, then hundreds, then thousands, and finally millions who worked for his success.

And tonight he stands before you—nominated for President of the United States of America.

After Reagan's first-ballot defeat in Miami, I assumed that I would return to teaching at Dartmouth. I bought a second-hand Volvo in Sacramento, packed my bags and launched forth along southern Route 66. I know that Joseph Wood Krutch, Barry Goldwater and others share a deep love for the great Western American desert, but I never want to see it again. Mile after mile, hour after hour of blazing antihuman wasteland, a god-awful representation of the indifference of nature. I stopped off for a beer at a lonely desert bar in the midst of what seemed to be an Army missile testing range, Hunter Thompson country, and put in a phone call to the governor's office in Sacramento to check for messages. There were some, including a request to call Nixon headquarters in New York City. I immediately called the number and got Jim Keogh on the line. He had taken leave from his job as an editor of *Time* and was in charge of the Nixon speechwriting operation. Would I come aboard for the campaign against Humphrey and the Democrats? The answer was yes, and I reset my course for Manhattan, and Nixon campaign headquarters at 450 Park Avenue, on the corner of 57th Street.

It was there, finally, that the whole American political picture of the post-World War II period finally became clear to me. It became clear that seismic changes had taken place in the social and political landscape, despite the persistence of all the old labels, Republican and Democrat, liberal and conservative. In 1956,

President Eisenhower had wanted to replace Nixon on the ticket as a means of expanding the Republican Party in the direction of Catholic ethnics and southern conservatives. He had seriously considered running with Frank Lausche of Ohio, a conservative Catholic Democrat, or else with Robert Anderson of Texas. Nixon had blocked all of this at the time, thwarting Eisenhower once again, but this time it was all happening in Nixon's 1968 headquarters. The place was full of ambitious Catholics and Jews whose parents had undoubtedly voted for Franklin Roosevelt. They were lawyers, economists, nascent politicians. This was not the old country club, chamber-of-commerce Republican party. And it was overflowing with talent. Many of these younger Nixon workers were not well known in 1968, but they certainly have become so since then.

Bill Safire was one of the speechwriters, a clever, witty New York Jew who had come over from Javits, Rockefeller, and liberal Republicanism. He is now a major columnist for *The New York Times*. Patrick Buchanan was there, having joined forces with Nixon two years earlier. After his White House years, Pat would become an important syndicated columnist. He was a lapsed Catholic, disgruntled by the changes that followed Vatican II, but a Georgetown Irishman nevertheless. Kevin Phillips, now a major political analyst and author, was across the street, installed in a semi-secret office under John Mitchell, giving advice on ethnic and other voting patterns. In charge of campaign research was Alan Greenspan, an economist, Jew, and admirer of Ayn Rand. He would become chairman of the president's council of economic advisors. His assistant was Jeff Bell, a young political professional who would upset the liberal Republican senator, Clifford Case, in the 1976 primary, then lose to basketball star, Princetonian and Rhodes Scholar, Bill Bradley. These and other very bright and rising young men created the excitement of the 1968 Nixon campaign. This must have been the way it was in 1932, I thought, when the ambitious young talent of the nation flowed out of the law firms and universities and into the Roosevelt campaign and then into the New Deal. A mild liberal Republican presence at 450 Park was George Gilder, a Rockefeller speech writer and founder of the liberal Ripon Society. He had, without giving much indication of it then, commenced a long intellectual and political journey to the right, and in 1981, his *Wealth and Poverty,* a major work on free market economics, would sell half a million copies.

In 1966, in a moment of exasperation, President Johnson had called Richard Nixon a "chronic campaigner," but Nixon's extensive campaign experience served him well in 1968. From the primaries through the general election, the whole enterprise was a technical masterpiece, every detail in place, every schedule met, the headquarters at 450 Park in constant touch with the "tour," that is, the candidate out across the country in *The Tricia*. Back in Sacramento, the speech-writing effort had been relatively casual. You would produce some material on a desired theme. Reagan would look it over, use some ideas, reject others, add some thoughts of his own, chat casually with you about it. Then he would reduce the whole thing to topic phrases on file cards and deliver it magnificently, often ad libbing.

A 1968 Nixon speech was about as casual as the Apollo moon landing. At 450 Park Avenue, the principal writer assigned to produce a speech would know exactly where and when it was to be delivered, and what the deadlines were for drafts. About a week before a major Nixon speech, the writer would join *The Tricia*, wherever it might be, for the final work with Nixon himself. I had the principal responsibility, for example, for the major domestic Nixon speech of the campaign, on law and order. It was to be delivered in Philadelphia, in a key state. In preparing it, I consulted daily with Nixon's crime task force in Washington, headed by Rep. Richard Poff of Virginia, a man of great intelligence and a careful student of the subject who later declined a nomination to the Supreme Court. I also consulted a legal task force in New York which had been assigned to process policy recommendations. Should there be a law enforcement academy, similar to West Point? Could the role of computers be enhanced? What about gun control? The process went through innumerable drafts, Jim Keogh discussing the evolving speech with Nixon on the phone.

When I joined the tour aboard *The Tricia*, I found the plane to be a technological marvel. It was a regular commercial jet, completely refitted for the campaign. Nixon had a private cabin near the front. The midsection of the cabin was full of sophisticated electronic equipment. There were several rows of seats for staff, complete with individual air-to-ground phones. You could phone anybody, anywhere. While working with Reagan in Sacramento, I had rented my house in Vermont to an actor from Berkeley who had a temporary job at Dartmouth—a mistake. I tried to call my house from the plane only to discover that the home phone had been disconnected, the actor having left a three-hundred-dollar phone bill.

Nixon worked carefully on a major speech like this one. He annotated it in his small and precise handwriting. At the time, I was still naive enough to believe that we were working on actual public policy, at least making serious recommendations, and that something here might actually matter where crime was concerned. In fact, despite the prominence of the law and order issue in the 1968 campaign, and despite the ingenuity of some of the ideas in the speech, nothing much was done—or could have been done—about crime in America. The whole point of the speech was political, and it was successful. George Wallace was talking about "law and order" and about running his car over those protesters. Hubert Humphrey was saying liberally that you had to have "justice" before you could have order, a nonsensical idea. We split the difference, weighing in with "Order and Justice Under Law." I played some variations on a Winston Churchill World War II speech on the theme of "have we come all this way" only to etcetera, in this case, see our cities go up in smoke and our campuses become hostage to fanatics and our streets become muggers' heaven. We talked about the Forgotten American, a phrase coined by Herbert Hoover, the citizen who goes to work and pays his taxes—that is, who is not a hippie, a Black Panther, or a war protester. I drew these themes together with a single line over which Nixon was practically ecstatic. Ramsey Clark, Lyndon Johnson's attorney general, always seemed to be saying that crime was the fault of society. The criminality belonged not to the perpetrator, but to the victim! Clark was also a Vietnam dove, so I called him a "conscientious objector in the war against crime." The crowd in Philadelphia loved it, and so did Nixon, so much so that he ad libbed into the speech a nonsensical promise to the effect that "When I am president, we will have a new attorney general." Wild applause. As if any incoming president would keep the previous administration's cabinet members. Our instincts in that speech were absolutely correct, though no one in his wildest dreams could have foreseen that the improbable Clark would find himself making propaganda for the North Vietnamese over Hanoi radio. (I recently discovered that LBJ had at least as much contempt for Clark as we did in the Nixon campaign.) But, alas, we lost Pennsylvania, the Democrats turning out enough blacks in Philadelphia to carry the city by a solid margin, the state by a narrow one.

I have mentioned the "new men" who appeared in the 1968 Nixon campaign, the talented men and women, many of them young, many of them Catholics and Jews, who represented something new and important in the Republican equation. But if you put the 1968 campaign in a certain historical perspective, its enormous significance quickly becomes clear. The 1968 campaign constituted a bridge between Eisenhower in the Fifties and Reagan in the Eighties. The Republican party in the Sixties was in the process of turning West and South, and it was Nixon's historic role—which he did not entirely comprehend—to provide the bridge between past and present. In 1960, Nixon had run with Henry Cabot Lodge, a Brahmin from Massachusetts. In 1968, he ran with Spiro Agnew, a border state governor and also an ethnic. The shift symbolized profound economic and demographic changes and responded to them.

In 1960, running with Lodge, Nixon also felt obliged to submit to Nelson Rockefeller's demand that he include in the Republican platform praise for the black sit-in protesters in the South. In 1968, any such gesture would have been out of the question, and not only because George Wallace would have leaped on it gleefully.

Consider the following enormous political facts. During the entire post-Civil War period, including the first half of the twentieth century, the South was the nation's most Democratic region, the Solid South, as it was called. FDR could count on sweeping the electoral votes of the entire region, adding some big states, and coasting home to an easy victory.

At the same time, the Northeast—Cabot Lodge, Tom Dewey country—was the most consistently Republican part of the nation. Today, the Northeast is the most *Democratic* region, and the South votes heavily for Ronald Reagan. The regions have more or less reversed their historic post-Civil War political identities.

Take another large set of facts. During the post-Civil War and New Deal periods, the South was the nation's poorest region, hookworm headquarters. During the depression, when I was a child, my Brooklyn grandparents had relatives in the South to whom they often sent shipments of food and used clothing. In its impoverished condition, the South went for New Deal programs like TVA, rural electrification, road building, the CCC. A place like Atlanta was a sleepy backwater where chickens walked in the streets. Today, the Sunbelt is booming and prefers Reagan's economics to government programs. The Northeast has declined economically, becoming more Democratic in the process. Again the regional identities have been reversed.

Franklin Roosevelt's New Deal coalition survived 1948, though in Truman's upset victory over Dewey, signs of breakup were plain to see. At the 1948 convention, the young mayor of Minneapolis, Hubert Humphrey, made a fiery civil rights speech that brought him national attention, but also produced a schism on the right, with Strom Thurmond running on the States Rights ticket. This foreshadowed the eventual Southern defection from the Democratic coalition. The same year, Henry Wallace ran on the Progressive ticket, breaking with Truman over policy toward the Soviet Union. A young history teacher named George McGovern worked for the Wallace ticket: trouble ahead for the Democrats from the Left. In 1948, Dewey lost to Truman very narrowly. It would probably be more accurate to say that he lost to the ghost of Franklin Roosevelt. Millions of voters had never voted for anyone for president but Roosevelt, had never voted anything but Democratic, and the Democratic habit was strong.

In 1952, Eisenhower's immense popularity enabled him to break into the formerly solid South, and he was also able to make big gains among Catholics in the suburbs. Increasingly, these elements of the FDR coalition were up for grabs. As we can see now in his *Diaries* and from much other evidence, Eisenhower wrestled with the political problem of bringing these voters and interests into the Republican party. He had detached them—but he did not succeed in permanently re-attaching them to the Republicans, though his Frank Lausche-Catholic scheme might have worked. In 1960, instead of Lodge, Nixon might have done far better to have picked either a Catholic or a Southern running mate, and fought Kennedy either for the suburban Catholics or the suspicious Southerners. Lodge could not even help him against Kennedy in Massachusetts, his home state.

The year 1964 was pivotal. Of course, Goldwater went down to overwhelming defeat, but he scored heavily in the states of the old Confederacy, and his defeat of Rockefeller at the Republican convention represented the Appomattox of Northeastern Republicanism. The old Republican establishment was finished. It was politically vulnerable in its power base of New York, Massachusetts, Pennsylvania, and Ohio. But new opportunities were opening to the South and West. Manhattan and the Rockefellers were still powerful, so was Chase Manhattan, but in Houston, Los Angeles, and at the Bank of America, all the vectors curved upward.

In 1964, the establishment Republicans of the Northeast, people like Rockefeller, Lindsay, Scranton, either ignored the Goldwater campaign or were openly hostile to it. It would not be long before most of them had retired from politics or crossed to the Democrats. Today, almost nothing is left of that breed of Republican. But Nixon did not ignore the Goldwater campaign. He worked hard for it, endorsing Goldwater and speaking all across the country. Nixon was negotiating his own transition from the older Republican party to a new one that was in the process of being born. Only weeks after his defeat, Goldwater endorsed Nixon for 1968, when he would run with a "Southern strategy" and a running mate from Maryland.

The Ford and Carter presidencies were aberrations connected with Watergate. Had Nixon served until 1976, a full eight years, he certainly would have engineered the nomination of John Connally, a Texan, the 1972 leader of "Democrats for Nixon." The 1976 Republican convention would have been held in San Diego, down the beach from San Clemente. It did not happen that way, but the Watergate aberration cannot alter deep running trends. Instead of Connally, we have Reagan—from Pacific Palisades, which is up the beach from San Clemente.

The beach at San Clemente is a dazzling strip of sand backed by lion-colored cliffs. The colors of living flora and fauna are sharper there than in the East, the deep greens and purples of the shrubbery, the tiny flitting birds colored bright yellow or light green. Half a dozen college kids were surfing. A freighter inched its way along the horizon. Four silvery Navy jets screamed southward toward their San Diego base. That morning I had visited Nixon at La Casa Pacifica. A year-and-a-half earlier, he had resigned from the presidency, but he had recovered his spirits and was working on his memoirs. Contrary to some reports, the Nixon compound bustled with activity—visitors, phone calls, congressmen on the line. The low Spanish-style house is magnificent perched on its cliff overlooking the Pacific.

I asked Nixon about the tapes. Connally had told him to destroy them.

"Yes," Nixon said. "I should have followed his advice. But, I didn't. And here we are."

We chatted about foreign affairs, about China. Nixon had a jade Chinese backscratcher dating from 600 B.C. The Pacific glistened outside the picture window.

The Pacific! As a child, I possessed the Pacific imaginatively, even though I had never laid eyes on it. My Pacific was this vast expanse of blue water under cloudless skies. It should have been painted by Raoul Dufy. Then my mental focus would narrow, "pan in," as movie directors say, upon an island with golden sands and palm trees, and with a blue lagoon on which there was always landing one of those Pan Am flying boats. See the white spray as it touches the blue water of the lagoon. The pilot and co-pilot, stepping off onto the quays, always wore starched white cotton uniforms, with epaulettes and gold braid. It was important in this vision that their shirts always had short sleeves. Tanned, tropical. They called each other "Mister."

I asked Nixon about the local legend that back before World War II he had walked along the beach here with Patricia Ryan, his future wife, and dreamed about owning La Casa Pacifica, one of the notable mansions in Southern California. Nixon could not remember doing this, but the idea has a poetic rightness. He had dreamed about those trains in the night as a boy, and he had come a long way from the lemon groves and from his father's grocery store to fame, global achievement, disaster, survival, riches.

In the 1952 Checkers speech, Nixon had painfully exposed his meager assets and tried to make a virtue out of them with the symbol of his wife's plain Republican cloth coat. Things would change drastically. After his 1962 defeat for the California governorship, he headed back East again and joined the Wall Street law firm of Mudge, Stern, Baldwin and Todd, which soon became Nixon, Mudge, Rose, Guthrie, and Alexander. As a practicing lawyer, his salary was around $100,000 a year. He bought a ten-room Fifth Avenue apartment, which he sold for $311,023 when he entered the White House, further augmenting his capital with $250,000 from his book *Six Crises*. He had stock holdings of $371,000.

From then on, he never looked back financially. This capital became the basis for some startlingly successful real estate ventures. Within the first seven months of his election, the President purchased two expensive and elaborate new estates—at San Clemente, California and Key Biscayne, Florida.

In Key Biscayne, the transaction involved a cluster of houses on Bay Lane, a pleasant road stretching along the Biscayne Bay. In the fall of 1968, Richard Nixon had stayed in the brick and stucco ranch house of an old friend, Senator George A. Smathers. On December 20, 1968, Nixon bought this house on 500 Bay Lane for $125,527. A second house on 516 Bay Lane was sold to Nixon for $127,800 through a transaction between the owner, Manual Area, Jr., and Nixon's close friend, Bebe Rebozo, who also conveniently owned a house at 490 Bay Lane.

The transactions at the San Clemente property involved a fourteen-room Spanish-style hacienda and 26 acres, for $1.4 million. Nixon, unable to finance this transaction, borrowed $450,000 from his millionaire friend Bob Abplanalp, a Swiss who had invented the aerosol spray. Nixon put $400,000 down on the estate and assumed a $1 million mortgage on the rest. He hoped to sell all but 5.9 acres to a suitable buyer, perhaps the trustee of a proposed Nixon Presidential Library.

On December 15, 1970, unable to sell land to the trustees of the projected Nixon Library, Nixon resold the unwanted land to the B & C Investment Company headed by Bob Abplanalp and his silent partner, Bebe Rebozo. This purchase cancelled Abplanalp's earlier loans to Nixon, now totalling some $625,000, and Nixon paid $600,000 of the $900,000 remaining on the original San Clemente mortgage. After all of these intricate dealings, Nixon emerged owning one of the most beautiful homes on the California coast for a total expenditure of $374,514. During the Watergate furor, it came out that he had also improved San Clemente at some substantial public expense, though this may at least in part have been the effort of zealous subordinates eager to please the boss.

And there were deals upon deals in Florida, arranged by Bebe Rebozo. In 1967, Nixon purchased 199,891 shares in one of Rebozo's companies which controlled Fisher's Island, an undeveloped island located between Miami Beach and Key Biscayne. Nixon paid one dollar per share. In 1969, Rebozo bought 185,891 of these shares, but at two dollars per share, almost doubling Nixon's investment. Nixon bought two undeveloped lots in Key Biscayne from the Cape Florida Development Company, paying $38,000. In 1972, he sold the lots to William S. Griffin, an officer in Bob Abplanalp's Precision Valve Company, for $150,000, nearly quadrupling his investment.

Nixon also tried to handle the tax problems on all this through the use of his congressional and vice presidential papers, donating them to the National Archives. The trouble here was that LBJ had achieved a huge tax deduction with his papers, and the Congress had passed a law against this type of thing. Nixon's tax accountant apparently beat the legal deadline by falsifying the date on the donation documentation, a maneuver that emerged during Watergate. Nixon took an $80,000 tax deduction for his congressional papers, and a deduction of $570,000 for the vice presidential papers. He took $60,000 of this on his 1969 return, with the remainder to be spread over the next five years. Thus, in 1970 Nixon paid an income tax of $792.81, and, in 1972, $873.03, about what a family earning $8,000 a year normally pays. Eventually, Nixon was required to pay $465,000 in back taxes.

In 1978, his memoir, *RN: The Memoirs of Richard Nixon,* climbed onto the bestseller lists and stayed there for an extended period, both in hardcover and softcover. The Nixon offices in San Clemente provided his publisher, Grosset and Dunlap, with a list of Nixon supporters compiled from his presidential mail and other sources. And Grosset and Dunlap mailed out 100,000 letters to them. Instead of the regular trade edition, they could, for $50, get a copy with a book plate autographed by Nixon; for $250, they could get a leather-bound copy with 22 karat gold ornamentation. Nixon made a financial killing on the *Memoirs.* In 1980, his global strategy book, *The Real War,* sold very well and was intellectually impressive.

By that time, he had sold the estate at San Clemente for a handsome profit—though he had to take some flak about those government financed improvements—and bought an elegant town house on East 65th Street in Manhattan. He paid $750,000 for this, and sold it two years later for $2.6 million, buying a country estate in New Jersey for $1.2 million. As a former president, he enjoys an office, staff and secret service protection at government expense, and has an annual pension of $69,000.

The personal curve has been mostly up, but not entirely. Nixon has spent around $1 million defending himself against law suits arising out of Watergate, and he settled out of court a law suit brought by A. Ernest Fitzgerald, a Pentagon official who had challenged military costs and been fired; this cost $144,000. And in October 1981, when police cracked the murderous Kathy Boudin radical underground circle, they uncovered plans to assassinate Nixon at his recently acquired New Jersey estate. But Nixon is finishing a new book, certain to be a best seller, about famous figures he has known—Chou En-lai, Mao, De Gaulle, Churchill, Eisenhower, and numerous others. He has been in the foreground of twentieth-century politics since 1946, when he was first elected to Congress.

Richard Nixon is a battle-scarred veteran of the political wars. He has been the "man in the arena," as he likes to say, the man of action who dares greatly and risks great defeat. In private life, he is delightful company, thoroughly versed in American history and full of anecdotes, often racy and earthy. He has come a long way, in his current relative serenity, from that plain Republican cloth coat of the 1952 Checkers speech. Despite Watergate—or, well, perhaps including it—he has had a remarkable career.

SINATRA

Frank Sinatra stood there in the banquet room at the White House with tears in his eyes, looking at the President of the United States. In their very different ways, both Sinatra and Nixon had been among the dominating figures of American life in the middle decades of the twentieth century. Sinatra struggled to speak. It was a stag dinner for Pierre Trudeau. Earlier that evening, the taxis and limousines had pulled up at the elliptical driveway before the entrance. Not far away the Washington Monument was a gleaming needle in the dusk. Men in evening clothes strolled past the Marine guards and went upstairs to the reception and cocktails. Waiters circulated with trays of cocktails. Bob Haldeman roamed around taking home movies. Henry Kissinger chatted with John Connally. After a while, the eight-member Marine band suddenly went into action, playing "Hail to the Chief." The double doors slid open, and Richard Nixon and Pierre Trudeau strode into the room. Nixon waved his hand in an oddly constricted and tentative greeting. There was a receiving line. Trudeau was urbane and courtly, and very French. The president and the prime minister chatted with the guests.

The dinner later on was socially heterogeneous. Frank Fitzsimmons, head of the Teamsters, was there. He was a Nixon supporter. A banker introduced himself to D. Keith Mano, the novelist. "What line of work are you in," asked the banker. "Cement," replied Mano. The novelist actually owns a cement factory in Long Island City. Frank Sinatra was having an animated conversation with the vice president, Spiro Agnew.

After dinner, Nixon thought we should have some brief remarks by Agnew and Connally. They were hot news. Connally was widely regarded as angling for Agnew's spot on the 1972 ticket. "I was in San Francisco the other day," said Agnew. "I phoned my office. There was a man with a Texas accent on the other end of the line."

Nixon asked Frank Sinatra to sing a few songs. The Marine band came into the room and accompanied Sinatra. He sang "Tea for Two," "Smoke Gets in Your Eyes," "Nancy With the Laughing Face," "Ol' Man River."

Sinatra's energy filled the room. His voice was not the famous voice of the Forties, but the presence had become more powerful, partly because of his legend. He is a sexual Houdini, a Tarzan. During the Fifties, he had a tumultuous affair with a famous movie actress. She had bounced off an affair with Dominguin, the bullfighter, and landed on Frank. Sinatra began to experience a loss of artistic energy. He began to fade as a singer, but then made a comeback as a movie star. He introduced Judy Exner to Jack Kennedy and Exner became a regular visitor to the White House.

Standing there at the president's party, Frank sang "The House I Live In." This is a song drenched in Forties patriotism, World War II stuff. "The house I live in," sang Sinatra, "the people that I meet, the girl I left behind me, the policeman on the beat. . . ."

At that time and place, this was especially moving. Outside, across the country that year, the nation seemed to be pretty heavily populated with war protesters and dope fiends. The papers were full of Charlie Manson.

"That is America to meee," Sinatra concluded. He meant it. He meant every word of that World War II patriotism, dying for apple pie and the Brooklyn Dodgers.

The president of the United States stood up in his place at the table.

"That was wonderful, Frank," he said. "We are all honored to hear you sing. I myself found your last song deeply moving, and I wonder if you would sing it again for us as an encore."

Sinatra had trouble replying.

"Mr. President," he said, "I grew up in Hoboken. . . . When I was a boy, I never thought I would be standing here in the White House, singing in the White House, talking with the President. Well, maybe that *is* what America is to me, what America is about." Sinatra began to cry. Then he got control of himself, the Marine band began to play. "The house I live in, the people that I meet," sang Sinatra, "the girl I left behind me, the policeman on the beat. . . ."

CHAPTER TEN

Real Witches

"That's the most unheard of thing I ever heard of."

> Senator Joseph McCarthy
> during a Senate committee
> investigation of Communism.

One evening in the fall of 1962, I was having dinner with the late Lionel Trilling at the Faculty Club at Columbia. We had known each other for years. He had been an important professor for me when I was an undergraduate at Columbia, and, after the Korean War, when I came back to teach English there, he was a friend. That evening, over dinner, he said something very odd.

I had been doing some research, and I had been surprised to find that another of my influential professors, Frederick W. Dupee, an exceptionally cosmopolitan and suave lecturer on modern European literature, had been some kind of Communist during the 1930s. I had come across, in *The New Masses,* a review by Dupee of Joseph Stalin's 1936 *Soviet Constitution.* I was amazed. There was Dupee, praising the homely peasant virtues of Stalin's prose—as if the dictator had personally written this fraudulent document himself. Not only this, but I found that Dupee's close friend, the late Richard Rovere—in 1962 the urbane Washington

correspondent of *The New Yorker*—had also been a Communist:
youth editor of the same *New Masses*.

"Oh," said Trilling, "everyone was a Communist during the
Thirties."

I knew that this was not true. None of the people I had grown up
among were Communists. Even Trilling had not been; he had at
that time considered himself a Marxist and a Freudian.

Trilling said one other strange thing during that dinner. I had
met William F. Buckley, Jr. socially, through a student in one of
my summer courses at Columbia, and, while we chatted about this
at dinner, I actually had a book review in the mail to Buckley. I still
remember the book, Aldous Huxley's prescient account of chemically induced mysticism, *The Doors of Perception*. In the midst of
this conversation, Trilling said:

"You wouldn't ever write for *National Review*, would you?"

This was an intimidating question. My review *had* been mailed.
I did *not* have tenure at Columbia. And Trilling was a very senior
and powerful professor, even a world figure. But I subsequently
thought about both of these remarks a good deal. It was clear from
Trilling's nonchalant attitude toward Dupee, Rovere, and Communism on the one hand, and his anxious question about *National
Review* on the other, that he evidently considered Buckley and
National Review in some way *worse* than *The New Masses* and
Communism and a rave review of Stalin's phony Constitution. It
seemed to have some connection with that other odd remark, "Oh,
everyone was a Communist during the Thirties."

Everyone?

I subsequently reviewed all of my contact with Communists and
Communism while growing up in the Thirties. It was minor, but in
various ways significant, and I touch upon it briefly here both to
establish my own attitudes in the matter and to give some background for the discussion that will follow of the Communist issue
during the Fifties. The Fifties were hardly apolitical. The Communist issue was boiling.

Sometime around 1934 or 1935, I was walking with my father,
the out-of-work architect, in Brooklyn's Prospect Park. He
pressed my hand—I can feel him still. A circular roadway, busy
with cars, runs around the park near its margins. All of a sudden, a
crowd of young people and some adults walked out into the
roadway. The adults raised their hands, interrupting traffic that
had the green light. I was surprised, impressed by their arrogance.

"The Young Communist League," my father explained. I vividly recall the incident, even now and it has since come to be symbolic to me of the arrogance and antidemocratic character of Communism. We moved to Queens when I was about five, and I began kindergarten. Before I went to high school, I met, so far as I know, only one Communist. This was an architect friend of my father who lived in Jackson Heights and had a Russian name. Sometimes my father would visit him on a Sunday afternoon, and, after some kidding about "sharing the wealth," they would both get drunk. Still, one Communist architect hardly qualified as "everyone" being a Communist during the Thirties.

At the end of the decade, when I was nine or ten, I followed the Finnish-Soviet war as a partisan, a passionate one, of the Finns. *Life* magazine was my source, with its superb photographs of those white-clad Finnish ski troops, and the Russian corpses frozen in the Finnish snow. The Russians, in contrast, entirely lacked style. Their equipment looked tinny. When the Russians won the war, and the Finnish pavilion closed at the New York World's Fair, I was crushed. And everyone—*everyone*—I knew had rooted for the Finns.

In 1943, I entered Stuyvesant High School, and there things changed a good deal. Stuyvesant was a special high school, one of the three in New York which required an entrance examination for admission, and it took the students with the best scores from all over the city. And at Stuyvesant, Communism was a very big deal. Communist Party Headquarters was a couple of blocks away in Union Square, and Communist literature ubiquitous. Over in Union Square, indeed, the various Communist factions had orators who harangued each other with endless venom and erudition. A lot of the students at Stuyvesant took their Marxism with the utmost seriousness, and for the first time in my life I listened to impassioned arguments about the dialectic, the role of the bourgeoisie, the merits or lack of them of the Hitler-Stalin Pact, of Trotsky, of Stalin. These students also knew all about things like Wagner's music, and most of them seemed to want to go to Harvard and become doctors. It was a fascinating world, utterly unlike any I had known. In the class that graduated the year before mine, Otto Eckstein was the number one student. He went on to Harvard, M.I.T., and the Council of Economic Advisors. In the New York State elections of 1946, Tom Dewey was running against former Governor Herbert Lehman. Stuyvesant decided to stage a debate on the election. The students had next to no interest in the major party candidates. I was the only student willing to speak for Dewey, and, as I recall, they had to come up with a shop teacher to speak for Lehman. All the student excitement revolved around left-wing and Communist minor candidates.

I entered Dartmouth in 1947 and found little or no Communism around that campus, though there was a lot of sympathy for Henry Wallace's 1948 Progressive Party candidacy. I do remember being temporarily moved by a student production of Koestler's *Darkness at Noon*. The single illuminated cell on a dark stage in which Rubashov lived and suffered seemed to me the epitome of political evil, as indeed Koestler had intended.

In 1950, I transferred to Columbia, studied with Trilling, Dupee, Barzun, Van Doren, listened to Niebuhr and Tillich. While at Columbia, as it happened, I met an authentic Communist functionary. I heard about him through a campus friend of mine, a philosophy-theology student who considered him an interesting character and took me over to meet him. Sam, the Communist—I have forgotten his foreign-sounding last name—had been a movie cameraman but now he was living in a dingy cold-water flat on the black and Hispanic East Side. He was a romantic and nocturnal character, nervous, sallow, always in motion. He was trying to agitate among the local blacks, so far as I can tell with no success at all. He admired the poet Kenneth Rexroth and the painter Ben Shahn, and he had known Kenneth Fearing. He believed fervently in "scientific socialism," and he gloated over the fact that the Russians now had the atomic bomb—but he had a good sense of humor. The last time I saw Sam, I had brought a rather classy debutante around to his dingy flat to see this character, and for some reason the girl was carrying a small piece of modern sculpture, one of those wiry things. "Is that," Sam asked her, "some new kind of a contraceptive?" She found Sam rather charming, which he was, but after that I never saw or heard of him again.

In June of 1952, I was graduated from Columbia and thrust into the midst of the Korean War. It was as a naval intelligence officer in Washington that I first seriously engaged the issues we are about to deal with here.

I had absolutely no desire to enter the armed forces. The stalemated Korean War seemed a dreary, even a ghastly thing. But letters from my local draft board hit my mail box with horrible regularity. Anything would be better than the infantry, I thought, and so I enlisted in the Navy, put in for officer training, and found myself in Naval Intelligence—as a matter of fact, in the Naval Intelligence School on the large naval base then in Anacostia, Maryland. We took courses on a large number of things pertaining to the duties of an intelligence officer, but I was fascinated by the controversies then taking place about internal security, the McCarthy charges, and the assorted investigations that had been going on in this area. I turned myself into a scholar of the whole controversial question, and the names *Amerasia,* Hiss, Owen Lattimore, Oppenheimer, Igor Gouzenko, Klaus Fuchs, Judith Coplon, took on concrete and vivid reality for me. I read and summarized the entire fifteen volumes of the senate investigation into the nature and influence of the Institute for Pacific Relations.

Again, like Stuyvesant High School, Anacostia was a very different world from the one I had grown up in, the world I had known. And looking back now, I think I can give a reasonable interpretation to Trilling's observation that "everyone" had been a Communist in the Thirties. That world was different from mine— but it was *not* different from the one in which Trilling had spent his formative years. Trilling had *known* Whittaker Chambers as an underground Communist. What Trilling meant is that "everyone"—a casual exaggeration, of course—in certain circles in New York intellectual life had been a Marxist or Communist of some kind; and the generalization could have been extended south to Washington and maybe north to Boston and Cambridge. Trilling's generalization could not have been extended to Queens, Long Island, of course. It was because he had grown up in that milieu— though most of his friends had long since ceased being Communists—that Trilling considered it okay to have written for *The New Masses,* but by no means acceptable to be writing for *National Review*. His historical and social pieties were deeply involved.

Anyway, it was during the early Fifties, when I went deeply into the literature on the question of American Communism, that I arrived at the following conclusions. Based on all of the available material, and there was an enormous amount of it, serious and honest scholars might well disagree over the extent, if any, of Communist influence on American policy making. That was one of the great controversies of the late Forties and early Fifties.

Thus, when Republicans and conservatives began complaining about the presence of Alger Hiss at Yalta and at the San Francisco conference which founded the United Nations, Harry Truman exploded that the issue was a "red herring." For this he was much ridiculed. But I now understand that when he screamed "red herring," Truman did not mean that Hiss was not a Communist and an agent. We now know that Igor Gouzenko, a defecting Soviet code clerk in Canada, had informed the Royal Canadian Mounted Police interrogators about numerous Soviet agents, and that the Prime Minister, Lester Pearson, had informed the White House that Hiss was one of them, and that the Truman White House had moved with alacrity to shunt Hiss off to the Carnegie Foundation for World Peace, out of the flow of classified material. Truman's "red herring" remark meant that the Republicans were making Hiss a *partisan* issue, whereas the national security problem had been solved. Indeed, by that time, John Foster Dulles, a trustee of the Carnegie Endowment, certainly knew that Truman and Acheson knew that Hiss had been a Communist. Nixon later learned that Truman, after reading the dossier on Hiss, had remarked to a Justice Department aide, "Why, that son-of-a-bitch has betrayed his country."

As I say, honest scholars can disagree over the importance of Communist influence on American policy making. What they cannot disagree about is the presence of actual Communists and proven Communist sympathizers in positions of great importance both inside and outside government.

Everyone now knows the essential details of the great headline-after-headline cases, like those of Hiss and the Rosenbergs. They have been the subject of countless books and articles and even movies and plays, and there is no need to go back over that material here. In any case, Allen Weinstein, in *Perjury,* has, in my opinion, settled once and for all the verdict on Hiss: guilty of perjury, in fact of espionage. And Louis Nizer appears to me to have settled the matter of the guilt of the Rosenbergs.

I would like, instead, to return to two almost forgotten cases of the period, forgotten now but important then, indeed consequential. They are interesting in themselves and invaluable as a key to the mood of the times. These were the *Amerasia* and "Institute of Pacific Relations" cases.

First, however, something that seems to me necessary for today's readers, most of whom are aware that there were congressional investigations of Communism in the early Fifties, but who probably have only a vague idea of what such hearings were like.

To set the stage for the two cases I have chosen, therefore, I would like to take a moment to reconstruct, with the help of the political philosopher James Burnham, a typical interrogation—not one of the famous and celebrated confrontations, but, more usefully, a routine hearing. This scene—"In the Caucus Room"—comes from Burnham's book *The Web of Subversion* (1959):

"A few minutes before 10 o'clock on the morning of May 1, 1953, my wife and I entered room 213, Senate Office Building. Like many other rooms on Capitol Hill—in the splendid Capitol building itself, in the two House Office Buildings and the Library of Congress—No. 318, the Senate Caucus Room, caught the look of dignity and measured purpose that marked the Republic's early days. It is large, noble in proportions, high-ceilinged, with handsome, light-colored paneling.

"Across one end was a long, fixed table, like a judge's bench. Several chairs were in back of this, and a few in front. Farther out, at right angles, were a half dozen tables for reporters. Off to each side were small groups of chairs for such special visitors as the relations or close friends of senators. All this occupied about a third of the room. In the remainder, there were three or four hundred chairs for whoever might enter, for the citizens of a free country who might want to watch their representatives carrying out their duties, for the merely curious, or even for enemies who for whatever purpose of check-up or intimidation might want to come.

"As we entered, television equipment was being adjusted. There was no excitement. It was plain that nothing special was expected, that all was routine. A few reporters, wandering casually in, chatted with each other. The general audience was never numbered more than sixty or seventy. Half of them we recognized from other similar hearings that we had watched: specialists; professionals in subversion (on one or the other side); observers for the military intelligence services, the FBI, the Central Intelligence Agency; informal representatives of four or five foreign governments. The rest were Public, just anyone who happened to open the door, tourists from Nebraska, high school seniors from Nashville who had won a bus trip to Washington, a couple of old men who had nothing else to do. All through the hearing that soon began, the Public drifted in and out. Some had only a few minutes allotted to this official "sight" of a conducted tour. Others were quickly bored. There were a few, though, who came, who realized, with a tightening of the face, what was unfolding there, and who stayed.

"Senator William E. Jenner of Indiana, in a fresh, grey double-breasted suit, took the chair in the middle of the front table, or bench. The Subcommittee on Internal Security of the Senate Judiciary Committee was about to begin its session. When the Democrats had lost control of Congress, Senator Jenner, replacing Democratic Senator Pat McCarran of Nevada, had become the subcommittee chairman. He was joined that morning by Senator Herman Welker of Idaho; the subcommittee's director of research, Benjamin Mandel; and the subcommittee counsel, Robert Morris.

"Two men entered from a side door and took chairs immediately in front of the senators, across the bench. One, obviously the witness, was slight, rather nervous in manner, with close-cropped hair. He was dressed in a dull suit of greenish cast. He was Anybody, Nobody. There would have been no reason to notice him, for good or ill. The other was, by his manner and briefcase, the attorney.

"The TV lights and cameras started, along with the opening of the hearing. The witness, whose name turned out to be Edward J. Fitzgerald, was questioned principally by Robert Morris, occasionally by one of the senators. His voice was undistinguished, low and hard to follow.

"There was nothing remarkable in the official story of his career, as this emerged under Robert Morris' steady questioning, supplemented by the documents that Benjamin Mandel had always exactly at hand. After study at the University of Vermont during the depression days, and a brief job on a "Eugenic Survey," Edward Fitzgerald went to work, as many a young man has done, for "the government." And, as some do, he prospered. He climbed, indeed rather quickly for one who had had no special training and no highly placed family connections.

"Fitzgerald began in 1936 with an agency called the National Research Project. This was a branch of the Depression-born Works Progress Administration (WPA), and was located in Philadelphia. Most of the few citizens who ever noticed the name of the National Research Project have long ago forgotten it. But let it now be remembered. It is not unimportant for our story. Its director was a man named David Weintraub, whose chief assistant was one Irving Kaplan. Those names also we shall frequently meet again.

"Fitzgerald's initial salary was a modest $1,800 a year, but it rose fast for those depression days. By 1941, always with David Weintraub's kindly sponsoring, it had reached $4,000. In that year Fitzgerald accepted a reduction to $3,200 when he shifted first to the Federal Security Agency and then to the Federal Works Agency. His modesty was soon rewarded. By 1942, a year later, he had completed a shift to the War Production Board, where, as "Principal Economist," he was drawing $5,600. His advance continued through a period in the Foreign Economic Administration and then the Department of Commerce. When he resigned from Commerce in September 1947, he had topped $8,000.

"There Edward Fitzgerald might seem to be—in appearance, manner and the framework of his career—indistinguishable from ten thousand others. Why, then, was he in that chair that morning? The record gives the incredible answer.

"In November 1945, two years before Fitzgerald resigned from his last government job, the Federal Bureau of Investigation prepared a top secret memorandum that was circulated a few weeks later among high government officials. It was this memorandum to which Attorney General Brownell referred in the speech on the Harry Dexter White case that he delivered in Chicago, November 6, 1953. One paragraph of the memorandum read as follows:

> The head of the next most important group of Soviet espionage agents with whom Bentley has maintained liaison was Victor Perlo of the War Production Board. Members of this group were introduced to Bentley in 1944 at the apartment of John Abt, General Counsel of the Amalgamated Clothing Workers of America, CIO, in New York City. The individuals in this group include Charles Kramer; . . . Henry Magdoff of the War Production Board; Edward Fitzgerald, formerly of the Treasury Department and then with the War Production Board. . .

"*Soviet espionage*—that is, *spying:* the unauthorized transmission of information to a government that is officially dedicated to the destruction of the United States government and the American form of society. A generation or even a decade ago, the suggestion of such a charge would have seemed to most Americans unbelievable, absurd. Did Edward Fitzgerald, then, at once and most indignantly deny it? Let us consult the record:

MR. MORRIS: Were you a member of the espionage ring described in that memorandum?

MR. FITZGERALD: I decline to answer on the ground it might tend to incriminate me.

MR. MORRIS: Did you know Mr. Victor Perlo who was named here as head of the ring?

MR. FITZGERALD: I decline to answer on the same ground.

MR. MORRIS: Do you know that Mr. John Abt named in this memorandum?

MR. FITZGERALD: I decline to answer on the same ground.

And so on.

"Mr. Fitzgerald was no less reticent on many other subjects about which he was questioned that morning. He declined (on the same ground that it might tend to incriminate him) to explain the circumstances leading to his job in the National Research Project. He declined to state whether he had been aided by David Weintraub or Irving Kaplan, then or later, or even whether he knew if he had known them. He declined to explain any of his transfers from one agency to another, or, whether anyone had suggested these transfers or helped in securing them.

"He declined to say whom he had listed as references in connection with his transfers. Documents were, however, introduced to supply some of the answers on this point. His superior officers on the National Research Project, David Weintraub and Irving Kaplan, could always, apparently, find a good word for their subordinate. Not only was Weintraub a recurrent reference. He spared no pains in writing letters of recommendation for Fitzgerald. He found Fitzgerald a man of 'excellent judgment . . . capable of assuming responsibility, ingenious, many good ideas, pleasant disposition, highly cooperative, diligent, straight-forward, loyal.' He gave an unqualified 'yes' as answer to such questions as: 'Is this person efficient and industrious? Is this person temperate in habits? Is this person of good moral character?'

SENATOR WELKER: While you were with the War Production Board did you give away any secret material to any known Communist or any espionage ring operating in Washington?

MR. FITZGERALD: I decline to answer that question on the ground it might tend to incriminate me . . .

SENATOR WELKER: Did you ever transfer any secret information, top secret information to William Remington while you were in the Department of Commerce?

MR. FITZGERALD: I decline to answer that question on the same ground . . .

SENATOR WELKER: Mr. Fitzgerald, as of this moment, are you a member of a secret espionage or sabotage ring against the interest of the Government of the United States?

MR. FITZGERALD: I decline to answer that question on the same ground as before.

"In 1947, Mr. Averell Harriman, then Secretary of Commerce, suggested to Fitzgerald that he take a leave of absence. 'I said I preferred under the circumstances to resign.' The subcommittee displayed interest in what Fitzgerald has been doing since his resignation from government service. He has become, he testified, a freelance writer. He has written some fiction for *Confession Magazine* (sic), but principally he has been a book reviewer, assigned most often to novels. For an economic analyst he seems to have taken readily to this new field of interest. His main clients have been three of the nation's most important book-screening media: the *New York Times Book Review;* the New York *Herald Tribune Book Review;* and the *Saturday Review*. In the first four months of 1953, he had six reviews published in the *Times,* 53 in the *Saturday Review,* and about 50 in the *Herald Tribune.*

"In connection with the *Saturday Review* there was a rather strange colloquy during the hearing:

MR. MORRIS: Did you know Mr. Norman Cousins? (Editor of the *Saturday Review*)

MR. FITZGERALD: I do.

MR. MORRIS: Did he know about your having been identified in Washington as a member of a wartime espionage ring?

MR. FITZGERALD: May I consult?

MR. MORRIS: You may. (Witness confers with counsel.)

MR. FITZGERALD: I discussed the matter with Norman Cousins.

MR. MORRIS: Did you make any explanation to him?

MR. FITZGERALD: I decline to answer that question.

MR. MORRIS: Did you deny the allegations in the published testimony about your participation in the war espionage ring?

MR. FITZGERALD: I decline to answer that question on the same ground as before."

The *Amerasia* case is one of the most unusual cases in the history of espionage, and it sheds a great deal of light on what might be called "the acceptability of Communism," both Soviet and American, among important journalists and intellectuals at the end of World War II.

The magazine *Amerasia* was started in 1936 by Frederick Vanderbilt Field, a millionaire Communist, and Philip Jaffe, a greeting-card manufacturer and close friend of Earl Browder. Jaffe had run the Communist publication *China Today* with Frederick Vanderbilt Field under the pseudonym J. W. Phillips, and during the investigation was identified under oath as a Communist. He had written a book on China called *New Frontiers in Asia*. According to the testimony of Professor Kenneth Colegrove, an Asian specialist from Northwestern University and no partisan of the Left, who had been a member of the original *Amerasia* advisory board, the ostensible purpose of the magazine was to translate into popular terms what the specialists were saying about Asian affairs. Colegrove and other scholars felt that this would be a genuine service to the American people. Around 1940, however, Colegrove found that an increasing number of the pieces published followed the Communist line, many of them published over his protest. In 1942, Colegrove resigned from the board of *Amerasia*.

Early in 1945, this obscure little journal became nationally famous as the focal point of the *Amerasia* case. It came about this way. On February 28, 1945, Archbold Van Beuren, the security officer for the Office of Strategic Services, visited the New York office of Frank Bielaski, Director of Investigations for the OSS.

He showed Bielaski a document that had been prepared by Kenneth E. Wells of the OSS Research Division. It was an analysis of conditions in Thailand and carried a "Secret" classification. Wells, then reading the January 26 issue of *Amerasia,* came across an article on British-American relations in Thailand. He had the sudden realization that he had seen a lot of this article before, that, in fact, he himself had written much of it. Checking it against his secret report, he discovered that entire paragraphs from the secret government document had been carried over into the *Amerasia* article. Frank Bielaski was assigned the job of discovering the source of the leak, a difficult job since the secret report had been disseminated to at least thirty government officers.

Bielaski decided to have a look at the *Amerasia* offices in Manhattan. On Sunday night, March 11, 1945, five agents and a lock expert from the Office of Naval Intelligence entered the building and gained access to the offices through a superintendent. They noticed that for a tiny-circulation magazine, *Amerasia* possessed a remarkable quantity of photocopying apparatus. The reason for this soon became clear. Searching through the offices, Bielaski and his agents found dozens of photocopies of government documents, some of them marked "Top Secret."

"I was, of course, nonplussed after seeing all this stuff," Bielaski later testified. One of the investigators said to me, 'You haven't seen anything yet. Let me show you what is in the envelope.' So he opened the envelope and pulled out about, I would say, a dozen or fifteen documents which were the same as those lying around the place. I didn't read them particularly. It was when I started to look at them he said, 'Wait a minute. You are looking at the wrong place; look in between them.' And here, in between these documents we found six typewritten documents . . . and all six of them were marked 'Top Secret.'

"Of the six, I remember only two. . . . The first dealt with the disposition of the units of the Japanese Navy subsequent to the Battle of Leyte. . . . It showed them by name and the ports where they were hiding or place where they were hiding, and if they were disabled.

"The second document was one which was headed, to the best of my knowledge, the bombing program or strategic bombing program for Japan; and it said in effect that the targets would be the principal industrial cities of Japan. I don't remember the cities named, but my recollection is that they would be bombed progressively, until they reached the point where they couldn't stand it any longer, and that would be the end of it. It was a progressive plan of bombing for Japan.

"I went back to Jaffe's office, and the men there had listed four or five of these documents. About that time, we happened to pull the office door back, and I discovered, behind that door, a very large bellows suitcase which had the initials of P.J.J. as I recall on it, which we believed to be Jaffe's initials. I had the lock man immediately open that, and that was stuffed so full of documents that we just dropped everything. I knew it was impossible to make a list of all of them, and told the men we might just as well discontinue making the list, and we would have to decide what we were going to do. We had only, by the way, about an hour and a half in that place. We had agreed to get out, and thought there was time enough.

"I have tried to estimate . . . how many documents we saw there . . . and it was a conservative number to say there were 400. I didn't believe that anybody would believe me if I made a written report on what we saw and what we did. . . . So I decided to take enough with me to show them what we had found.

"I took between twelve and fourteen documents. I took either four or five OSS documents and . . . documents which had initials or something on them which would permit us to trace the channels through which they had come . . . the State Department, Military Intelligence, Naval Intelligence, Bureau of Censorship, British Intelligence, OSS, and possibly some others. . . . Also, those that I saw also were marked to the effect that 'The possession of these documents by an unauthorized person constitutes a violation of the Espionage Act.'

"Among these documents was a lengthy document detailing the location of the units of the Nationalist Army of China, their strength, how they were armed, where they were located.

"Before we left the office of *Amerasia,* we found five typewritten copies of the document we were looking for. We did not find the original, but found five unfolded and perfectly clean typewritten copies. I think that is significant, if I may digress for a moment, for this reason. We felt, or we considered, this thing that we had stepped into was a well-established and going wholesale business in stealing government documents, and that there was every means there for reproducing. The fact that the original document of the

OSS was not there, but that five typewritten copies were there, made us believe that a batch had come in ahead of our trip, our visit to the office, they had moved out, the originals had gone back to Washington, and these five copies were found, that was all that was left.

"I came down here, went to the office of Mr. Van Beuren, and handed him the five copies of the document he was looking for, and told him where I got it. He was very much pleased.

"Then I proceeded to hand him, one by one, the four or five additional documents that had been stolen from OSS, documents that originated from OSS, and one of them, he told me, was of such secrecy that it was almost calamitous. It was a document that was marked for the Chief of Naval Intelligence only, a secret document. I don't know what it was about . . . I brought it with me, and it was an original, as well as the others that I brought, original documents of varying degrees of secrecy."

The foregoing testimony was given in executive session to the Senate Internal Security Subcommittee, at that time under the chairmanship of Senator Millard Tydings, a Maryland Democrat. Tydings asked his Republican colleagues not to make known what had transpired in his hearing room, but there was no way to keep the cork in that particular bottle, and a typical sequence of events quickly followed. Senator Joseph McCarthy knew the whole story and was being used by FBI Director J. Edgar Hoover as a conduit to the press. McCarthy gave the *Amerasia* story to Frederick Woltman of the Scripps-Howard newspapers, and it hit the streets at 11:00 A.M., in stunning and accurate detail, in the Washington *News*. Here is the story amazed Washingtonians found in their morning paper:

Capitol Hill was rocked today by the disclosure that the *Amerasia* documents, now under scrutiny by the Tydings Senate subcommittee, contain startling military and high state secrets of a nature hitherto unrevealed. . . . Today, for the first time, the contents of a tiny fraction—five out of 1700—are public property. Their authenticity as part of the *Amerasia* collection is affirmed by Senator Bourke B. Hickenlooper (R., Ia.), a member of the Tydings subcommittee.

Here is the nature of at least five of the secret *Amerasia* documents stolen from government wartime files:

The Navy's formal wartime 'organization plan' for setting up counterintelligence operations throughout the United States. It was sent by the director of Naval Intelligence to the ranking intelligence officers of the nation's 14 naval districts.

A highly confidential forecast of the trends of the war in the Pacific, delivered by Assistant Secretary of State Joseph C. Grew to top officials in the Department. It gave the location of twenty-five American submarines then in Pacific waters. And it outlined the government's policy with respect to the Japanese emperor.

A document setting forth in detail the composition of allied troops in Malaya.

Details about two messages from President Roosevelt to Generalissimo Chiang Kai-shek. In them, the President proposed that General Joseph Stilwell be made commander of all armies in China, including the Communist armies. The messages, delivered in July 1944, were routed through the U.S. Army commander in Chungking, then General Stilwell. The report itself bore the top secret classification for 'Eyes Only.' That phrase meant it was to be read by no one except the person to whom it was addressed.

A message addressed to the American Embassy in China, and sent by the State Department over the name of former Secretary of State Cordell Hull . . .

Last week Senator Millard Tydings (D., Md.), chairman of the subcommittee, announced it had testimony that 99 percent of the *Amerasia* documents were 'casual and routine.' The rest, he added, were only of 'some importance.'

Thus the storm swirled around the investigation being conducted in 1951 by the Tydings subcommittee. Let us return to the spring of 1945 and the bizarre events that followed the discovery of the document cache in the *Amerasia* offices.

As we have seen, Frank Bielaski took his samples of stolen government documents to Archbold van Beuren, the security officer of the OSS. Van Beuren was shocked by the sensitivity of the documents he examined. After a conference with the chief legal counsel of the OSS, it was decided to take the matter directly to the head of the agency, General "Wild Bill" Donovan. He, in turn, immediately conferred with the Secretary of State, Edward Stettinius, who consulted Secretary of the Navy James V. Forrestal. The case was removed from the jurisdiction of the OSS and turned over to the FBI, whose investigation turned up still more stolen documents.

The FBI also established the identities of the principal figures involved in and around the *Amerasia* offices. Philip Jaffe and Kate Mitchell were identified as the editors, and FBI surveillance indicated that they were in frequent contact with a man named Emmanuel Larsen of the State Department, Lieutenant Andrew Roth of the Office of Naval Intelligence, and a writer for *Collier's* magazine named Mark Gayn. Lieutenant Roth functioned as a liaison between the State Department and the Office of Naval Intelligence. Within a month, the FBI informed the State Department and the Navy Department that it was prepared to turn its evidence over to the Justice Department for prosecution. The two departments, however, requested that the indictments be delayed, presumably to allow for further investigation into the possibility that other personnel might be involved in the apparent espionage network.

Political considerations, however, were also playing a role in delaying prosecution under the Espionage Act. In his diary entry for May 28, 1945, Secretary of the Navy James Forrestal indicated that considerations of international politics were impinging upon the *Amerasia* case:

> Major Correa reported to me that the Department of Justice has evidence to the effect that Lieutenant Andrew Roth has been furnishing confidential and secret documents to a man named Jaffe, head of a publication named *Amerasia* in New York City. Jaffe has had intimate relationship with the Russian consul in New York. . . . Major Correa reported that it was proposed that Lieutenant Roth should be taken into surveillance Wednesday. He said that the FBI thought that unless speedy action were taken important evidence would be dissipated, lost and destroyed. I pointed out that the inevitable consequence of such action now would be to greatly embarrass the President in his current conversations with Stalin, because of the anti-Russian play-up the incident would receive out of proportion to its importance.

That Forrestal, a Catholic and an anti-Communist, felt that international considerations were more important than the *Amerasia* espionage case is a powerful indication of the government's priorities in the spring of 1945. Reinforcing the administration's political caution, no doubt, was the fact that the San Francisco conference to organize the United Nations was taking place at the same time. (Alger Hiss, of the State Department, was playing a prominent role in San Francisco.) Forrestal's position, in any case, amounted only to keeping President Truman informed about the *Amerasia* case.

The prospective indictments also ran into legal problems. On May 29, 1945, representatives of the FBI met with James M. McInerney of the Justice Department to lay out the case against Jaffe, Mitchell, Larsen, Gayn and Roth, and also against John Stewart Service of the Department of State. Service had given government documents to Jaffe, explaining that Jaffe had been "interested" in them. But of the three categories of information possessed by the FBI, two were not admissible in court. One was a recording of a conversation between Jaffe and John Stewart Service which had been obtained by bugging a hotel room in which Jaffe had been staying in Washington. The conversation concerned U.S. military policy in the event of an American landing in China. The second inadmissible body of evidence was the material that had been discovered in Frank Bielaski's illegal entry into the offices of *Amerasia,* and in an FBI search of the apartment of Emmanuel Larsen. This meant that the only admissible evidence available to the prosecutors would be the results of the continuing FBI surveillance of the principals, information about whom they had seen and where, and for how long, information that might establish inferences but not much more. Nevertheless, on June 2, 1945, informed about the state of the case, President Truman telephoned the FBI and ordered that the arrests be made and the case brought to prosecution. The FBI made the six arrests in the late afternoon of June 6, 1945, finding some six hundred government documents in Jaffe's office and another two hundred in Larsen's apartment, plus forty-two in Mark Gayn's home. They came from the State Department, the Navy Department, the OSS, the War Department, and other key agencies. Nevertheless, the attitude of the Justice Department seems to have been oddly lethargic. McInerney, Assistant Attorney General in charge of the Criminal Division, regarded the government's case as tainted by the earlier illegal entries, and he tended to downplay the importance of the government documents involved: "Little above the level of teacup gossip in the Far East," he said.

When the government presented its case to the grand jury, no-bills were voted for Mark Gayn, John Stewart Service, and Kate Mitchell. Gayn's participation, on the basis of the admissible evidence, was minor, and neither Mitchell nor Service had been in the possession of any documents when arrested. Indictments were voted against Jaffe, Larsen, and Roth, not for espionage, but for the illegal possession of government documents. Jaffe immediately opened negotiations with the government. Emmanuel Larsen filed a motion to quash the indictment on the grounds of the illegal searches. The Justice Department struck a deal with Jaffe according to which he would plead guilty and pay a fine, in the amount of $2500. Larsen pleaded *nolo contendere* and was fined $500, which Jaffe paid. Lieutenant Andrew Roth was discharged from the Navy the day before the arrests, thus ruling out the embarrassment of a court martial, and the indictment against him was not pursued by the Justice Department, even though five copies of State Department documents in Roth's handwriting had been found in Jaffe's office.

Legally speaking, the *Amerasia* case was over by February 15, 1946, when the Justice Department no-prossed the Roth indictment. In the eyes of the law, several thousand government documents, most of them classified and many of them Top Secret, had passed through the offices of *Amerasia* with its elaborate photocopying equipment. Well, why? As far as the law was concerned, it all must have been done to boost the circulation of a magazine with 2,000 subscribers.

The *Amerasia* case ended legally in 1946, but it came roaring back politically in 1951. The Tydings committee, with its Democratic majority, issued a broad and general clearance to the security arrangements of the State Department, and minimized the importance of the whole *Amerasia* episode. But the glaring discrepancies between the facts in the case and its treatment by the government in 1945–46 ultimately could not be glossed over. The bottom line here was clearly espionage. And the decade of the Fifties opened with angry questions being asked about the attitude of the federal government toward Communist penetration.

The *Amerasia* case itself was only a tiny corner of the larger picture. As the various investigations rolled forward, the emerging implications were startling.

FLOYD PATTERSON

Most of the people in Chicago Stadium that November evening in 1956 figured that the ageless Archie Moore would defeat the inexperienced young fighter. There was some betting action on whether or not Moore would knock him out and in what round. Going into the ring Moore was a 2-1 favorite.

Patterson had been born in 1935 in Waco, Texas. His parents, a manual laborer and a domestic servant, had moved North seeking opportunity, and Patterson grew up in the Bedford-Stuyvesant section of Brooklyn.

He found the existence there in the violence-filled streets unbearable and retreated into himself. He refused to speak, and he could not look other people in the eye. Once, he carved three X's with a knife into a photograph of himself. He was a chronic truant. He could not read.

He was sent to the Wiltwyk School, near Esopus, New York, where a gifted teacher somehow reached him. He was, it turned out, very intelligent. The athletic director awakened in him an interest in boxing. He returned to Brooklyn in 1947 and began to work out regularly at the Gramercy Gym on the lower East Side of Manhattan. Cus D'Amato owned the place. Patterson also continued to go to school.

He entered the Golden Gloves when he was fifteen and lost in the second bout. The next year he won the Golden Gloves middleweight title. In 1952, he won nine amateur titles and won the Olympic middleweight gold medal. He turned pro. When Rocky Marciano retired undefeated in April 1956, the stage was set for Patterson.

Patterson had an unorthodox peek-a-boo style, holding his gloves in front of his face and peering between them, but he was a fine combination puncher. At six feet and 185 pounds, he had a panther-like grace and could score sudden knockouts.

By the middle of the fifth round Patterson had established tactical dominance over the clever Moore. With thirty-one seconds left in the round, Patterson hit Moore with a dozen punches climaxed by a vicious left hook. "The end came with dramatic suddenness," reported *The New York Times,* "Patterson setting his man up with a left hook that was truly artistic in its delivery." Moore went down, took a six count, and struggled to his feet. Patterson was all over him and knocked him down again. At twenty-one, Patterson became the youngest heavyweight champion in history.

D'Amato then proceeded to match him against a string of also-rans.

On June 26, 1959, however, disaster struck an overconfident Patterson in the third round of a fight with Ingemar Johansson of Sweden. Nothing much happened for the first two rounds. Then Johansson hit Patterson with a slow left, followed by a bone-crushing right to the face, Johansson's "toonder punch." Patterson got up, but Johansson knocked him down six more times in that round before the referee stopped the fight.

Patterson came back to defeat Johansson and regain the crown on June 20, 1960, using two devastating lefts to win in the fifth round. "It was worth losing the title for this," Patterson said. "I never for a moment thought of losing, but to win this way, it's just perfect."

Floyd Patterson was a disturbing champion. He was gentle. He once said that he would rather lose a fight than seriously injure his opponent. People did not expect a heavyweight champion to be a complex man, especially a black heavyweight champion. A black was supposed to be like Jack

Johnson, Sonny Liston. But Patterson was thoughtful, divided about the violent sport he practiced, a Catholic convert. He was a peculiar heavyweight.

Today, his shrewd investments have made him a millionaire. He has a forty-acre ranch in upper New York State, boxes for fun, coaches young fighters, and is one of the most widely-respected figures in the history of the sport.

CHAPTER ELEVEN

More Real Witches

An investigation into something called The Institute of Political Relations may sound like a bore, but, believe me, it wasn't. I had been astonished by the details of the *Amerasia* case, and, after hours at the Intelligence School, all through that sweltering summer of 1952, I studied the fifteen volumes of testimony in the Institute of Political Relations case. The legal and even the political case came to very little in the end, as it had in the *Amerasia* case. What casual and even interested people had heard were broad-brush charges. Senator McCarthy, at the storm center of these issues, had wildly exaggerated. He had called one of the Institute's principals, a scholarly man named Owen Lattimore, then teaching at Johns Hopkins, the chief Soviet agent in the Pacific. Lattimore was supposed to be a master spy, someone like Richard Sorge, the romantic Communist in Tokyo who had used his Japanese sources to keep the Soviets informed, often precisely, of German military moves. The Soviets never believed Sorge, and the Japanese executed him. Meeting McCarthy's charges, Lattimore's defenders cried "witch hunt"—so far as my research reveals, Lattimore was the first to exploit that term—and also cited the various threats to civil liberties and academic freedom posed by the investigation.

My own reading of the Senate documents and my follow-up on

the surrounding controversies led to different conclusions. Lattimore was not any sort of chief Soviet spy, not even a spy at all. I read the fifteen volumes with a sense of discovering the "culture of Communism" in the West. It was not really something that Senate committees and government instrumentalities could deal with at all.

The Institute of Pacific Relations, hereafter IPR, was one of many similar scholarly organizations. It had been founded in 1925 in Honolulu by a group of business, educational and religious leaders who, gazing out across those broad expanses of blue water, knew that enormous economic and civilizational interests were involved there, but that there existed a vacuum of knowledge about the Pacific peoples.

Nothing could have been more natural or useful than the founding of such an institute. In its way, it was a symptom of the end of American isolationism. American troops had reached the Rhine in 1918, foreshadowing an American interest in Europe. In the war of 1898, America had won the Philippines with the help of Admiral Dewey. America and the West needed serious sources of information about the Pacific area, but the general intellectual tilt was toward Europe. The IPR tried to fill the vacuum. It sponsored major research, it made possible the publication of authoritative books, pamphlets, papers and surveys. It held international conferences, helped to create important academic careers, and published an influential quarterly called *Pacific Affairs*.

When the Japanese attacked Pearl Harbor, the United States government was caught embarrassingly short of concrete knowledge of the Far East. We did not even know, for example, the character of the beaches on important invasion sites—and often suffered unnecessary slaughter as a result of such ignorance—much less the politics of the various countries, groups, and factions. The government turned in its need to the IPR for expertise, and IPR people flowed into official positions. Unfortunately, there was a sort of spiritual and political interlock between the small group of people who ran IPR, the group of espionage agents who ran the magazine *Amerasia*, and the unblushing Communists who ran *China Today*.

The hearings before the Senate Internal Security Committee, contained in those fifteen volumes, constitute a Balzacian canvass of the culture of Communism, and touch on everything from the Sorge spy ring in Japan to the open activities of the millionaire Communist, Frederick Vanderbilt Field, American Secretary of

IPR for ten years between the mid-Thirties and the mid-Forties. The central figure in the hearings, the scholarly Owen Lattimore, was the moving force and the editor of *Pacific Affairs* during the same period. What came to the surface in the Senate hearings was the extraordinary interface between the "respectable" scholarly organization, IPR, the propaganda-espionage outfit over at *Amerasia*, and other Communist publications.

A number of the figures who came to be central to the investigation of the IPR had led rather spectacular pseudonymous existences. Frederick Vanderbilt Field, American secretary of IPR and heavy financial contributor, had long been active on such Communist publications as *The New Masses, The Daily Worker, The Communist* (the name of which was later changed to *Political Affairs*). Sometimes Field wrote under his own name, sometimes as Frederick Spencer or Lawrence Hearn. He appeared under his real name, however, at a banquet honoring the Communist publication *China Today*—the chief speaker at the banquet was Earl Browder. Hans Mueller, the German Communist, also known as Heinz Moeller, wrote under the byline "Asiaticus." The Chinese Communist, Chi Chao-ting, wrote as "Hansu Chan."

From my own perspective as an American academic, reading through all this, I experienced a sense of vertigo. Neither side, IPR nor openly Communist, seemed to be honest. Certainly the readers on either side did not know whom they were reading, or just who was abusing the authority of published material for ulterior and secret goals. Surely, even a *Communist* reader deserved to know whom he was reading! It seemed to me that potential graduate students like myself, once I got out of the Navy, and professors who depended on IPR material, were at the mercy of a Communist-sympathizing bunch of conspirators and scholarly impostors. Was IPR material checkable? Could you find "Asiaticus" or "Hansu Chan" in any phone book or any university catalogue?

Did it matter? The more I dug into it, the more serious it seemed, and not primarily from the point of view of federal policy making. It still seems to me serious. I did not then believe that Communists in and around the State Department and in the media defeated Chiang Kai-shek's Nationalists. Theodore White has remarked to me that the Kuomintang government was only dust, administratively speaking, on an ocean of people and unmanageable military and ideological politics. From our perspective today, in effective alliance with Peking against Moscow, all those old controversies seem anachronistic. But I also believe that the Communists in and around the IPR and the then power structure desired, and would have brought about, a Chinese Communist victory in 1949 had it been in their power to do so. They by no means foresaw the Chinese-Soviet break. They would have been scandalized. At no point did the ideological management of the IPR, a relatively small group, ever criticize Moscow.

Some of the material in those fifteen Senate investigation volumes is extraordinary. Mr. Edward C. Carter, executive IPR director, in 1938 recommended American Communist leader Earl Browder to a Canadian group as "100 percent American." He recommended to President Roosevelt's personal emissary to Chiang, Lauchlin Currie, that he visit Chou En-lai as soon as possible. During the Hitler-Stalin Pact period, he arranged a luncheon between Lattimore and the Soviet ambassador to inform the Soviets of Lattimore's impending assignment as special American advisor to Chiang. At the time of that luncheon, neither Chiang nor the State Department knew about it. One of the most famous exhibits to surface during the Senate hearings was the so-called "cagey letter," written by Lattimore to Edward Carter, in which Lattimore laid down the IPR line for this supposedly objective and scholarly organization. It is an exercise in extraordinary arrogance and scholarly duplicity:

> I think that you are pretty cagey in turning over so much of the China section of the inquiry to Asiaticus, Han-seng, and Chi. They will bring out the absolutely essential aspects, but can be depended on to do it with the right touch.
>
> For the general purposes of this inquiry it seems to me that the good scoring position, for the IPR, differs with different countries. For China, my hunch is that it will pay to keep behind the official Chinese Communist position—far enough not to be covered by the same label—but enough ahead of the active Chinese liberals to be noticeable. For Japan, on the other hand, hang back so as not to be inconveniently ahead of the Japanese liberals, who cannot keep up, whereas the Chinese liberals can. So the chief thing is to oppose the military wing of Japanese aggression in China, counting on a check there to take care of both the military and civilian components of aggression in Japan. For the British—scare the hell out of them, always in a polite way, but usually in a way that looks as if it might

turn impolite. The British liberal groups are badly flustered; but being British, the way to encourage them to pull themselves together is to fluster the Tories. For the U.S.S.R.—back their international policy in general, but without using their slogans and above all without giving them or anybody else the impression of subservience. . . .

This Lattimore letter blew the IPR cover. For all of its prestige and for all of its respectable support, for all of its heavyweight backers—General George C. Marshall was a trustee, but never knew it (apparently, he was simply named to the board)—the supposedly scholarly organization had become a Communist advocacy conspiracy with no pretense, at the core, to objective scholarship. Professor Kenneth Colegrove, who had resigned from *Amerasia* because of its Communist slant, described the "cagey letter" as "one of the most intellectually dishonest academic documents that I have ever seen. This is the complete negation of what the IPR said to professors and teachers all over the country that it was."

Owen Lattimore's own performance as editor of the prestigious quarterly *Pacific Affairs* can only be described as grotesque. The editors of *Pacific Affairs* passed on, to *Amerasia,* articles which were too obviously slanted in a Communist direction. Lattimore declined to join the editorial board of the Communist magazine *China Today* for purely tactical reasons: "My position as an editor of *Pacific Affairs* makes it impossible for me to join the editorial board of *China Today*." In an editorial shoot-out with anti-Stalinist William Henry Chamberlain, Lattimore defended the infamous Stalin purge trials. Prominent Soviet generals and politicians were forced to confess to being fascist spies and were shot. Said Lattimore, "That to me sounds like democracy." He argued that the Soviet seizure of Outer Mongolia was not aggression, but that the Japanese seizure of Manchuria was.

Lattimore beat the Communist party drum as a book reviewer. Soviet imperialism in Central Asia was wonderful. He reviewed a book by Joshua Kunitz called *Dawn Over Samarkand* enthusiastically, commenting especially on the word "dawn" in the title, because what "is taking place in Central Asia undoubtedly is like a dawn and rebirth." He went on to comment that the author's "different sections are also prefaced by selections from the statements of Bolshevik leaders, notably Stalin, and these illuminate, in a remarkably effective way, the theories that underlie current processes, so that the reader is not deluged with marvels, but given a connected line of reasoning to account for them."

Of course Lattimore, as a writer and as an editor of an independent magazine, had every right to say what he wanted. But his work makes clear that he was an almost open apologist for Soviet imperialism, and that he had subscribed (see above quotations) to the ideological basis for it. He was also editing the most influential journal in the area of Pacific studies, trying to promote academic careers and ideologically-slanted books on Asia, trying to influence government policy. He was doing it all under false colors, and when the spotlight was turned on him, he wrote it all up in a book called *Ordeal by Slander*.

Lattimore, in fact, seems to have been ideologically in love with the Soviet Union. In 1936, Anna Louise Strong, a lifelong Communist, who stayed in China after Mao's revolution and died there, published a book called *This Soviet World*. Lattimore reviewed it in *Pacific Affairs,* and his review, a collector's item, follows in its entirety:

This is one of the best books Miss Strong has written. She has always had a warmth of emotion which makes her one of the great contemporary reporters, but this book is notable for its direct presentation of profound ideas with complete simplicity and no loss of depth. Her answer to the charge that the Communists are 'painfully definite' in the way in which they 'take refuge in formulae' is an admirably concise statement of the 'dialectical' method of splitting and resplitting formulae so as to destroy dogma by converting it into science. Her book as a whole is a good confrontation of the Soviet ideas of democracy, originality, and individuality and the foreign idea of 'regimentation.'

One of her best passages is the comment on the 'strange paradox' that in the Soviet Union 'every achievement costs infinite effort, yet mighty achievements are won in an incredibly short time.' Another good passage is the exposition of Stakhanovism, in which the distinction between the liberation of the worker's technical adeptness is convincingly distinguished from the employer-fostered 'speed-up.'

The book is intended primarily for American readers, and comparisons are accordingly in American terms; but as the problems themselves are all of international significance, they can be understood anywhere, in any language.

One searches almost in vain through the pages of other scholarly journals for some notice of this Anna Louise Strong book to which Lattimore gave such praise in his own authoritative quarterly. In his performance as editor, Lattimore reviewed an extraordinary quantity of Communist propaganda hardly noticed elsewhere, and reviewed it favorably. A content analysis of *Pacific Affairs* under Lattimore's leadership exhibits, to put it mildly, a Communist tilt. Not at all surprisingly, he was invited to join the editorial board of *Amerasia,* but declined. It would have blown his cover.

Well, what do we conclude?

My opinion today is not much different from the opinion I reached when I first read the record. I see no evidence that Lattimore was, as McCarthy charged, a master Soviet spy. He was, however, fervently pro-Soviet. He saw the possibility of adding his also beloved and long-studied China to the Soviet empire. He used every power available to him to do so, promoting rotten books, creating pro-Soviet academic careers, bending the evidence, conspiring, interacting with the Communist spy group at *Amerasia,* lying about his intellectual loyalties when caught, all the while being defended by liberals.

I conclude that Owen Lattimore, *Pacific Affairs* under his leadership, and the IPR insofar as he could influence it, were part of the *culture* of Communism. I consider that an empirical datum, established by the evidence.

The Fifties' perception of these things could not fail to be powerfully affected by unfolding events in the world arena. Eastern Europe had fallen to the Red Army, and the Soviets immediately imposed totalitarian puppet regimes on the nations of what was once known as Central Europe. Winston Churchill, with his immense international prestige, sought to alert the West. On March 5, 1946, at Westminster College in Fulton, Missouri, introduced by President Truman, Churchill declared that an "iron curtain" had "descended across the Continent," with the U.S.S.R. establishing "police governments" and also using "Communist parties and fifth columns" to extend its domination. On February 25, 1948, the Soviets staged a coup in Prague, murdered the democratic statesman, Jan Masaryk, by throwing him from a window, and Czechoslovakia went behind the Iron Curtain. The next year saw the fall of China to Mao's Communist armies and the flight of the Nationalists to Formosa. On June 25, 1950, the North Koreans attacked across the 38th parallel, sent the South Korean army reeling backward and quickly seized the capital of Seoul. Alger Hiss was sentenced for perjury—the trial had really been about espionage—and Klaus Fuchs was convicted as an atom spy in England. Fuchs' American confederate, Harry Gold, got thirty years in prison. Julius and Ethel Rosenberg were convicted as atom spies and sentenced to death in the electric chair; their co-conspirator, Morton Sobell, got a thirty-year sentence.

In addition to all of this, there was a murky area where accident, nightmare and speculation created a peculiar atmosphere. People familiar with the Communist phenomenon knew very well that murder was simply another political technique. Trotsky had been killed by an axe-wielding agent of Stalin. The anarchist, Carlo Tresca, had been shoved onto New York City subway tracks and killed by an onrushing train. The Communist propaganda genius, Willi Munzenberg, had been murdered on Stalin's orders, for obscure reasons. And now, in the United States in the late Forties, as the government began to crack down and as witnesses were being subpoenaed, a number of key figures died under questionable circumstances.

Alger Hiss had turned over a Ford car to the Cherner Motor Company without payment, an important item in the chain of evidence against him. The man who had notarized the Hiss signature on the transfer of title, W. Marvin Smith, a Justice Department lawyer and a longtime friend of Hiss, fell, jumped, or was pushed to his death down an office stairwell. Harry Dexter White, a former Assistant Secretary of the Treasury, and a principal figure in the background of the Hiss case, died suddenly during the Hiss investigation. White's testimony would have been important. His body was cremated without autopsy. Lawrence Duggan, a former State Department official and friend of Hiss, jumped, fell, or was pushed from the sixteenth floor of a Manhattan office building. Duggan hit the pavement wearing one galosh. The other galosh remained on the floor of his office. Sumner Welles, Assistant Secretary of State, sent a telegram to New York Mayor William O'Dwyer stating that it was impossible to believe that Duggan had killed himself. Welles demanded a thorough investigation. Four days later, Welles suffered an apparent heart attack on his Virginia plantation and was discovered almost frozen to death. Canadian diplomat Herbert Norman, then ambassador to Egypt, discovered to be a Communist and about to be exposed, fell to his death from a window in Cairo. Harvard professor F. O. Matthiessen, a major literary critic and prominent teacher of American literature, died under peculiar circumstances. He was a Communist sympathizer and had recently returned from Czechoslovakia. Matthiessen was due to be questioned under oath by investigators. On April 1, 1950, he rented a hotel room near Boston's North Station. He plunged to his death from the window of his room.

There exists no evidence at all that any of these deaths were "executions" from the Communist side. They may all have been suicides or accidents. F. O. Matthiessen, for example, had his full share of personal problems as a homosexual, neurotic, on top of it all an Episcopalian, and a fellow traveler. On the other hand, "defenestration"—meaning throwing you out of a window—was a favored method of "executive action" by the Soviet secret operators in the late Forties and early Fifties. Thus, Jan Masaryk, son of a great Czech liberal hero, "fell" out of a window in Prague during the 1948 Communist take-over.

An impressive body of literature meanwhile created a widespread and profound awareness that in Communism, we were facing something quite different from traditional dictatorships and tyrannies. Arthur Koestler's *Darkness at Noon,* written in 1941, became a bestseller and was adapted for a successful Broadway play. Koestler convincingly depicted circumstances, based on the great Stalin purge, in which loyalty to the Communist revolution took precedence over truth and even over self-preservation. The revolution could not only overthrow government; it could also overthrow the human mind as well. Orwell's *1984* appeared in 1949, presenting a world in which totalitarianism has triumphed and is now conducting mop-up operations against all traces of human decency. In *The Captive Mind* (1951), the Polish exile Czeslaw Milosz—the 1980 Nobel Prize winner—described the eagerness of intellectuals to swallow a mind-altering pill which provided the illusion of certainty but destroyed the intelligence. The pill was a metaphor for Communist doctrine.

In the same year, 1951, there appeared a magisterial and highly erudite work called *The Origins of Totalitarianism* by Hannah Arendt. It provided a historical and theoretical analysis of totalitarianism, which Arendt concluded is a novel form of government. It is based on terror and achieves its ideal form in the concentration camp. Wherever totalitarianism "rose to power, it developed entirely new political institutions and destroyed all social, legal and political traditions of the country. No matter what the specifically national tradition or the particular spiritual source of the ideology, totalitarian government always transformed classes into masses, supplanted the party system, not by one-party dictatorships, but by a mass movement, shifted the center of power from the army to the police, and established a foreign policy openly directed toward world domination. Present totalitarian governments have developed from one-party systems; whenever these became truly totalitarian, they started to operate according to a system of values so radically different from all others, that none of our traditional legal, moral, or common-sense utilitarian categories could any longer help us to come to terms with, or judge, or predict their course of action."

The next year, 1952, saw the publication of Whittaker Chambers' great autobiography, *Witness,* which focused on the Hiss case against the background of the global struggle against Communist totalitarianism. In a prefatory "Letter to My Children," Chambers wrote: "For it was more than a human tragedy. Much more than Alger Hiss or Whittaker Chambers was on trial in the trials of Alger Hiss. Two faiths were on trial. Human societies, like human beings, live by faith and die when faith dies. At issue in the Hiss case was the question whether this sick society, which we call Western civilization, could in its extremity still cast up a man whose faith in it was so great that he would voluntarily abandon those things which men hold good, including life, to defend it. At issue was the question whether this man's faith could prevail against a man whose equal faith it was that this society is sick beyond saving, and that mercy itself pleads for its swift extinction and replacement by another. At issue was the question whether, in the desperately divided society, there still remained the will to recognize the issues in time to offset the immense rally of public opinion to distort and pervert the facts.

"One day in the great jury room of the Grand Jury of the Southern District of New York, a juror leaned forward slightly and asked me: 'Mr. Chambers, what does it mean to be a Communist?' I hesitated for a moment, trying to find the simplest, most direct way to convey the fact of this complex experience to men and women to whom the very fact of the experience was all but incomprehensible. Then I said:

When I was a Communist, I had three heroes. One was a Russian. One was a Pole. One was a German Jew.

The Pole was Felix Djerjinsky. He was ascetic, highly sensitive, intelligent. He was a Communist. After the Russian Revolution, he became head of the Tcheka and organizer of the Red Terror. As a young man, Djerjinsky had been a political prisoner in the Paviak Prison in Warsaw. There he insisted on being given the task of cleaning the latrines of the other prisoners. For he held that the most developed member of any community must take upon himself the lowliest tasks as an example to those who are less developed. That is one thing that it meant to be a Communist.

The German Jew was Eugen Levine. He was a Communist. During the Bavarian Soviet Republic in 1919, Levine was the organizer of the Workers' and Soldiers' soviets. When the Bavarian Soviet Republic was crushed, Levine was captured and court-martialed. The court-martial told him: "You are under sentence of death." Levine answered: "We Communists are always under sentence of death." That is another thing that it meant to be a Communist.

The Russian was not a Communist. He was a pre-Communist revolutionist named Kalyaev. [I should have said Sazonov.] He was arrested for a minor part in the assassination of the Tsarist prime minister, von Plehve. He was sent into Siberian exile to one of the worst prison camps, where the political prisoners were flogged. Kalyaev sought some way to protest this outrage to the world. The means were few, but at last he found a way. In protest against the flogging of other men, Kalyaev drenched himself in kerosene, set himself on fire and burned himself to death. That also is what it means to be a Communist.

That also is what it means to be a witness.

THE CARDINAL

On the evening of December 26, 1948, Cardinal Josef Mindszenty was arrested by a Hungarian Army colonel, with the support of a large contingent of police. He was brought immediately to the police interrogation and torture center at 60 Andrassy Street in Budapest. A police major, an officer in the secret police, stripped him of his clothes and ordered that he be dressed in a clown's outfit. A group of jailers and police shouted obscenities.

At about 11 P.M. that night, the Cardinal was taken to his first interrogation and asked to sign a confession. When he refused, he was taken back to his cell and beaten with police clubs until he fainted. He was interrogated again three times that night.

The guards who accompanied him to his cell continually used filthy language. The Cardinal was not allowed to sleep, and he refused the food he was given because he thought it might be drugged. The interrogations and beatings lasted for more than a month.

On some occasions, the torturer forced Mindszenty to run ahead of him, pursuing him with a truncheon and a sharply pointed knife. The splinters in the wooden floor lodged in the

Cardinal's feet. Though disciplined by prayer, Mindszenty began to lose the ability to recall events consecutively.

He was brought to trial on February 3, 1949, before a People's Court. The charges were treason, misuse of foreign currency, and conspiracy. After a three-day trial he received a sentence of life imprisonment. The Pope issued an eloquent protest.

During the revolution of 1956, the Cardinal got out of jail. When Soviet tanks crushed the revolution, he sought refuge in the American embassy. He remained there for fifteen years.

During the 1960s, both the United States and the Catholic Church tried to improve relations with Moscow and with the Eastern Bloc generally. *Detente.* The Cardinal wrote to President Nixon and learned that he would no longer be a welcome exile in the American embassy. He left Hungary on September 29, 1971. In 1974, Pope Paul VI declared Mindszenty's See vacant; Mindszenty published his memoirs. Everything he had tried to uphold seemed a shambles. He died after a heart operation on May 6, 1975.

In what was routinely described as a "moving tribute," Paul VI declared: "Death has now come to extinguish on earth a flame which has illuminated with its brilliant light these last few decades in the life of the Church." Paul himself, and Richard Nixon, had rendered that flame politically irrelevant.

In 1980, the first Polish Pope, John Paul II, declared that he would "go to Poland" if the Soviets invaded. Lech Walesa, a daily communicant, visited the Vatican and received John Paul's blessing. Not long after that, a Turkish assassin with KGB connections shot the Pope and nearly killed him.

The British actor Alec Guinness starred in a 1954 movie called *The Prisoner,* based on Mindszenty's experiences at 60 Andrassy Street. Jack Richardson played the Communist prosecutor with great intellectual force. Nothing could stand in the way of the Revolution, the Dialectic, Soviet power.

One result of the movie was that Guinness became a Catholic.

CHAPTER TWELVE

The Art Capital of the World

The Cedar Tavern does business on the west side of University Place in New York's bohemia, Greenwich Village. It is a few blocks north of New York University's main campus, a few blocks north, too, of Washington Square. The Cedar Tavern has a dark, 1890s atmosphere. When you walk in out of the bright sunlight, it takes several moments before you can distinguish anything in its dark interior. Then you see the long dark-wood bar along the right wall, the Tiffany overhead lights, the tables on the left and the booths in the rear.

When you go to the Cedar Tavern today, you see students from New York University, local businessmen, and assorted Greenwich Village types. You see a lot of beards, jeans, and sandals. If you come at lunch time, you might well run into Nat Hentoff, a quintessential Village personality who writes for *The Village Voice*. The bottom line for Hentoff is individual freedom. He wears a large and bushy beard.

Today, the Cedar Tavern is a good Village bar, but, of course, there are others. Yesterday, back in the Fifties, it was the hangout of the New York School of painters, also known as the Tenth Street School, the Abstract Expressionists and the Action Painters. They made New York the Art Capital of the World in the Fifties, and, as a group, as a movement, made the first real advance since the

Twenties in artistic consciousness. In the Fifties, the Cedar Tavern was to art what the Dome and the Select had been in the Paris of the Twenties. At the Cedar, you ran into Jackson Pollock, Willem de Kooning, Mark Rothko, and their younger colleagues, New York painters like Larry Rivers, Helen Frankenthaler, Robert Motherwell, Robert Rauschenberg, Joan Mitchell. During the Fifties, the most exciting creative ideas and the most intense artistic energies were being generated within a few blocks of the Cedar Tavern.

The radical modernism of the New York School of the Fifties has to be understood against the background of the 1930s, when the modernist movement launched by Picasso, Braque and others was virtually suspended. From about 1930 until the mid-Forties, the propagandist style known as Social Realism dominated the art world. No longer was the artist supposed to be a bohemian free spirit from Montmartre. He was supposed to be an anticapitalist militant and an antifascist who attended protest meetings. Painters like Ben Shahn and William Gropper, now almost forgotten, were for a time considered major figures. This style of painting celebrated The People, who were always depicted as having thick wrists and necks and abnormally small brain cavities. Diego Rivera and José Clemente Orozco were imposing their garish cartoons on public buildings.

And then, poof!—with the end of the war, all of this Popular Front art disappeared. All of a sudden, everyone had more than enough of peasants and Okies and Mexicans and blacks, and thick wrists and even tractors had become a bore. Intelligence, experiment, the sense of possibility, the fresh air of intellectual and artistic freedom had returned. Stalin lived in Russia. He no longer lived in the art galleries of Manhattan.

Even during the heyday of Social Realism, to be sure, outposts of modernism resisted the thick-wrist trend. One important tender of the modernist flame was Hans Hofmann, a middle-aged German painter who had taught in Munich and who knew the great modernists of the Twenties. Hofmann ignored the Stalinists and ran a modernist art school in Greenwich Village. An aspiring artist could enroll in Hofmann's art school on Eighth Street and associate there and at the Cedar Tavern with other artists in the new movement, de Kooning, Pollock, Franz Kline.

In the early days of the New York School, both Hofmann and de Kooning were inspirational figures. De Kooning held his first one-man show in 1948 and established himself as a major modern artist, in reputation the only rival to Jackson Pollock. He was admired for his absolute artistic integrity, which was a felt force in his paintings. De Kooning was also a brilliant and passionate conversationalist, his talk full of wit, and abounding with insights about art and modern experience. Hans Hofmann did not match de Kooning or Pollock in reputation as a painter, but he was widely thought to be America's best art teacher. He was affable and always encouraging, and he gave his students, whom he treated as colleagues, the sense that they were all embarked on a historic adventure.

The modern movement in the arts, and perhaps especially in painting and sculpture, stresses freshness and invention. It expresses a sense of living intensely in the present, and of responding to ideas and impressions and experiences which have become available only in our time. The modern artist, characteristically, is willing to press further, to take risks, to risk failure in ways that would have been inconceivable in an earlier day because of fixed rules and conventions about the nature of art.

Earlier in the century, always pressing against the conventions, Picasso had moved painting decisively away from representation and created a dozen new styles. The New York School took up where Picasso and his contemporaries of the Twenties had left off. They shifted the idea of painting from imagery to expression, to invention and construction. Their painting was not "about" some external subject. A painting was an "event." It symbolized the passion and the freedom of the artist. "The consciousness of the personal and spontaneous in the painting and sculptures," wrote Meyer Schapiro in 1957, "stimulates the artist to invent devices of handling, processing, surfacing, which confer to the utmost degree the aspect of the freely made. Hence the great importance of the brush, the drip, the quality of the substance of the paint itself." Despite popular misconceptions, these artists did not paint "out of control." They demanded that a work possess an individual order or coherence, a quality of unity, that the forms and colors possess and express quality, that the painting speak to us as a whole charged with intense feeling. No one ever mistook a Pollock for a Kline, or a Motherwell for a Rothko.

Of course, within the larger enterprise, differences of temperament and theory existed. Hans Hofmann, for example, was more cerebral, and perhaps it would be fair to say that he was more "European." He had lived in Paris from 1904 to 1914, had lived through the birth of modernism, he had known the originators of Fauvism and Cubism, and he had opened his own art school in Munich in 1915. When Hofmann spoke, he spoke with the art history of the twentieth century behind him. His conception of art had a metaphysical, even sacerdotal quality. He believed that art reflected universal laws which also governed nature, and that art at its highest was a spiritual revelation. He aspired to create suggestions of depth and space which were realizations of spiritual reality. De Kooning, in contrast, painted canvasses that were restless, raw, violent. His visual rhythms suggested the direct experience of the modern city, of New York. He communicated a sense of risk, of "going for broke" that was quintessentially American. He paid a heavy spiritual price for this directness, this pursuit of the absolute aesthetic experience. "I saw him in Easthampton," recalls a friend, "starting something, and after the first week people would sneak in to take a look. 'Beautiful,' they'd say, it looked absolutely right. And then over the next two months, day by day, whatever was right he would slowly destroy, out of this incredible pride."

But de Kooning and Hofmann agreed on important principles. They insisted that the modern artist approach his subject matter in a way very different from past artists. Today's reality was a *Gestalt*, and it could be grasped only through a total experience made up of glimpses and hints. The painter was to translate the volumes and voids of "real" experience into a pictorial language that would be *flat*, as appropriate for the picture plane. They looked back to Cezanne and the Cubists as progenitors, and, for all their radicalism, the sense of traditional reference was never far from their canvasses.

The New York School, all of it south of 23rd Street, really consisted of several loosely-related circles of artists. One, which called itself "American Abstract Artists," included Ad Reinhardt, Josef Albers, and a sculptor named Ibram Lassaw. Mark Rothko, Adolph Gottlieb, and Milton Avery were in a group known as "The Ten." A group gathered around John Graham including de Kooning, Arshile Gorky, Stuart Davis, and David Smith. Jackson Pollock hung out with Robert Motherwell, Roberto Matta, and William Baziotes. Out of this ferment, there arose after the war the movement that would dominate the Fifties and be known variously as Abstract Expressionism, Action Painting, or American-Type Painting.

The New York School had a strong theoretical bent. Some artists, like Robert Motherwell, who had taught philosophy at Harvard, were themselves articulate theoreticians. But several important New York art critics, who frequented the downtown art scene, undertook to explain to the public what the Tenth Street School was doing. These critics were Clement Greenberg, Harold Rosenberg, Hilton Kramer, and Professor Meyer Schapiro of Columbia.

In his 1957 essay, "Recent Abstract Painting," for example, Schapiro had a number of interesting things to say about the relationship of this art to the surrounding social reality. That reality is increasingly organized, increasingly a product of bureaucratic teamwork. "Paintings and sculptures," said Schapiro, "are the last handmade personal objects within our culture. Almost everything else is produced industrially, in mass, and through a high division of labor. Few people are fortunate enough to make something that represents themselves, that issues entirely from their hands and mind, and to which they can affix their names." Against that kind of social reality, "The object of art is, therefore, more passionately than ever before, the occasion of spontaneity or intense feeling." Just because it is connected with a particular living human being, the brush stroke, the drip, even the accident, take on enormous meaning. "Modern painting," Schapiro observed, "is the first complex style in history which proceeds from elements that are not pre-ordered as closed articulated shapes . . . While in industry, accident is that event which destroys an order, interrupts a regular process and must be eliminated, in painting the random or accidental is the beginning of an order. It is that which the artist wishes to build up into an order, but a kind of order that in the end retains the aspect of the original disorder as a manifestation of freedom."

Perhaps the most influential critic and theorist associated with the New York School was Clement Greenberg, and his 1955 essay, " 'American-Type' Painting," asserted in convincing terms the importance of this group of artists. Greenberg located them in the mainstream of modernism, which he described lucidly and succinctly: "Though it may have started toward modernism earlier than the other arts, painting has turned out to have a greater number of *expendable* conventions imbedded in it, or at least a greater number of conventions that are difficult to isolate in order to expend. It seems to be a law of modernism—thus one that applies to almost all art that remains truly alive in our time—that the conventions not essential to the viability of a medium be discarded as soon as they are recognized. This process of self-purification appears to have come to a halt in literature simply because the latter has fewer conventions to eliminate before arriving at those essential to it."

As Greenberg saw it, the New York School had moved beyond the earlier Cubists in the direction of self-purification, particularly in their dedication to "the integrity of the picture plane"—their recognition of the essential fact that the paint is applied to a flat, two-dimensional surface. Jackson Pollock stood first in Greenberg's pantheon. "Pollock's strength," in his opinion, "lies in the emphatic surfaces of his pictures, which it is his concern to maintain and intensify in all that thick, fuliginous flatness which began—but only began—to be the strong point of late Cubism . . . It is the tension inherent in the constructed, recreated flatness of the surface that produces the strength of his art."

Harold Rosenberg, another critic closely associated with the New York artists, focused on the "act" of painting, on the spontaneity which was one feature of this kind of art. Rosenberg called the new school "Action Painting." "At a certain moment," he wrote, "the canvas began to appear to one American painter after another as an arena in which to act. What was to go on the canvas was not a picture but an event." Though they focused on different features of the new painting, the descriptions of Greenberg and Rosenberg were not mutually exclusive. Both critics had perceived things that were true.

As early as 1950, Robert Motherwell was stressing the area that Rosenberg was to explore: The "process of painting . . . is conceived of as an adventure, without preconceived ideas, on the part of persons of intelligence, sensibility, and passion. Fidelity to what occurs between oneself and the canvas, no matter how unexpected, becomes central . . . no true artist ends with the style that he expected to have when he began . . . it is only by giving oneself up completely to the painting medium that one finds oneself and one's own style." To such assertions about the centrality of spontaneity, Meyer Schapiro added the necessary complement of form: All "these elements of impulse which seem at first so aimless on the canvas are built up into a whole . . . The artist today creates an order out of unordered variable elements to a greater degree than the artist of the past."

Of all the Abstract Expressionists, Jackson Pollock had the greatest reputation and the widest notoriety. His famous interlaced skeins of flung paint were denounced as fraud and hailed as an artistic breakthrough. In his disdain for theory and for intellectualization, and in his evident raw passion, Pollock seemed an extreme embodiment of tendencies we recognize as characteristically American. A younger painter, Jane Freilicher, describes Pollock's role as an exemplar of freedom, asserting that "his achievement brought a glamor and authority to American painting which inspired younger painters . . . If you can bring it off, 'make it work,' it might be possible to do anything."

Robert Goodnough provides this description of Pollock's studio at his home in Easthampton, Long Island: "To enter Pollock's studio is to enter another world, a place where the intensity of the artist's mind and feelings are given full play. . . . At one end of the barn the floor is literally covered with large cans of enamel, aluminum, and tube colors—the boards that do show are covered with paint drippings. Nearby a skull rests on a chest of drawers. Three or four cans contain stubby paint brushes of various sizes. About the rest of the studio, on the floor and walls, are paintings in various stages of completion, many of enormous proportions. Here Pollock often sits for hours in deep contemplation of work in progress, his face forming rigid lines and often settling into a heavy frown. A Pollock painting is not born easily, but comes into being after weeks, often months, of work and thought. At times he paints with feverish activity, or again with slow deliberation."

Pollock was also a heavy drinker, and on his trips to New York he would invariably show up at the Cedar Tavern, get drunk and frequently become violent. One night he arrived drunk at Peggy Guggenheim's, in the midst of a chic party. He disappeared for a moment into an adjoining room and then re-emerged naked. Whereupon he urinated into her fireplace. It pleased him to be admitted to the 21 Club or the Stork Club without a necktie, but he often got so drunk and abusive that he was thrown out anyway.

By 1954, Pollock had ceased painting, and, in a state of severe depression, went to a psychoanalyst, visiting both the analyst and the Cedar Tavern on his regular trips to Manhattan. In July of 1956, his wife, Lee Krasner Pollock, sailed to Europe for a vacation. A mistress named Ruth Klingman moved in with Pollock in Easthampton. Pollock was drinking heavily, and his friends thought he looked exhausted. Shortly after 10 P.M. on August 11,

Pollock's 1950 Oldsmobile convertible careened off an East-hampton road, crashed into some trees and overturned. Ruth Klingman broke her pelvis. Her friend Edith Metzger and Pollock died instantly.

Arshile Gorky was another painter who played a pivotal role in starting the New York School, and now, more than thirty years after his death, Gorky's work is undergoing re-examination and reevaluation. In short, Gorky's paintings *seemed* to be abstractions. They were hailed as such, and thus exerted their original influence. But recent work on them has made a persuasive case that Gorky's real subject was his own bizarre and melancholy life.

He was born in Turkish Armenia in 1904, and his name was Vosdanik Manoog Adoian. His early years were passed under the grim shadow of Turkish persecution. His father had fled to America in 1908. Gorky survived the slaughter of the Armenian population by the Turks during World War I, but his mother died of starvation in 1919, at the age of 39.

The next year, Gorky and his younger sister Vartoosh came to America and lived for a while with their older sister Akabe in Watertown, Mass. In 1925, at the age of 20, he settled in New York and took the name Arshile Gorky. Arshile is a variant on the heroic name Achilles; and Gorky in Russian means "the bitter one."

Though he was a self-taught artist, he was immensely talented, a fact that was quickly grasped by the director of the Grand Central School of Art, Edward Graecen, who gave him a job teaching a class in sketching. During the depression, he endured extreme poverty, sometimes being unable to afford to buy paint. In 1935, the Federal Arts Project came to his rescue, and he produced a mural called "Aviation," which for a time decorated the Newark Airport. He sold his first painting to the Whitney Museum in 1937. Gorky's art went through a protracted apprenticeship. He immersed himself for years in the great European modernists—Cezanne, Picasso, Miro, Kandinsky—and it was not until 1945 that he had produced enough nonderivative work to be able to hold a one-man show. Before 1941, Gorky could produce first-rate imitations of Matisse, of Cezanne, of Picasso; after 1941, he produced a succession of Gorkys which are among the greatest paintings produced in this century.

It was during the summer of 1941 that everything came together for him. He evolved a style that combined form with abandon, humor with tragedy, organization with dream, in a sort of exquisite balance. He developed several unusual concepts of the picture space. In his "Good Afternoon, Mrs. Lincoln," we find ourselves in an interior organic convulsion. In "The Orators," one enters and exits from all directions. "The Limit" . . . has no limits. His mature art possesses a strange and dreamlike fluidity. As he once said, "New organisms, like new embryos, require a fluid matrix in which to evolve."

While he was at the peak of his powers, and creating the paintings which would win him a permanent place in the history of art, a series of Job-like misfortunes overtook him. In February 1946, a fire in his Connecticut studio destroyed much of his most recent work. Three weeks later, he discovered that he had cancer; the surgeon took two paintings for his work. Gorky's marriage fell apart, and his wife left with their children. In February 1948, he fractured his neck in an auto crash, and when he returned from months in the hospital he found that his right arm was numb. Desperately, he tried to draw with his left hand. On the morning of July 21, he phoned several friends and chatted. It was a last act of communion. Then he hanged himself in a woodshed near his house. Written on a wall near him were the words "Goodbye My Loveds."

"When they started out," writes Clement Greenberg, "the 'abstract expressionists' had had the traditional diffidence of American artists. They were very much aware of the provincial fate lurking all around them. The country had not yet made a single contribution to the mainstream of painting or sculpture. What united the 'abstract expressionists' more than anything else was their resolve to break out of this situation. By now [1955], most of them (along with the sculptor, David Smith) have done so, whether in success or failure. Whatever else may remain doubtful, the 'centrality,' the resonance of the work of these artists is assured.

"When I say, in addition, that such a galaxy of strong and original talents has not been seen in painting since the days of Cubism, I shall be accused of chauvinist exaggeration, not to speak of the lack of a sense of proportion. But I make no more allowance for American art than I do for any other kind. At the Biennale in Venice in 1954, I saw how de Kooning's exhibition put to shame not only the neighboring one of Ben Shahn, but that of every other painter his age or under in the other pavilions. The general impression is still that an art of high distinction has as much chance of coming out of this country as a great wine. Literature—yes, we know that we have done some great things in that line; the English and French have told us so. Now they can begin to tell us the same about our painting."

It may be taken as suggesting the variety of America—and the variety of the Fifties—that a very great artist who had nothing to do with the Abstract Expressionists or with the Tenth Street School, was actually living and working at the time in the same Greenwich Village neighborhood. Any evening in the Village, you might see Edward Hopper, often with his wife, having a bite to eat in the local Nedick's, a fast-food forerunner of MacDonald's.

Edward Hopper stood very much apart from the revolutionary things going on around him in the New York art world of the Fifties, and he had no use for the New York School. But he also accomplished something absolutely unique. Through his mastery of light and composition, he elevated realistic representation to the level of metaphor and created a pictorial poetry of isolation. Individualism is a dominant theme in all of American culture, and Hopper himself was a supreme individualist, but he got onto canvas the emotions, often painful, of the isolated individual.

Hopper was born in 1882 in Nyack, New York, into a solidly middle-class Baptist family. His mother encouraged her children in their theatrical and artistic interests, and Hopper began to sign and date his drawings by the age of ten. By the time he was graduated from Nyack High School, he had decided upon a career as an artist. His family supported the decision, but, as a prudent measure, insisted that he attend a school of commercial art in New York.

After two years of studying illustrating, Hopper had enough self-confidence to transfer to the New York School of Art, known as the Chase School, located at the corner of Sixth Avenue and Fifty-seventh Street. There he worked with the famous art teacher William Meritt Chase, but, in his opinion, more decisively with Robert Henri, a star of the New York "Ash Can" school of realism, who joined the Chase faculty in 1903.

People like Chase and Henri were artistic innovators and had their quarrels with the academicians, but they did stress the import-ance of the tradition of Western art. Sometimes they held classes at the Metropolitan Museum of Art, and they demanded that their students absorb the tradition. Chase taught that "Absolute original-ity in art can only be found in a man who has been locked in a dark room from babyhood. . . . Since we are dependent on others, let us frankly and openly take in all that we can. We are entitled to it. The man who does that with judgment will produce an original picture that will have value." Edward Hopper absorbed these lessons well.

In the fall of 1906, he sailed for France, really for Paris. Culturally and artistically, Paris was a revelation. "Every street here is alive with all sorts and conditions of people, priests, nuns, students, and always the little soldiers with their wide red pants." ("Little soldiers": Hopper was a bony six-footer.) He absorbed the Louvre, visited the exhibitions and the galleries; he went to Berlin, Brussels, London.

He returned to America in 1907 to work as an illustrator, but also to contribute one oil painting, *The Louvre*, to the Exhibition of Independent Artists, the Armory Show, of 1910, which had been organized by John Sloan and Robert Henri in opposition to the art establishment of the time.

In December 1913, Hopper moved his New York studio down-town from East Fifty-ninth Street to Three Washington Square in the Village, where he would live and work for the rest of his life. Curiously, though he did not at all admire the experiments of the New York School of the postwar years, Hopper's Washington Square Studio was about a five-minute walk from the Cedar Tavern.

Hopper paid his bills as a commercial illustrator, but over the years he exhibited regularly as a serious and developing artist, indeed a major artist. He explored many modes. A pattern appears in the careers of major modern artists, whether they write fiction or compose musical scores or paint on canvas. They have to absorb and master the past before they can launch forth into a new and distinctive creation. Hopper explored many modes, in the realistic tradition he had chosen. For a while, he worked in the French tradition. His *Soir Bleu* of 1914 represents a variation on Wat-teau's *Gilles* of 1714, Watteau's sad clown wittily transposed to the Paris of the early twentieth century in the form of a sad waitress.

As we see it now, however, as a whole, Hopper's career had a goal. It would express with unique intensity a common perception. In the service of that perception, he would produce, perhaps, five great paintings. He himself sensed this inner dynamic, fed in part by unconscious sources, of his own career: "In every artist's development," he wrote, "the germ of the later work is always found in the earlier. The nucleus around which the artist's intellect builds his work is himself: the central ego, personality, or whatever it may be called, and this changes little from birth to death. What he was once, he always is, with slight modification. Changing fashions in methods or subject matter alter him little or not at all."

On May 15, 1967, at the age of 84, Hopper died in his old studio at Three Washington Square. By then he had achieved something absolutely unique in the history of art, a poetry of isolation, a strange poetry about the beauty of living in that cold and sceptical Eastern American light, so unlike the light of Paris or London.

In my opinion and the opinion of many others, Hopper's 1930 oil, *Early Sunday Morning,* is one of the most powerful paintings ever committed to canvas. It shows the facade of a run-down, two-story, red-brick urban building. There are empty store windows below, empty room windows above. There is a striped barber pole and a fire hydrant. No human beings are visible. In a way, it seems that no human beings could really inhabit this scene. There is something about it that is resistant to humanity. It looks as if a neutron bomb has gone off. Above the red brick row, the sky is a clear pale blue. This painting possesses an implicit tendency to abstraction. Most of the lines are horizontal. The window shades hint at Cubism. And in the upper right hand corner, mysteriously interrupting everything, is a dark rectangle. We are here in the world of T. S. Eliot's "Waste Land," of Wallace Stevens' similarly titled "Sunday Morning."

The theme of isolation, whether against an urban or a rural or seaside landscape, was the central theme of Hopper's last period, from about 1930 to his death in 1967.

Hopper's *Morning Sun* of 1952, for example, bathes a waking woman wearing a red chemise in that hard American light. She sits on her bed and gazes out through her window at a red-brick factory row, pale red brick in that hard light. Never has flesh or mind seemed so isolated and vulnerable. Though Hopper used a realistic technique and painted immediately recognizable subjects, his art possesses a powerful metaphysical and even religious resonance. *This* is metaphysical loneliness. One wishes that we could have had the response of T. S. Eliot to Edward Hopper masterpieces like *Excursion into Philosophy* (1959) or *Sunlight on Brownstone* (1956).

Not surprisingly, the meticulous and controlled Hopper had no time for the Tenth Street School of Abstract Expressionists. His entire tradition was completely different. Hopper perfected his own art, alone. But also not surprisingly, the artists over at the Cedar Tavern admired him enormously, for his use of color and light and for his exploitation of the abstract qualities of his compositions.

In the Fifties, that allegedly boring decade, New York was the Art Capital of the World.

BISHOP FULTON SHEEN

He had taught philosophy at Catholic University in Washington and had written such books as *God and Intelligence, Philosophy of Science, The Mystical Body of Christ,* and *Philosophy of Religion.* During the 1930s, he conducted "The Catholic Hour" on prime time radio in competition with "Amos 'n' Andy." The Catholic press in Milwaukee demanded that he be taken off the air and replaced by two men who would sounded like Amos and Andy and the Kingfish, but who would expound Catholic doctrine. Nevertheless, he stayed on the air and held his own.

But in 1951, the question remained. Could he go on television and compete with Milton Berle? The show was a commercial one, and he was paid $26,000 a night. Millions of dollars came in unsolicited through the mail. He gave it all to the Society for the Propagation of the Faith, a Catholic missionary organization.

He appeared on the screen in a black bishop's cassock and purple cloak, and he wore a large cross on his breast. He had piercing eyes and Irish good looks, he spoke without notes, and his only prop was a blackboard, on which, before drawing, he would write JMJ near the top: Jesus, Mary, and Joseph.

On television, he later wrote, his approach was ecumenical. It was "directed to Catholics, Protestants, Jews, and all men of good will. It was no longer a direct presentation of Christian doctrine but rather a reasoned approached to it, beginning with something that was common to the audience. Hence, during those television years, the subjects ranged from science, to humor, aviation, war, etc. Starting with something that was common to the audience and to me, I would gradually proceed from the known to the unknown or to the moral and Christian philosophy. It was the same method Our Blessed Lord used when He met a prostitute at the well. What was there in common between Divine Purity and this woman who had five husbands and was living with a man who was not her husband? The only common denominator was a love of cold water. Starting with that He led to the subject of the waters of everlasting life."

The handsome bishop on the television screen addressed some of the most profound questions. "Is it possible," he asked, "for the rain and the phosphates and the carbon, moisture, and sunlight to enter into the higher life of a plant? To do so, the plant must go down to the chemicals to absorb and assimilate them. If the plant could speak, it would say to the moisture and the sunlight, 'Unless you die to your lower existence, you cannot live in my kingdom. You are not blotted out; you are not destroyed, for if you were destroyed, you would never live in me and nourish me. Surrender this lower form of existence, and find yourself in me a living thing.'

"If plants are ever to live in the animal kingdom, the animals must come down to the plants and consume them. But the second law must also function: the plants must surrender their lower existence. They must be pulled up from their roots, ground beneath the jaws of death. They are not destroyed; otherwise they would never nourish the animals. . . .

"Why should the law stop with man? Is there not something higher that can come down to man, on the one condition that man die to himself? The rose has no right to say there is no higher life than itself. . . . There is something higher than man in this universe, namely, God. But if man is ever to be elevated to partnership with the divine, God must come down to man. But there is a difference between man going down to lower creation, and God coming to man. These things have no personality, no freedom, no liberties, and no rights; only persons have rights. Animals need never consult the plants; plants need never consult the chemicals. . . . But no one can ever lay hold of man without exercising or abusing man's freedom. Even God will not do that. He will not come into the order of humanity without first asking man if he will freely receive him. . . .

"Tremendous hidden reserves of power are available to anyone who desires them. But one must desire them. The door is open only to him who knocks. The Divine only entreats, pleads, and offers, but He will not use force, even to save us from our shortsighted preference for a meaner and lower form of life."

The bishop received twenty-five thousand letters a day. He received thousands of letters indicating interest in the Church. He conducted large catechism classes in school buildings in Washington and New York.

The television show was holding its own against Milton Berle.

CHAPTER THIRTEEN

The House of Intellect

Contrary to current opinion, the Fifties were years of intellectual ferment and intense excitement, of intellectual births and deaths, controversy and resolution. I will always consider it my great good fortune to have become aware of serious ideas, to have been a young man and a college student, just as this decade was commencing. In the autumn of 1950, I arrived on the Columbia University campus as a junior, a transfer student from Dartmouth, drawn to Columbia because of its superior English department, the best in America at that time, with the possible exception of Yale. During my first two college years, at Dartmouth, I had read and used Mark Van Doren's book on Shakespeare. He was teaching at Columbia. I had read essays by Reinhold Niebuhr, and a book on Matthew Arnold by Lionel Trilling. They were teaching at Columbia. I had read a book on Melville by Richard Chase. He was teaching at Columbia. To do my second two undergraduate years there seemed a natural idea. It was at Columbia that I began to understand that a great many important things were happening in the life of the intellect during the Fifties. They were happening in the Columbia English department itself, where I later became a professor, and in the university beyond the department, and in the intellectual life of America.

In this section, we will be focusing on four professors, all of whom were at the peak of their influence during the Fifties. They were distinctive, indeed unique individuals, but also representative, I think, of the particularly rich intellectual life of that decade. Naturally, I could have chosen other men and women, but I chose these because they were connected with Columbia, were part of my own experience of the Fifties, and two of them were my friends. During the Fifties, these two, Lionel Trilling and Mark Van Doren, were the leading members of a powerful English department. Across Broadway, two blocks away, at Union Theological Seminary, Reinhold Niebuhr and Paul Tillich were presences not only for the university but for the intellectual life of the nation.

I had found Dartmouth to be a New England campus out of Central Casting, with its elms, its red-brick Georgian buildings, its library with white-spire clock tower booming the hours, its nostalgia-drenched songs. But the Columbia campus had its own kind of beauty. The geometrical severity of its walks and plots of grass, the columns of Butler and Low libraries, the symmetrically placed fountains, all have a classical quality about them. There are brisk autumn days, and long and silvery spring afternoons when students stroll indolently along the walks. Even the old McKim, Mead and White buildings, like so many long-established things, have something aesthetically and even morally moving about them. I also found that at Columbia the life of the mind really *mattered,* that books and ideas were enjoyed, yes, but also ruthlessly examined. Lionel Trilling would remark to me that Columbia was not so much *alma mater* as *dura mater,* which was true.

Lionel Trilling had the most intelligent-looking face I have ever seen, a face of extraordinary refinement. He had white hair, dark deep-set eyes, and deep curving lines running from his nose to the corners of his mouth. He was physically slight, his body appearing to be merely something that carried his exquisitely intelligent head around, and his suits were tailored and looked English. For any student of literature at Columbia, Trilling's senior-year course in nineteenth-century English literature was a climactic event, something to be looked forward to, prepared for, and remembered. He taught it in the Socratic fashion, asking questions, demanding serious answers, constantly smoking cigarettes like some kind of French intellectual. When I first encountered him in a classroom, his intellectual intensity along with his personal elegance and his almost British manners—though he was Jewish—struck me as bordering on the un-American. The students in his senior-year course cared about their grades, of course—the best hoped for fellowships to Oxford or Cambridge—but they cared even more for Trilling's esteem. Because of who and what he was, his approval really meant something. And I think it is true that, in comparison with other Ivy League schools, more Columbia students hope for careers in writing, publishing, journalism and the arts. Robert Gottlieb, now chief editor at Knopf, was in Trilling's course; and so was Richard Howard, the poet and translator; Norman Podhoretz, now editor of *Commentary*; Eliot Zuckerman, who writes on music; Jason Epstein, who founded *The New York Review of Books*; and John Rosenberg, the novelist, an eccentric who then called himself Rupert and frequently came to class in white pancake makeup and a pajama top. Students of this sort desperately wanted Trilling's approval, but they also meant to test and challenge him. Though they were then only college students, they had the power to do so, and, three days a week in Hamilton Hall this made for some extraordinary sessions.

In 1930, under a pseudonym, Trilling had published a brilliant essay—now long-forgotten and uncollected—on the special quality of Columbia, its peculiar intellectual intensity, which he connected with the powerful Jewish presence there, though he maintained that the "account of Columbia's Jewishness must be a matter of tone and atmosphere rather than of numbers." And he cited, persuasively, one of the Jewish stereotypes: "he is a man who is solely interested in his work, a skeptical and searching man, absorbed in text or tube. . . . There are Gentile scholars of such sort, of course; but the type, the 'pure intelligence,' the almost disembodied mind, is something that has been much identified with the Jew. Music and visionary politics have their analogous Jewish stereotype." Trilling concluded that this type exerted a powerful influence at Columbia, "Dura Mater," and his 1930 view was still correct in the Fifties. I have found that I miss that intensity in much of the rest of American academic life.

In 1950, Trilling published the book that made him for the first time something more than a very distinguished academician. He had established himself as a reviewer and essayist. He had published a major book on Matthew Arnold, a shorter study of the British novelist E. M. Forster, a novel called *The Middle of the Journey*, featuring a character named Gifford Maxim who was based on Whittaker Chambers, and a couple of brilliant short stories, but it was *The Liberal Imagination* that made him the premier American intellectual of the Fifties. Intellectually, it was a high-risk enterprise. In effect, Trilling was declaring that in 1950 liberalism was intellectually and emotionally bankrupt, even while occupying all the seats of power—but that he, Trilling, could save it. He thus established himself as a powerful critic of liberalism, but he did so while remaining *within* liberalism. He wished to clean out of liberalism its Stalinist residue, which was still a strong presence in 1950. Only two years before, the former New Dealer, Henry Wallace, had run for president on what almost amounted to a Stalinist ticket. But Trilling also wanted to deepen and complicate the liberal tradition that had come down from the British and American nineteenth centuries, eliminate its simplicities and sentimentalities. He undertook to do this by bringing to bear upon liberalism a literary and intellectual tradition which was nonliberal and often antiliberal. In order to save the patient, he proposed serious transformation, deep surgery. I am not sure that he fully understood how drastic the transformation would have to be, nor am I certain that he entirely believed that the patient could really be saved. Nevertheless, he was utterly determined to remain, himself, within liberalism, even if it went down politically and intellectually. He was very much aware of T. S. Eliot, of Yeats, of Nietzsche, of Ortega y Gasset—but they were, so to speak, over there, culturally, while he was here. For Trilling himself there were no possibilities outside liberalism. If the liberal confederacy were to die, he had no conception of what might come after it.

Trilling's title, *The Liberal Imagination,* was something of a joke, since the central point of the book was that liberalism did not have much imagination at all.

What especially worried Trilling was the inferior quality of the novels, poems, and essays being written by liberals. "If we now turn and consider the contemporary literature of America," he wrote, "we can see that wherever we describe it as patently liberal and democratic, we must say that it is not of lasting interest. . . . This question is the most important, the most fully challenging question in culture that at this moment we can ask." Trilling saw that his negative judgment on contemporary liberal writing was also, clearly, a judgment on the liberal ideas and emotions that informed it—a judgment that these ideas and emotions were inadequate and inferior. Once the matter was put this way, it was also obvious that the very greatest writers, the best novelists and poets and critics, had simply *not* been drawn to liberalism. In *The Liberal Imagination*, Trilling did not say so openly, but there was only one inference to be drawn from that set of observations, a chilling surmise: that unless something could be done about it, liberalism might be finished, *kaput*.

Yet the facts were indisputable. Works of liberal tendency by Sandburg or Steinbeck or MacLeish could scarcely be mentioned in the same sentence with works by Yeats, Eliot, Faulkner, or Hemingway. And Trilling was well aware of the achievement of the powerful group of critics who derived from the conservative southern agrarian tradition, men such as Allen Tate, John Crowe Ransome, Robert Penn Warren, Cleanth Brooks. To make matters worse, these southern critics derived much of their inspiration from the criticism and poetry of T. S. Eliot, a troubling figure for Trilling, who had described himself, with intentional provocation, as an Anglo-Catholic, a Classicist, and a Royalist. For Trilling, who was determined to write as a liberal, this situation amounted to a cultural and political emergency. He had been struggling with it for a decade.

In 1943, for example, he had tried to counterbalance the fact of Eliot by attempting to promote the British novelist E. M. Forster as a liberal alternative, and he published a short, elegant book on Forster. But though Forster is indeed a considerable novelist, the whole tactic proved worse than ineffective. Eliot, drat him, had just published one of the greatest religious poems ever written in English, "Four Quartets," and he bestrode the literary world like a colossus. "No one since," as Donald Hall has written, "has embodied, or seemed to embody, such authority." For all of his gifts as a novelist, Forster simply did not measure up to Eliot's intellectual or emotional power, or to his technical virtuosity. There was a difference of *scale*. To put Forster forward against Eliot was simply to throw in your hand at the start. Trilling might have used Frost—except that Frost was a conservative of another kind; and Trilling was very slow to grasp Frost's real achievement, if in fact he ever did. The only figure in the American tradition potent enough to pit against Eliot was Whitman, as poets later in the Fifties would demonstrate, but Trilling never reached for Whitman. Their differences in temperament and style were simply too enormous. So, in *The Liberal Imagination*, which consisted of sixteen essays written over a period of ten years, Trilling tried a different strategy. The individual essays had appeared in places like *Partisan Review* and *The Nation,* and they had been much admired, but when he brought them together in this volume, the whole was much greater than the sum of the parts. This was a book, not a collection, and it had point and coherence. It was about literature, but about much more than literature. It carried the subtitle "Essays on Literature and Society," and it was Trilling's distinctive strength as a critic that he operated so effectively precisely at the juncture between literature and society; he was a critic, but also a great instinctive sociologist. And *The Liberal Imagination* came forward with a heroic ambition, nothing less than to resuscitate an apparently sick or even moribund liberal tradition. Trilling was trying to recover a viable position between, on the one hand, the Stalinists and fellow-travelers, and, on the other, Eliot, the agrarians and other conservatives.

This goal determined the structure of the book. There were the great deflations, masterful discussions of accepted liberal literary heroes: the influential literary historian V. L. Parrington, Theodore Dreiser, Sherwood Anderson, and sex researcher Alfred Kinsey. With cool and intelligent precision, Trilling demonstrated exactly where they were inadequate—and how, moreover, this inadequacy was rooted in the culture of liberalism:

> Parrington does not often deal with abstract philosophical ideas, but whenever he approaches a work of art we are made aware of the metaphysics on which his aesthetics is based. There exists, he believes, a thing called *reality;* it is one and immutable, it is wholly external, it is irreducible. Men's minds may waver, but reality is always reliable, always the same, always easily to be known.

> To James no quarter is given by American criticism in its political and liberal aspect. But in the same degree that liberal criticism is moved by political considerations to treat James with severity, it treats Dreiser with the most sympathetic indulgence. Dreiser's literary faults, it gives us to understand, are essentially social and political virtues. . . . It is as if wit, and flexibility of mind, and perception and knowledge were to be equated with aristocracy and political reaction, while dullness and stupidity must naturally suggest a virtuous democracy, as in the old plays.

> The salvation that Anderson was talking about was no doubt a real salvation, but it was small, and he used for it the language of the most strenuous religious experience.

The Kinsey Report, we may say, has an extravagant fear of all ideas that do not seem to be, as it were, immediately dictated by simple physical fact. Another way of saying this is that the Report is resistant to any idea that seems to refer to a specifically human situation.

But what was to be done about the inadequacies and flaccidities of the liberal mind so relentlessly exposed in Trilling's deflationary essays? There Trilling had a serious problem on his hands. As he saw it, America simply did not possess a flourishing conservative intellectual tradition. Had it possessed one, such a tradition could be drawn upon as an alternative, used to put corrective pressure upon liberalism, called upon for analysis and insight. But there *was* no conservative tradition. In the famous Preface to *The Liberal Imagination*, Trilling wrote, in tones that admitted of no disagreement: "In the United States at this time liberalism is not only the dominant but even the sole intellectual tradition. For it is the plain fact that nowadays there are no conservative or reactionary ideas in general circulation."

Trilling, therefore, used literature as a kind of substitute for a living conservative tradition. It was in literature that one could find the required sense of complexity, an expression of the full range of human possibility and human limitation, and a sense of style, intellectual energy, and refinement of thought and perception—everything, in short, that Trilling found lacking in the liberalism of 1950. But the literature he invoked was not that of the standard liberal authors. He went to James, Proust, Wordsworth, the Mark Twain of *Huckleberry Finn*, Tacitus, and Freud. These were the sources of power; these were the truths and the minds that might resuscitate liberalism, if anything could. And, finally, there was the style of *The Liberal Imagination* itself. Trilling had evolved a style of great power and flexibility, and, above all, *precision*. There were no liberal evasions in a Trilling sentence. The style derived from Matthew Arnold, about whom Trilling had written his first book, and perhaps also from James and Eliot. The Trilling style, by its very success, declared that you didn't have to write like Dreiser, you didn't have to write like *The Nation*, in order to be a liberal.

Great excitement surrounded this book in the early Fifties. In its method and in its politics, it represented a challenge to the dominant school of New Critics. They concentrated upon a careful analysis of a literary text, often going line-by-line through an

A major presence on the Fifties movie screen, now faded from memory, starring in *The Cattle Queen of Montana*, 1955. (*RKO Radio Pictures, Inc.*)

Ed Sullivan, the personality who presided over the Fifties entertainment revolution.

Frank Sinatra and Ava Gardner, when the going was especially good. (*UPI*)

Lucille Ball. More people watched Lucy's childbirth on TV than watched Eisenhower's inauguration the following day.

Allen Tate and T. S. Eliot. Eliot was an overwhelming intellectual presence during the Fifties.

Reinhold Niebuhr rediscovered sin as a theologian but was slightly embarrassed by the Resurrection.

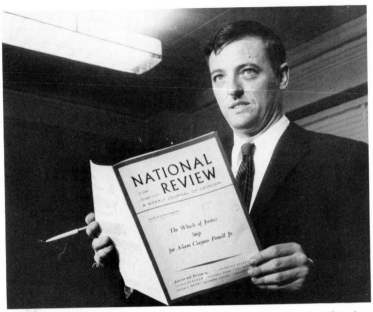

William F. Buckley, Jr., in the early days of *National Review,* now favorite reading of President Reagan. (*UPI*)

The House of Intellect at Columbia: Charles Everett, Andrew Chioppe, Richard Chase, Mark Van Doren, Lionel Trilling. Chase isn't really reading. (*Columbia College Today*)

Jackson Pollock was central to the art scene when New York was the art capital of the world. He stands in front of his 1953 painting, "Portrait and a Dream." (*Hans Namuth*)

Mary Martin and Ezio Pinza in *South Pacific*. The old music went out in a blaze of Rogers and Hammerstein glory. (*John Swope, King Features*)

Elvis had a remarkable pelvis, and the songs were also changing.

James Dean gears up on the road to infinity. (*American Weekly*)

Poet Allen Ginsberg trying to return poetry to the people in his revolt against the Fifties, Eliot, Ike, and heterosexuality. (*Wide World Photos*)

The Beatles made their American debut on the "Ed Sullivan Show." "The day the music stopped" with the death of Buddy Holly proved transitory. (*Wide World Photos*)

entire poem. They tended to exclude biographical and historical considerations, concentrating only on the text. Trilling read literature with full awareness of history, biography, and surrounding culture. Of course, the New Critics had a program, which was part of their method. They had a quarrel, from a traditionalist point of view, with much of modern culture, and they wished to recover the tradition. This involved a deliberate exclusion of surrounding history, a lifting of the literary work out of history, and the establishing of it as a part of a literary canon. Then, from the perspective of the canon, the New Critics would conduct their wars with liberalism and with much in modern culture.

Serious, even furious intellectual fights were waged over the whole question of critical method. Just what relevance, demanded Trilling's bright Columbia students, did a biographical or historical fact have in the discussion of a poem? Suppose the poem had floated up on the beach in a bottle? We wouldn't know anything about its author. Literature should be studied *as literature,* not as something else. Trilling was always interested in the moral, the cultural, the political implication. The partisans of rival methods and rival critics fought these issues out at Columbia and elsewhere. The atmosphere, although this was the early Fifties, was anything but apathetic.

There also arose at Cambridge University, in England, a powerful literary critic who was a Trilling rival and adopted by many students as a standard-bearer and challenger. F. R. Leavis was a brilliant and acerbic Cambridge don who attracted a wide following, and he had a stunning impact on the teaching of literature in England. He edited a powerful magazine called *Scrutiny,* in which he and his followers laid down the law according to Leavis. It was to be expected, given Leavis' personality, that he was, throughout his career, in a state of total war with the faculty and administration of his university. In 1952, he published a collection of his principal essays entitled *The Common Pursuit,* a book of criticism which, like Trilling's, had implications beyond literature or critical method. The partisans of Leavis conducted a heated controversy with the partisans of Trilling, and it was, intellectually, very lively.

Leavis could analyze a poem or a passage of prose with great skill, and, like the New Critics, he tended, when he did that, to stick to the text. For that reason, many literary people preferred him to Trilling. But, like the Puritan preachers who were his spiritual forebears, Leavis found occasion in the texts for a particular kind of moral instruction. And Leavis' morality was Puritan. He would seize upon a slight sneer in a comment by Lord David Cecil about George Eliot, and reply in downright Puritan fury. "And her standards of right and wrong," wrote Cecil, "were the puritan standards. She admired truthfulness and chastity and industry and self restraint, she disapproved of loose living and recklessness and deceit and self-indulgence." That bit of mild superiority had no chance of getting by Dr. Leavis, no chance at all. "I had better confess that I differ (apparently) from Lord David Cecil in sharing these beliefs, admirations, and disapprovals, so that the reader knows my bias at once. And they seem to me favorable to the production of great literature. I will add (exposing myself completely) that the enlightenment of aestheticism or sophistication that feels an amused superiority to them leads, in my view, to triviality and boredom, and that out of triviality comes evil."

In his writing on the novel, to which he chiefly turned during the Fifties and Sixties, Leavis pursued these moral preoccupations. He found them best served in the "great tradition" of the English novel which he isolated with what most would consider eccentric exclusivity. The "great tradition" consisted of Jane Austen, George Eliot, Henry James, Joseph Conrad, and D. H. Lawrence. Period. But it was Leavis' genius, exercised through analysis and, especially, apt quotation, that made his position even plausible. He had the power to persuade you, whatever you thought of Dickens or Trollope, say, that his five authors did constitute a tradition, and one of power and excellence. All of these controversies and all of this achievement occurred during the Fifties, when nothing much was supposed to be happening.

Trilling's influence was also exerted through a famous graduate seminar he taught with Jacques Barzun, a course which many students found to be a decisive experience, and through which passed many who have since had distinguished intellectual careers.

To this seminar, a Ph.D. student had to be admitted by Trilling and Barzun, who examined samples of his written work and then conducted a formidable interview in Trilling's office in Hamilton Hall. No more than a dozen students were admitted. It met for two hours on Wednesday evenings, and the subject was "cultural history"—by which was meant the discussion of a major work of great cultural importance, a book by Nietzsche, Hegel, Bagehot, Blake, Hazlitt. On the weekly agenda was the book, but also a paper on some subject written by a student in the course, which was criticized and argued about with great, and often illuminating, intensity. Barzun must have spent hours writing his comments on these essays, at every level of importance and seriousness. He vastly improved my own writing, though I remember today only two of his more whimsical comments. He took me to task for calling Dickens' *Pickwick Papers* a "Victorian novel," observing that it had come out in the year before Victoria came to the throne. That expressed his sense of accuracy, and also a certain donnish wit. He also won a debate with Trilling over the question of whether, in a typed manuscript, the line under a title should be continuous or broken. It should be continuous, Barzun successfully argued, since it italicized *one title*.

In September 1975, before Trilling learned that he was mortally ill of cancer of the pancreas, he began writing a personal memoir of Barzun. When he died on November 5 of that year, he had completed only a few pages, and his last words were about the seminars the two men had taught. "The course seemed to be designed as if its chief purpose was to give life such significance as derives from achievement against odds. It consisted of a series of [dramatic structures], each of which came to its climax on Wednesday evening. Thursday might conceivably accommodate gestures toward relaxation and well-deserved rest, but by Friday one had to be getting forward with next week's book, possibly with the illusion which might be maintained for the first day of the weekend, that one could get the work done at a reasonable, deliberate pace. But this was never possible—unfailingly one had to read faster and give more hours to reading as each day passed. Wednesday afternoon was given to desperate efforts to come to the end of the work, then to a call to reasonableness and the jotting down of salient ideas. A shower before dinner was fortifying." A few sketchy notes followed, including "Jacques and me/his ability/ music/science," and "J & me: my slovenliness—lack of system." Many of the student essays read and fought over in that seminar became chapters in important books, and many of the students passed on to major intellectual careers.

There was a good deal of pathos about Trilling's last years. He collected his often distinguished essays in volumes that were respectfully, even reverently treated, *Beyond Culture* and *The Opposing Self*, and he produced the final book, *Sincerity and Authenticity*, the Charles Eliot Norton lectures at Harvard, but despite the distinction of these works, something had been lost, and it was the direct and vital engagement of "society" with "literature" that had been so powerful a source of energy in *The Liberal Imagination*. All writers exist mentally and emotionally in a particular time and place, and Trilling—it is clear to say in retrospect—was a man of the Forties and Fifties, when he was an intellectual force. During the Sixties, he went out of focus, seemed beached. The attack upon liberalism as he understood it did not now come from any of the old familiar sources, not from Stalinism, not from any of the familiar kinds of stupidity, not from reaction, but from the New Left. In 1968, pointedly ignoring High Culture, intellect and precision, the New Left would turn Trilling's intellectual home, Columbia University, into a shambles. Columbia never recovered its Fifties authority. Othello's occupation was gone. The terms in which serious intellectual issues could be discussed had been permanently debased.

And the sad part of it was that Trilling did not go down fighting. He obliquely criticized the New Left in his attacks upon a mass "adversary culture." He taught a course in modern literature and reached the conclusion, in a rather dispirited essay, that writers like Joyce and Kafka were too radical to be taught to college students. In his final *Sincerity and Authenticity* (1972), he argued that the pursuit of authenticity was dangerous and destructive. But he might have tried a little authenticity himself and defended dramatically and in public his own university, yes, Columbia, against its tormentors. Did he fail to do so effectively because he was a "man of the Left?" Did he fail to do so out of a fear of more violence? He knew, intellectually, that there is a time when discourse ceases and action begins, but in 1968 at Columbia, when his whole life was trashed, he was not an effective force at all. It was too bad, but a man does what it is in him to do, and when he was going well during the Fifties, Lionel Trilling was a major and exciting figure in the life of intellect.

It will be worth returning one last time to that famous 1949 Preface to *The Liberal Imagination*. "In the United States at this time liberalism is not only the dominant but even the sole intellectual tradition. For it is the plain fact that nowadays there are no conservative or reactionary ideas in general circulation."

First of all, to the extent that this was true—and it did have some truth in it—it was a remarkably provincial statement. "In the United States. . . ." It certainly was not true of, for example, France. Wherever one would place, say, Maritain or Gilson on the political spectrum, theirs was not the "intellectual tradition" to which Trilling was referring. If, in 1950, Trilling believed that the liberal intellectual tradition was seriously bankrupt, well, there were other intellectual traditions. Was it foreordained that he remain forever in the old neighborhood?

Second, that announcement about liberalism being the sole American intellectual tradition depended upon some sleight-of-hand with the venerable word "liberal." On several occasions I discussed these sentences with Trilling. What it seemed to come down to is the view that all of American politics, at least insofar as it appealed to ideas, was "liberal." Thus in 1950, Trilling argued that Senator Robert Taft was a "liberal," by which he meant that Taft's free-market, small-government ideas derived from nineteenth-century liberalism. By a genuine conservatism, Trilling seemed to mean some European-style ecclesiastical and aristocratic establishment, which of course we do not have in America. To Trilling, Hamilton was a liberal, and so were Washington and Madison. An intellectual case can be made for placing them in the liberal tradition, but a case can also be made, and has often been made, that both the *Federalist Papers* and the *Constitution* are profoundly conservative documents, based upon eighteenth-century conservative distrust of popular sentiment and upon a conservative and anti-utopian view of human nature. To go no further, to forego discussion here of the traditions of American local government, jurisprudence, state government, church history, and so forth, Trilling appeared to place American history within the "liberal" tradition only by stretching the word "liberal" so wide that it covered virtually everything, obscuring useful distinctions both in the past and in the present.

Operationally, however, Trilling knew exactly what a liberal really was. Throughout his career, his work appeared only in certifiably liberal publications, or else apolitical academic ones. Though he might call Robert Taft a liberal, there was no chance of Trilling supporting Taft. What Trilling really meant by "liberal" were political positions one might imagine as being acceptable to his friends in New York and at Columbia.

But the 1949 preface was answered in ways that Trilling would not have anticipated. The appearance of Russell Kirk's *The Conservative Mind* in 1953 and the founding of the magazine *National Review* in 1955 were events of great importance. Kirk succeeded in demonstrating the existence of a conservative intellectual tradition "from Burke to Santayana"—he later made T. S. Eliot the terminus. Examining and recommending the thought of John Adams, Walter Scott, Coleridge, John Randolph, Calhoun, de Tocqueville, Paul Elmer More, and Santayana, among others, Kirk showed that the culture of the West, with its habits and assumptions, beliefs and moral imperatives, had been defended in the past with powerful intellectual weapons, and his point was clear: it was possible to do so in the present and in the future. It was also important that Kirk defended a tradition that was in no way crassly materialistic, one that could in no way be confused with the embarrassing figure of George F. Babbitt. The conservative position, this book demonstrated, could be articulated with graceful intensity.

Kirk himself was a spectacular figure in the early Fifties. A learned bachelor and eccentric, a bohemian figure who sometimes sported a cloak, he possessed panache and had a considerable impact as an itinerant speaker on the campuses and elsewhere. When the magazine *National Review* came into existence in 1955, it was the logical place for Kirk's columns to begin to appear. And the *National Review* conservatives, not only Buckley himself, but James Burnham and Wilmoore Kendall, political philosophers of very different kinds, and the others associated with the magazine, would make important contributions to the political culture of the Fifties. Both Burnham and Kendall made permanent contributions to political philosophy itself.

By 1981, *National Review* had surpassed *The New Republic* in subscribers, seemed much surer of its sense of direction, its senior editors were all publishing books, and it was the favorite reading of the 39th President of the United States. Trilling's 1949 sentences, perhaps defensible in some terms then, had a distinctly anachronistic ring in the Eighties.

At Columbia during the Fifties, the complementary figure to Lionel Trilling was Mark Van Doren, another English professor, but poet, fiction writer, critic, and teacher of great distinction as well—in the opinion of many the best teacher ever to hold a post at Columbia. Trilling was intense, demanding, a tough grader, impa-

THE HOUSE OF INTELLECT   247

tient with student laziness or uncertainty. He seemed European in a way, somewhat British. But Van Doren's face and manner proclaimed his American identity. He had grown up in Urbana, Illinois and had gone to the university there before taking his Ph.D. at Columbia. He felt a special affinity for a fellow citizen of Illinois, Lincoln, and wrote a play about him. Van Doren was strikingly handsome, and his intellectual manners, his classroom behavior, were spiritually democratic. He behaved as if he expected his students to perform at his own level. He treated them as equals, though of course they were not. His major course during the Fifties was called "The Narrative Art," and in it he dealt with a small number of supremely great works: *The Iliad, The Odyssey, The Divine Comedy,* selections from the Old and New Testaments, *Don Quixote,* and *The Castle.* His lectures were conversations, launched casually with some observations, and then he would draw a student in the class into the conversation. He had a way of creating intelligence in the student through these exchanges. Responding to Van Doren's questions, the student would find himself saying things he had never thought of before about Hector, or Brunetto Latini. "My purpose," he later wrote, "was to examine the various ways in which the greatest story tellers had put divine things and human things together. The ultimate dimension, I suggested, was given to narrative by the presence in it of gods or their equivalent. In the case of Cervantes I promised that it would be difficult to say what the equivalent was, yet I supposed it was there, or else *Don Quixote* would not be the supreme novel it is. Reading it slowly in preparation for the course, listening to every word of it in Motteaux's joyful translation, I had fallen hopelessly in love with it as I continue every year to do. The Bible, too, became for me a boundless world of wonder, terror, wisdom, and delight. Dante and Kafka, the one finishing his thought, the other unable to do so, I likewise discovered to be bottomless in meaning as well as brilliant with ten thousand details that cannot tarnish. Homer, I need not say, remained for me what Dante said he was, the sovereign poet. In a subsequent year I cut the course in half to fit into one term instead of two; but I knew from the first that I would never want to stop giving it while I taught at all. One reason was the papers the students wrote. Many of these told me things I could not have learned alone: things never said before, nor said with such beauty and force."

Van Doren was also a fine poet, and part of his power as a

teacher came through his direct poet's perception of another poet's work:

> My great friends do not know me.
> Hamlet in the halls,
> Achilles by the river, and Don Quixote
> Feasting with the Duke see no one there
> Like me, like Mark Van Doren, who grows daily
> Older while they look not, change not
> Die not save deaths their masters made.

From 1920 until his retirement in 1957, Van Doren taught all of the best students at Columbia. In the first class he met, in 1920, he found a "young man who engaged me beyond the call of duty. This was Whittaker Chambers, whose eyes were always upon me as if he thought he had found in this strange place a person who would understand him. . . . He was passionate about poetry, philosophy and all manner of abstract things; and his poems were good." In 1927, Van Doren published an article about his Columbia students, and wrote finely-drawn sketches of Meyer Schapiro, Louis Zukovsky, Clifton Fadiman, John Gassner, and Lionel Trilling. He indicated in that article, however, that the best student he had had at Columbia in those seven years, "in the first class I taught," was Whittaker Chambers. Of Trilling he recalled that "starting brightly as a freshman, he grew more melancholy each year, and more beguiling. Something fastidious in his gentle nature kept him from irony and rendered him incapable of satire, though he was by no means unaware of absurdities. . . . He spoke diffidently, with a hushed and harmless voice; and though he wrote exceedingly well he found it hard to decide what to write about. I thought I detected in him a particularly sensitive and at the same time healthy set of nerves, and said to myself that this was equipment indeed for a storyteller or a poet. He became both—but was careful to maintain the amateur standing which his fastidiousness forced him to prefer. He took up this, he took up that, only to let both fall gracefully at his feet, which passed lightly on to other pleasant fields. He is a college instructor now in the Middle West, whence he writes back letters full of praise for a few persons and of blame for a few others. He is still feeling himself out—respectfully, with dignity, and with grace. What he will eventually do, if he does it at all, will be lovely, for it will be the fruit of a pure intelligence slowly ripened in not too fierce a sun." That was Van Doren on Trilling in 1927. In 1961, when I was teaching at Columbia, I heard them in a public discussion of Tolstoi's great story "The Death of Ivan Illich." Each of them brilliantly deployed his characteristic approach, and when Trilling concluded his remarks for the evening by saying that though it was a great story, he knew how it could have been made greater, everyone in the room believed him.

Van Doren was the most effective classroom performer I have ever seen, and his power lay in the relationship he established with the students in the room before him. One can sense his clear and fine intelligence in the sentences I have quoted from him about Trilling as an undergraduate; and he himself had an accurate sense of his own classroom manner. "If I speak of the students last," he wrote in 1958, "it is not merely because they were the crucial persons with whom I spent my time, as must be true in any college; it is also because no way exists of describing what really goes on in a classroom once the door is closed. What goes on is a kind of secret between him who stands and those who sit. I knew this from the first; it was my secret even more than it was theirs. They had their own responses which I could hear or see them make: they raised their hands, they laughed, they talked, they shook their heads, they laughed, and they looked bored; and special approval or disapproval they expressed—the custom is now obsolete—by stamping or shuffling their feet on the floor. But even then I could believe that if anything of true moment was happening in their minds there was no immediate way for them to show it, any more than I could show, except by talking in the maturest way I could, and following any new idea as far as it would take me, how much our conversations interested me, and how much I learned from them. From the beginning, I think, I assumed experience even in freshmen. . . . Perhaps the chief novelty consisted in my assumption that nothing was too difficult for the students. . . . Freshmen have had more experience than they are given credit for. They have been born, had parents, had brothers and sisters and friends, been in love, been jealous, been angry, been ambitious, been tired, been hungry, been happy and unhappy, been aware of justice and injustice. Well, the great writers handled just such things; and they did so in the basic human language men must use whenever they feel and think. The result, if no teacher prevented its happening, was that the freshmen learned about themselves. And so did the teachers, at least if they read and talked like men of the world, simply and humbly, without assumptions of academic superiority."

Van Doren indeed was a man of the world. His Columbia Ph.D. dissertation on John Dryden had been a major critical work, and had been reviewed by T. S. Eliot in the *Times Literary Supplement.* As literary editor of *The Nation,* he had known the principal American writers of his time. His books on Shakespeare, on epic poetry, on education were major and will last. Despite his ambition to write epic or at least narrative poetry, his best work was in shorter forms, and it was often very good. When he walked into his Columbia classroom, he brought all of that with him.

In his politics, Van Doren was an enigma to me. He was profoundly a man of the Western tradition, "from Homer to the present," as T. S. Eliot put it, and yet in his time Van Doren appeared to be oddly leftist. He despised Harry Truman, and, I believe, supported Henry Wallace in 1948. His politics were those of *The Nation.* In 1958, in his autobiography, he declared his belief in the innocence of Alger Hiss, in no way dealing with the evidence of the contrary. This side of Van Doren I found completely impenetrable.

The last time I saw him was during the late Fifties. He stopped in to my Columbia office on the fourth floor of Hamilton Hall. It was a warm spring day, the window was open, and two pigeons had landed on my window sill and then hopped into the room and landed on the floor, bathed in sunlight. Van Doren looked at them, and then at me. "St. Francis," he said, and smiled, and left.

Before he died in 1972, he put together a remarkable final volume of poems. He had once written,

> Eternity is now or not at all,
> Waited for, a wisp: remembered, shadows.
> Eternity is solid as the sun:
> As present; as familiar; as immense.

It is characteristic of Van Doren that his final volume, put together when he knew that he was dying, is entitled *Good Morning.*

THE AGE OF AQUARIUS

On a Thursday evening in 1958, a year after T. S. Eliot had read his poetry in McMillin Theater at Columbia, three Beat poets read their works from the same platform. The literary critic and Columbia professor, F. W. Dupee, provided urbane introductions, keeping a certain distance from these writers, whom many considered barbarians, but also providing them with a certain academic sanction.

Allen Ginsberg had cleaned up his act. This was his triumphant return to Columbia, where he had been an undergraduate during the Forties. He was neat in plaid shirt and clean blue jeans.

The blond and thin Peter Orlovsky was widely known to be Ginsberg's lover. In one of his two published poems, he had written, "If I should shave, I know the bugs would go away." Nevertheless, Orlovsky had shaved.

Gregory Corso had once announced that he never combed his hair. For that Thursday night, "Ginsberg's Return," he had combed it.

Jack Kerouac was supposed to be on the program. He had coined the term "Beat," had himself been a Columbia under-graduate, and was a kind of godfather to the movement.

Kerouac didn't make it. He was rumored to be in some personal crisis downtown.

As an undergraduate at Columbia during the Forties, Ginsberg had been in constant hot water. During his senior year, he had been suspended for tracing in the dust of his dormitory window the words "fuck the Jews." The Dean could not bring himself to repeat the three words in discussing the incident. He wrote them on a piece of paper. But Ginsberg had been disciplined, lectured, threatened with jail throughout his college career. Tonight he returned as a celebrity, a leader in a national movement of the young, the best-known poet published by City Lights in San Francisco.

Outside McMillin Theater there was a vast throng that had been unable to get in. They pounded on the doors and milled around. Ticket-holders entered between lines of police. People were showing up from Greenwich Village and from God-knows-what corners of the city. There was an excitement in the air that had little to do with poetry. Something new was stirring in the culture, all across the country, and tonight the focus was here, in McMillin Theater.

Present that night was Diana Trilling, who later wrote of "the shoddiness of an audience in which it was virtually impossible to distinguish between student and camp-follower; the always new shock of so many young girls, so few of them pretty, and so many blackest black stockings; so many young men, so few of them—despite the many black beards—with any promise of masculinity." A nascent mob of the young, academic-plus-bohemian.

The evening belonged to Ginsberg. Orlovsky and Corso were supporting cast, almost props. Ginsberg read a poem dedicated to Lionel Trilling, and about Trilling, called "Lion in the Room." It was about a lion in the room with the poet. Though the lion was hungry, it refused to eat him. When Ginsberg had been an undergraduate, Trilling had tried to keep him out of trouble and out of jail. Ginsberg read from *Howl*, the long cry of pain that had first made him famous:

> I saw the best minds of my generation destroyed by madness, starving
>   hysterical naked,
> dragging themselves through the negro streets at dawn looking for an
>   angry fix,

angelheaded hipsters burning for the ancient heavenly connection to
    the starry dynamo in the machinery of night. . . .

The distinctive thing about Ginsberg and the Beats seemed
to be their conviction that they could *do* nothing about the circumstances of the suffering they proclaimed. There was no
suggestion that they could change the society they attacked so
vehemently with their words. But the hatred of American society constituted a powerful communion with their bearded and
black-stockinged audience.

It was clear from Ginsberg's poetry that the decisive event
in his emotional life had been the death of his mother, who
had been in and out of mental hospitals. He read from what
may be his best poem, *Kaddish,* which was based on the Hebrew prayer of mourning:

down the Avenue to the South, to—as I walk toward the Lower East
    Side—where you walked 50 years ago, little girl—from
    Russia, eating the first poisonous tomatoes of America—
    frightened on the dock—
then struggling in the crowds of Orchard Street toward what?—toward
    Newark—
toward candy store, first home-made sodas of the century, hand-
    churned ice cream in backroom on musty brownfloor boards—
Toward education marriage nervous breakdown, operation, teaching
    school, and learning to be mad, in a dream—what is this life?

Ginsberg was the Jewish Whitman. He said that the Columbia English Department was stuck in the nineteenth century,
that he had carried Whitman and William Carlos Williams one
step further.

Much of the poetry read by Ginsberg, Orlovsky, and Corso
that night contained obscenities, words like "fuck," and "shit,"
and "bullshit," and "cunt." These appeared to have no effect
whatsoever on the young audience, no intake of breath, no
nervous laughter—just nothing, zero. Orlovsky's homosexual
prancing and kidding produced no shock either. Something
new was happening.

Ten years later, a bearded Columbia undergraduate sat in
President Grayson Kirk's chair in his "liberated" office. Outside, the police were battling mobs of students and nonstudents. Someone took a crap in Kirk's wastebasket. Columbia

athletes battled student revolutionaries. Someone burned ten years of research by Professor Oreste Ranum of the history department—it had dealt with the French Revolution. The math building, which had been "liberated" by SDS members led by nonstudent Tom Hayden, was renamed Smolny Institute. Hayden declaimed that there would be one, two, many Columbias. Fayerweather Hall was renamed the Menchevik Center.

Both the administration and the faculty completely caved in. Neither seemed able to define itself in terms of its institutional responsibilities. Neither possessed the will to simply clear out the mob, insist on classes, insist on *Columbia*. In the midst of the destruction, neither Lionel Trilling nor Mark Van Doren said anything that mattered.

The Columbia University of the Fifties, a great university, was finished, whatever else might eventually emerge on the same real estate.

When last heard from, Mark Rudd, leader of the insurrection, was reported to be teaching school in Colorado.

CHAPTER FOURTEEN

Wrestling With God

Across Broadway from Columbia University stands the Gothic structure of Union Theological Seminary, probably the most important Protestant seminary in America. It is a liberal seminary, but it has always had a strong scholarly faculty, distinguished church historians and biblical scholars and philosophers. During the Fifties, because of the presence there of Reinhold Niebuhr and—until 1955, when he went to Harvard—Paul Tillich, Union Theological Seminary became one of the intellectual foci of the United States, influential far beyond the boundaries of regular Protestant scholarship and ecclesiastical matters.

During the Fifties, Reinhold Niebuhr was a powerful presence. Bald, civilized, and possessing a wide range of intellectual reference, he was a force in the classroom, in his wide social life, and in his writings. Though he suffered a mild stroke in 1952, which slightly impaired his speech, essays, reviews, and books seemed to flow from him in an uninterrupted stream. Niebuhr was exciting. To put it simply, but also accurately, Niebuhr was breathing intellectual life into the ancient doctrine of Original Sin, proving that it was an "insight," using it to illuminate the actual issues and circumstances we were all living through. To put it another way, Niebuhr was exciting because he was demonstrating that ancient religious traditions had something to say, something that could not be said as convincingly from purely secular perspectives.

Original Sin, to put it mildly, was not an explosive concept in the early Fifties, but Niebuhr made it one. He was a powerful critic of idealism, of human illusion. What Niebuhr meant by Original Sin now seems almost to amount to common sense—that permanent felicity is not available within history, that human motives are mixed, that situations exist which are intractable and must be endured with patience, that within history the choice to be made is often one among mixed goods or even evils. Niebuhr's Protestantism issued in the insight that there is, or may be, a realm of the Divine, a realm of the absolute and pure, but that here, where we live, we must inevitably deal with the imperfect, the corrupt, the ultimately unsatisfactory.

It is not too much to say that Niebuhr made a major contribution toward diminishing what might be called the windbag content of American liberalism. He did not think that the world was run by manifestos, not even the manifestos issuing from the United Nations. Niebuhr believed in the reality of power. Power must be opposed to power, whether in the arena of American politics and economics or in the world arena. The use of power, indeed, was one way of restraining a universal predisposition to sin grandly, through pride, illusion, and greed, on a universal scale.

The opening paragraph of his 1952 book *The Irony of American History,* a characteristic Niebuhr production of the Fifties, faced the power realities squarely: "Everybody understands the obvious meaning of the world struggle in which we are engaged. We are defending freedom against tyranny and are trying to preserve justice against a system which has, demonically, distilled injustice and cruelty out of its original promise of a higher justice."

But Niebuhr also saw in American history, though in milder terms, the "irony" which operated between those lofty pretensions to a higher justice on the part of the Soviets and the "demonic" actuality of their political behavior. This irony, in fact, was central to Niebuhr's doctrine of Original Sin, in which ideal aspiration was continually undone by the facts of human nature, tragedy often rooted in the degree of disparity between fact and aspiration.

Niebuhr was astute in picking out the ironies. There was the irony of an age of scientific progress issuing in an age of mass slaughter and possible atomic warfare. There was the irony of American Fifties prosperity threatened by global poverty and instability. There was the irony that separated liberal rhetoric from actual accomplishment. Both liberal idealism and Soviet revolutionism were based upon simplicities. The liberals thought that social problems could be cured by education and improved social environment. They were sentimental. The Marxists believed that social problems could be cured by state ownership. This extreme form of innocence, if it was that, issued in, perhaps inevitably, criminal behavior. Niebuhr's sense of the irony of human existence did have religious roots. If man really does have an eternal destiny and transcendent longings, but is also tied to a historical fate, then the contrast is bound to issue in savage ironies.

"In any event," he wrote of communism in 1952, "we have to deal with a vast religious political movement which generates more extravagant forms of political injustice and cruelty out of the pretensions of innocence than we have ever known in human history. The liberal world which opposes this monstrous evil is filled ironically with milder forms of the same pretension. Fortunately they have not resulted in the same evils, partly because we have not invested our ostensible 'innocents' with inordinate power. Though a tremendous amount of illusion expresses itself in American culture, our political institutions contain many of the safeguards against the selfish abuse of power which our Calvinist fathers insisted upon. According to the accepted theory, our democracy owes everything to the believers in the innocence and perfectibility of man and little to the reservations about human nature which emanated from the Christianity of New England. But fortunately there are quite a few accents in our constitution which spell out the warning of John Cotton: 'Let all the world give mortall man no greater power than they are content they shall use, for use it they will. . . .' "

This was powerful stuff and congruent with reality, and Niebuhr was a powerful intellectual force working to change American liberalism from within. Rhetoric about the Century of the Common Man withered in the Niebuhrian atmosphere. Arthur Schlesinger, Jr., the Harvard historian, moderated his earlier enthusiasm about Jacksonian democracy and talked about countervailing forces and the "vital center."

In 1955, I heard Niebuhr preach at a Protestant service in the university chapel at Harvard. That day, he was an authentic Protestant clergyman, continuous with his tradition, utterly appropriate there in the Harvard chapel. God existed, and Niebuhr meant it.

God was the judge of nations and of history. And we are here, now, in this hour, wrestling with our perplexities. There was little enough joy in this religious vision, no *Te Deums,* but it was genuine enough. Niebuhr deployed a great deal of biblical scholarship, which was appropriate for this Harvard situation, and listening to him that Sunday morning you felt that you were listening to an authentic voice from the entire Protestant tradition.

But, in fact, you were not. Niebuhr had indeed made central to his thought one of the principal Protestant emphases, the doctrine of Original Sin. It affected all human behavior and all human institutions. This was essentially the case Luther and Calvin had urged against Rome. Niebuhr had showed how the old doctrine was relevant to his own century, and in doing so he made a major contribution to our understanding both of our own experience and of the Christian tradition. But curiously enough, within Niebuhr's own writings, Protestantism was dissolving. By 1958, he would decisively throw Christianity overboard. This would be an intellectual disaster, a personal calamity, but a development that was also richly instructive.

Some hint of all this can be sensed earlier, in some sentences quoted from *The Irony of American History.* Niebuhr was concerned to clean up—to "edit"—his ancestral Protestantism, in the interest of making it respectable. Thus we find him in that 1952 book discoursing upon the supposed fact that our "Calvinist fathers insisted upon" the political safeguards that are embodied in our constitutional arrangements. Baloney. The Calvinists wanted a theocracy in New England, no safeguards, and Niebuhr knew it when he wrote those sentences in 1952. The constitutional safeguards were not provided by Calvinist or Lutheran theocrats, but by hard-headed eighteenth-century political thinkers like Madison and Jefferson. It is quite possible that the eighteenth-century constitution-makers had absorbed Protestant insights, but those were not foremost in their deliberations. When he wrote those sentences, Niebuhr was using history in the service of a much larger personal project—the absorption of Protestants like himself into what he took to be the American mainstream. That this entirely failed intellectually might have appealed to Niebuhr's sense of irony. After a lifetime as a more or less orthodox Protestant, Niebuhr ended in 1958 with his only original contribution to theology, that is, his idea that Christ is relatively unimportant.

Paul Tillich, his great modernizing colleague, thought that Niebuhr's intellectual and religious behavior was indefensible. Tillich had his own peculiar theories about Christ, but at least he was in the great European tradition of serious reflection on Him. Tillich was so profoundly religious that, in the grip of nineteenth-century biblical criticism, he once wondered whether Christian faith would be valid if Christ had never existed historically. In those early writings, Tillich concluded that Christ existed as an idea, beyond all controversy and scholarship, that Christ *had* to exist as an idea, actualizing itself in religious experience.

Niebuhr arrived at his curious theological fate via a long and varied route. He was born in 1892 in the rural backwater of Wright City, Missouri, the son of an immigrant German-speaking Lutheran minister. His intelligence and academic ability led him to the Yale Divinity School, and then, upon completing his degree, he chose to be ordained in the Evangelical and Reformed Church. Installed in a Detroit parish, the young minister experienced at first hand the ethnic and economic power struggles of a teeming industrial city. He began to publish articles in national magazines, and his reputation spread. In 1926, he journeyed east to preach at Harvard. In 1928, he accepted a post at the Union Theological Seminary in New York, and through his teaching, writing, and wide social acquaintance became a major figure on the American intellectual scene. In 1939, he delivered the Gifford Lectures at Edinburgh, which were published under the title *The Nature and Destiny of Man*.

Niebuhr sometimes had a dramatic and decisive impact. For example, he changed the life of Will Herberg, a Jewish philosopher who had abandoned Marxism during the late Thirties. Herberg read Niebuhr's *Moral Man and Immoral Society* (1934). "Humanly speaking," Herberg recalled, "it converted me, for in some manner I cannot describe, I felt my whole being, and not merely my thinking, shifted to a new center." Herberg found that he could now "speak about God and religion without embarrassment, though as yet without much understanding of what was involved." Herberg and Niebuhr became close friends; Herberg considered becoming a Christian but settled on Judaism instead, and in 1955 published an important book called *Protestant, Catho-*

lic, Jew analyzing the three principal religious groupings in America. Niebuhr's wife, Ursula, the niece of an Anglican bishop and a formidable biblical scholar who also taught at Union, said that Herberg reminded her of St. Paul.

But St. Paul, after all, had become a Christian. The experience on the road to Damascus had in fact occurred. Paul had declared that in Christ there is neither Jew nor Greek. But Niebuhr said that he understood Herberg's decision in favor of Judaism—and he struggled intellectually to find some formula which would legitimate that genial understanding. The sticking point, of course, was Christ. Niebuhr went back and forth intellectually, analyzing the phenomenon of religious tolerance, wondering in public whether a certain scepticism in religious matters was not intrinsic to tolerance, seeking some solution in the virtue of humility. In 1958, he dropped his bombshell in the form of a now famous paper read before a joint meeting of the Jewish and Union Theological Seminaries. The paper was called "The Relations of Christians and Jews in Western Civilization," and what Niebuhr tried to do was repeal Christian universalism.

The American Christian majority, he said, must "come to terms with the stubborn will to live of the Jews as a peculiar people, both religiously and ethnically." All right, nothing sensational there. But then Niebuhr did it. He claimed that the relations between Christians and Jews could be satisfactory only if Christians ceased "to practice tolerance *provisionally* in the hope that it will encourage assimilation ethnically and conversion religiously." Niebuhr proposed "genuine tolerance," which was to be achieved in "both the moral and the religious spheres" but only if the Christian "assumes the *continued* refusal of the Jew to be assimilated." He adopted the position of Franz Rosenzweig, the German Jewish philosopher, that Judaism and Christianity are "two religions with one center, worshipping the same God, but with Christianity serving the purpose of carrying the prophetic message to the Gentile world." He argued that Christians must give up missionary activities directed toward Jews, and not merely on grounds of politeness, but *on principle,* because they are *wrong.* The two faiths are sufficiently alike, despite some differences, and the Jew may find God "more easily in terms of his own religious heritage than by subjecting himself to the hazards of guilt feeling" which would result from a conversion to Christianity. It was hopeless, Niebuhr concluded, to suppose that anything could "purify the symbol of Christ as the image of God in the imagination of the Jew."

Whatever the psychological truth of these observations, the striking thing is that the truth-value of Christianity is entirely ignored. Christ is viewed as a "symbol" which cannot be purified in the Jewish imagination.

What Niebuhr was attempting to inaugurate was, in fact, henotheism, a divine pluralism, a god for "us" and a god for "them." It was a theological regression, a move back beyond the universalism to the tribal theologies of the ancient world. Christianity had broken through the exclusiveness of the tribe, and Niebuhr was trying to reinstate it. Rabbi Arthur Hertzberg detected in all this "a new theology," and he was right, except that it was also a very old one. As Sam Nadler, an official of Jews for Jesus, declared in an interview, "To deny the gospel to the Jewish people is the worst form of antisemitism . . . if the gospel is true, you're not being loving in being tolerant."

Niebuhr's 1958 bombshell was an astonishing intellectual development. A man proclaimed to be the most important Protestant theologian in America had given up a vital part of the Christian position. In fact, he had given up Christ—and had thrown St. Paul overboard, along with two millennia of Christian theology and ecclesiastical tradition. As John Murray Cuddihy has written, Niebuhr in these transactions was a sentimentalist, and Cuddihy quoted Chesterton: "The sentimentalist . . . is the man who wants to eat his cake and have it. He has no sense of honor about ideas; he will not see that one must pay for an idea as for anything else. He will have them all at once in one wild intellectual harem, no matter how much they quarrel and contradict each other." As a matter of fact, Niebuhr's frivolous Christology cast doubt upon the seriousness of his thought about original sin, the fall and the redemption being dependent on one another for their true meaning.

Niebuhr, of course, was responding to the obvious social and political pressures involved in living in a pluralistic modern America. His remarkable departure may have been foreshadowed by his earlier scathing attack on Billy Graham, who, though appealing to mass audiences, was nothing if not an orthodox Protestant. From Niebuhr's standpoint, Graham's real fault may have been that he was too aggressively Christian. But although Niebuhr involved himself in an intellectual debacle, it was an exciting and instructive one. By pushing this undertaking to its logical conclusion, he demonstrated its intellectual impossibility. Christian universalism and henotheism are contradictory and incompatible, and it was useful to have that demonstration made so dramatically in 1958.

To Niebuhr's colleague, Paul Tillich, a more rigorous and indeed more traditional theological thinker, Niebuhr was involved in intellectual absurdity. Observing Niebuhr's increasing emphasis on the "biblical" content of Christianity—i.e., its common substance with Judaism—at the expense of its Greek content, Tillich attacked, saying that Christianity cannot "give a preference to the Jewish in contrast to the Greek encounter with reality," since it "transcends this conflict." He accused Niebuhr of trying to absolutize not Christianity but Judaism, and of doing so in violation of his own principles, since Niebuhr would never accept the absolute claim of any culture, "not even the Jewish culture over against other cultures." Tillich was correct, but his criticism did not deflect Niebuhr from his course.

Through his writings and as a teacher, initially at Union Theological Seminary in New York and later at Harvard, Paul Tillich was a powerful presence. He was an intellectual force, but also a moral one, an exemplar. Where the twentieth century was concerned, his every utterance seemed to say, in Whitman's words, "I am the man, I suffered, I was there." Tillich was a Christian, but his influence had a curious two-way-street character. From the standpoint of Christian orthodoxy, Tillich was doctrinally suspect. He was even dangerous to the degree that his positions prevailed. Taking up a position on the boundary, so to speak, standing, in his phrase, "on the boundary" between the Christian tradition and modern secular culture, his thought and his teaching could be viewed as a path that led out of Christianity. That was the real substance of his famous quarrel during the 1920s with the neo-orthodox theologian Karl Barth, in which the two great German thinkers defined their positions against one another. Among other things, Tillich did not believe in immortality. His conception of Christ was, from an orthodox point of view, oddly impoverished. He viewed Christ as a unique exemplar only, and thought that Christianity was based not on the historical Jesus but on the biblical portrait of him. His "protestant principle" was a radical doctrine about periods of vital change in history and the creation of new symbols and structures, but also, from an orthodox standpoint, allowed far too little for tradition and church continuities. Thus, the suspect, the dangerous Tillich.

But at the same time, Tillich represented an intellectual road away from secularism, and that is the way he appeared to many of us in the Fifties. If you had been brought up in a generally secular American way, and if you thought, without much reflection, that reality was pretty much the world of the five senses, the daylight world of common sense as it struck you when you walked down the street, then Tillich was very big news. As a student and professor in Germany, he had had a superb European education. Not only did he deal with Spinoza, Schelling, Fichte, Kant, Hegel, Nietzsche in an expert way, he dealt with them as equals. He existed in a continuing conversation with them. Nor was religion for him something "over there" while secular culture was "over here." Religion was pervasive. Tillich discerned the religious dimension of art, poetry, music. He lectured on the significance of religion for philosophy, sociology, psychoanalysis. "There is," he wrote, "no place *beside* the divine, there is no possible atheism, there is no wall between the religious and the nonreligious. The holy embraces both itself and the secular." Tillich's dialectical logic was powerful because it was rooted in actual human experience. He closed the gap between abstract formulation and the thinking and feeling individual person: "The situation of doubt, even of doubt about God, need not separate us from God. There is faith in every serious doubt; namely, the faith in the truth as such, even if the only truth we can express is our lack of truth." He liked to startle his theology students, but in order to make an important point. He would write on the blackboard, "God does not exist." Gasp. But what he meant was that God's existence is not of the same kind as the existence of *other* beings. They are contingent, while God is absolute, the "ground of being," as Tillich put it, without which there would be nothing. "God does not exist," he wrote in his *Systematic Theology* (1951). "He is being itself, beyond essence and existence. Therefore to argue that God exists is to deny him." Tillich found that revelation of being in art, in acts of love, in philosophy, in the oceans and the mountains, everywhere. He did distinguish degrees of revelation, but he found clues to being, to God, in all of experience.

This was powerful stuff for an American in the Fifties who had begun to have some intellectual intimation that the secular conception of reality was in fact inadequate and impoverished.

Beyond his powerful intellect and prodigious learning, Tillich had great personal magnetism—a power that has to be called, frankly, erotic. Everyone responded to this in some degree, but his effect upon women was awesome. He was handsome in a Germanic way, with a large leonine head, high forehead, and bushy hair. His strong bone structure gave his features a chiseled look, and he had a ruddy complexion. His source of power, however, was emotional. He was transparent to feeling. His face revealed, or seemed to, every current that was passing within. His student at Union Seminary and later friend, Rollo May, recalls that "he had a spiritual quality combined with sensuousness which women found highly attractive," and Tillich's romantic reputation became legendary. His "sexual urge," recalls Rollo May, "was in the service of another aim which I call, in its strict sense, eros. Paul's life was the clearest demonstration of eros in action I have ever seen. His relationships were always a pull toward a higher state, an allure of new forms, new potentialities, new nuances of meaning, in promise, if not in actuality. . . . He had a way of looking not *at* but *into* a woman, with his attention fully concentrated on her. This fascinated women. It was not a seducer's approach—or, if you wish to use the word, it was a spiritual seduction. . . . His way of speaking in conversation or in lectures, especially when he discussed love in its various forms, gripped one with the revelation of something new in one's own emotions; it seemed so profound and so true that women received an assurance which led them to advance toward him with a courage which surprised even themselves. . . . Given the Victorian age out of which he came and the Weimar Republic in which he matured, his sexual behavior was, by and large, a courageous pilgrimage on another frontier. We do not need to accept his specific forms of behavior in love or marriage. But he ventured greatly and was greatly rewarded. . . . With a few exceptions, I have rarely met a woman who did not prize and treasure the experience." Among these numerous women, according to May, "there was a remarkable lack of jealousy of each other. When Paul was in the hospital with the illness from which he died, women of whom I had never heard telephoned me from various parts of the country to inquire about him, and I always marveled about their lack of jealousy. It was not that they did not know there were others. But each spoke out of her conviction that she represented something special to Paul. . . . 'He had enough eros for all,' as one woman put it."

Tillich grew up amid the medieval towns of eastern Germany, the son of an orthodox Lutheran minister, attended the Gymnasium and the University of Berlin and studied theology at Halle. With the outbreak of World War I, he enlisted in the German army as a chaplain and served until 1918. "The World War," he later wrote, "in my own experience was the catastrophe of idealistic thinking in general." And, elsewhere, "history became the central problem of my theology and philosophy because of the historical reality as I found it when I returned from the first World War: a chaotic Germany and Europe; the end of the period of the victorious *bourgeoisie* and of the nineteenth-century way of life." Much of the power of Tillich's later thought lay in his ability to incorporate into it his own profound reaction to his experience of the catastrophic history of the twentieth century. From it he developed his central doctrine of the "protestant principle" or "kairos." Kairos involves a deep turning in the process of history. Just as the protestant principle rejected all human claims in the face of God's claims, so Tillich's doctrine of kairos maintained that none of man's cultural or institutional forms can claim final validity. They are valid for a time, and then they come into crisis, and new structures arise out of the historical process. The death of the old relentlessly accompanies the birth of the new. Tillich's sense of the kairos in history bears a strong resemblance to T. S. Eliot's *Waste Land,* also a product of the period after the war, in which, amidst death in various forms, a dead god is struggling toward rebirth. Tillich's incorporation of historical catastrophe into the structure of his thought allowed him to speak with great immediacy to another postwar era.

In 1933, with the Nazi accession to power in Berlin, Tillich lost his academic post at Frankfurt, and, at the urging of Reinhold Niebuhr, accepted a position at Union Theological Seminary. From then until his death at age 83, in 1965, he was, as both teacher and writer, a powerful presence in American life. He worked on his massive *Systematic Theology.* He published a steady stream of major works: *The Protestant Era, The Religious Situation, The Dynamics of Faith, The Theology of Culture, The*

Courage to Be. "When Tillich spoke on Sunday mornings in the chapel at Union Seminary," recalls Rollo May, "a motley crowd overflowed the main auditorium and balcony. In contrast to the white collars and banker-like gray mien of most church congregations, this audience was colorful to say the least: blue collars, open collars, and sometimes no collars at all. Many had long hair; a good many were German exiles—flamboyant persons from the intellectual or art worlds who probably went to church only when Tillich was speaking. . . . The titles of the sermons lead one to ponder: 'Loneliness and Solitude,' 'The Eternal Now,' 'Heal the Sick: Cast Out Demons,' 'On the Transitoriness of Life,' or 'Meditation: The Mystery of Time.' "

Some sense of the intensity of Tillich's presence can be grasped from the concluding paragraphs of his 1952 book *The Courage to Be,* the published version of a series of lectures he gave at Yale. He ends by talking of the "God beyond God"—by which he means the God who is not a being like others, the God who is in his phrase "the ground of being," the God who said "I Am."

"Absolute faith," wrote Tillich,

or the state of being grasped by the God beyond God, is not a state which appears beside other states of mind. It never is something separated and definite, an event which could be isolated and described. It is always a movement in, with, and under other states of the mind. It is the situation on the boundary of man's possibilities. It *is* this boundary. Therefore it is both the courage of despair and the courage in and above every courage. It is not a place where one can live, it is without the safety of words and concepts, it is without a name, a church, a cult, a theology. But it is moving in the depth of all of them. It is the power of being, in which they participate and of which they are fragmentary expressions.

One can become aware of it in the anxiety of fate and death when the traditional symbols, which enable men to stand the vicissitudes of fate and the horror of death, have lost their power. When 'providence' has become a superstition and 'immortality' something imaginary, that which once was the power in these symbols can still be present and create the courage to be in spite of the experience of a chaotic world and a finite existence. The Stoic courage returns but not as the faith in universal reason. It returns as the absolute faith which says Yes to being without seeing anything concrete which could conquer the nonbeing in fate and death. . . .

It returns in terms of the absolute faith which says Yes although there is no special power that conquers guilt. The courage to take the anxiety of meaninglessness upon oneself is the boundary line up to which the courage to be can go. Beyond it is mere nonbeing. Within it all forms of courage are re-established in the power of the God above the God of theism. *The courage to be is rooted in the God who appears when God has disappeared in the anxiety of doubt.*

Paul Tillich's orthodox Lutheran father would certainly have regarded important aspects of his religious thought with profound and thoroughly justified suspicion, but Tillich's expression of—his embodiment of—the European religious tradition and one religious possibility at least in the twentieth century was a powerful presence in the intellectual life of the Fifties. His theology does not achieve the sense of balance and completeness that we find in classical theology. There are gaps, disproportions, even incoherences. But he had done something special, unique. He had opened theology to the modern world, and he had internalized the negations of the modern world. As a theologian, he had literally come back from the trenches of World War I, but he had come back spiritually from the trenches of negation: two catastrophic wars, the collapse of a social and political order, Hitler, the death camps, Stalin, the Gulag, the abyss of meaninglessness. He had faced negation—what he called non-being—in all of its modes. Small wonder that his completed system had holes in it, like that of a wounded veteran. And yet, in spite of the negation, he made his affirmation. It was impressive, exciting, and it counted.

These major figures from the intellectual life of the Fifties have appeared somewhat arbitrarily, because I happened at the time to be in their presence. I could have written instead about Harry Levin and Douglas Bush of Harvard, or William Wimsatt, Maynard Mack, and Cleanth Brooks of Yale, R. P. Blackmur of Princeton, or the French philosopher, Jacques Maritain. But I will have to let these men I have dealt with here suffice as examples from a period when the life of the mind was particularly intense, various and exciting.

FRED

Frederick W. Dupee was an accomplished literary critic and one of the stars of the Columbia English Department. He had startlingly blue eyes, and his life represented a guide book to the successive trends through which he lived, from communism back before World War II, through the elegant criticism of the Fifties, the counterculture of the Sixties.

He had been some kind of a communist during the 1930s and a writer for *The New Masses*. When Josef Stalin promulgated a new Soviet constitution in 1936, Fred reviewed it as a *literary* event, praising the dictator's earthy peasant directness and his obvious integrity.

During the 1940s, Fred moved away from politics and became attached to the psychoanalytical theories of Wilhelm Reich. Reich maintained that the cosmos produces a kind of energy, which he called "orgone." If you can absorb this orgone, it greatly improves your well-being, particularly your sexual well-being—but, unfortunately, most people cannot absorb it very well. For some years, Fred sat regularly in an orgone box, a specially-designed, telephone-booth-like affair which was supposed to enhance one's orgone receptivity.

During the Fifties, he lectured at Columbia—urbane lectures on Proust and Gide and other modern writers. Fred made it sound almost as if he had known them. He favored conservative pin-striped suits and regimental ties, and listening to him in his Columbia classroom, you felt that Paris might be just outside the door. He also lectured on Mann, Joyce, Eliot, Yeats, central authors for the Fifties, and he was writing a book on Henry James, a favorite of the Fifties' critics.

In 1951, Fred spent some time in Paris, and something must have happened there because when he returned the pin-striped suits disappeared. He now favored Harris Tweed jackets and flannel slacks, much more Ivy League.

Fred had married one of his students at Bard, but that was not where the real action seemed to be. At one point, he found himself in love with a Columbia junior from Virginia, a rather preppy young man who wore tweed jackets and regimental ties just like Fred. Fred had him over to his New York apartment for drinks, and he took him swimming in the nude at the New York Athletic Club. One night, back at the apartment, he loaded the young man up with Jack Daniels and made his move. It was Andre Gide in full cry, Corydon on the upper West Side. But the young man said no. Fred was crushed. A couple of days later, the young man received a post card from Fred. The only thing on it was a drawing of a man hanging by the neck in a noose.

Fred published a book of literary criticism called *The King of the Cats*. He also got political again, briefly, during the Columbia riots of 1968. He sided with the rioters and against the Columbia administration. The rioters were filling the university president's wastebasket with shit and burning scholars' research and preventing professors from holding classes, but Fred began talking about it all in terms that made Mark Rudd sound like Danton or Camille Desmoulins. People said that Fred wasn't really being political at all, that he was drawn to the youthful rioters in a sentimental homosexual spasm.

Not long after that Fred retired and moved with his wife to Malibu. And not long after that he died of an overdose.

CHAPTER FIFTEEN

From the Clock at the Biltmore to LSD

"I remember," she said, "that I wore a camel's hair coat, a long wool scarf and a Fair Isle sweater. I must have had a dab of Arpege behind each ear. I had a Scotch-plaid skirt and green woolen socks that came up to my knees. It was Sunday around five o'clock. I forget whether I had come down for something like the Yale-Princeton game or just to go to the theater, but the Palm Court at the Biltmore was jammed. I usually drank a glass of something like sherry. The Biltmore was like a club in those days. Everyone seemed to know everyone else. There was a hum of conversation, cries of 'Hey, George, over here,' and 'Sue, for heaven's sake.' There was excitement in the air, especially on those cool autumn evenings—I think New York is at its best then. Of course, people were always meeting under the clock at the Biltmore, but the clock there had other uses too. It told you when seven o'clock was getting close, and people began leaving for Grand Central station to go back to New Haven or Hanover or Boston. In my purse, I might have had a theater or football program, or a swizzle stick from the Stork Club."

In 1981, of course, the Biltmore died. Its Grand Ballroom and Palm Court and all the rest crumbled to dust before the iron ball of the wrecker and progress.

But let us shift for a moment from that memory of the Fifties at the Biltmore to a somewhat later memory, some fifteen years later, in 1970. The spring term at Dartmouth was ending; in fact, it was final exam period. The students in my course in The Age of Johnson bent in earnest industry over their final exam blue books, writing their answers to a question about tradition and revolt in the literary culture of the late eighteenth century. *Bong . . . Bong . . .* The clanging bell in the tower of Baker Library began to toll the hour. The students began to close their exam books, get up out of their seats, come forward, and hand the blue books to me as they went out the door. When one of the students handed his book to me, he looked at me with an odd intensity and said, "This is the best essay I've ever written."

"Congratulations," I replied. "I look forward to reading it." And then he left too.

When I got back to my English Department office, I opened his exam book. The only mark in it was a single black horizontal line of ink across the top of the first page. He had written the whole essay or whatever it was on a single line at the top of that first page. LSD. The gift of Doctor Timothy Leary of Harvard to the students of America. By 1970, we were well into the Age of Aquarius, the era of turn-on, tune-in, and drop-out. Before it was over, some of my best students had disappeared into rural communes, into the Himalaya mountains, into—for some reason—Goa, in India. Students were walking out of second-story windows, falling into stairwells.

The incident of the one-line essay occurred not long after I had returned East from Sacramento, where I had been working as a speech writer for Ronald Reagan. Around the campus at Berkeley, I had seen teenagers having public sex in vacant lots, on benches, in doorways. I remember buying some paperbacks in a bookstore on Telegraph Avenue, about eight dollars' worth. I gave the clerk a ten-dollar bill, and he gave me seven dollars change. "That doesn't look right," I said. "Peace, brother," he said. That year a crowd of street people tried to occupy some university property in Berkeley, a vacant lot, and plant pot. They refused to leave. Women were nursing infants, others were having sex, people were playing guitars. They called it "The People's Park." Governor Reagan had them removed by the State Police as helicopters circled overhead. Across the Bay, in the Haight-Ashbury section of San Francisco, the Flower Children of the early Sixties had turned murderous. They begged for handouts, as before, but if you didn't give them something, you could be beaten up or worse. Of course, they were killing each other too. Charles Manson, the Symbionese Liberation Army—the important fact about both is that no one was *surprised* by these phenomena. They merely carried the whole thing to its nightmare conclusion.

And then, all of a sudden, the Sixties were over. Not only temporally, but the state of mind.

The great shift in style and emotion that came at the end of the Fifties had long been prepared for, had been gestating all through the Fifties themselves. Its tremors could be felt, faintly at first, as far back as the beginning of the decade. And it is important to notice that this shift gathered force long before the word Vietnam was present in anyone's consciousness. An important sequence of quite sober and widely-read books, for example, beginning with David Riesman's *Lonely Crowd,* in 1950, expressed in various ways a sense of impatience and irritation with American life. C. Wright Mills' *White Collar: The American Middle Classes* followed in 1951. Sloan Wilson's best-selling novel, *The Man in the Gray Flannel Suit*, came out in 1955, and William H. Whyte's comprehensive study of the bureaucratization of modern life, *The Organization Man*, appeared in 1956. These books, a kind of nervous beating of the feet, expressed a sense of impatience at what their authors felt to be the over-organization of life, a feeling that individuality had been somehow diminished, and that there had occurred a loss of intensity, adventure, surprise. Significantly enough, C. Wright Mills' 1951 book, *White Collar,* was only a way-station on his intellectual journey. Before he died in 1962, prematurely, of a heart attack, this Columbia sociologist had become a Castroite Marxist who routinely apologized for America's enemies but never forgave American sins, however venial.

David Riesman's *The Lonely Crowd*—actually, he was one of its three authors, along with Nathan Glazer and Ruel Denney— reflects a less hectic sensibility than that of Mills, and a far finer intelligence; of all these books, it is surely the one that will continue to be read by a wide audience. Though it is a work of sociology, it is also a work of literature, and it has a novelistic power in its grasp of social reality and in its concrete detail.

The central argument of the book, stated in its simplest form, is that a change had occurred in the character of the American people. In the past, American culture was dominated by people who were "inner-directed," but now "other-directed" people were the dominant type. By inner-directed, Riesman meant people who had internalized traditional authority and the demands of their parents, especially their ideals and expectations of achievement. Other-directed people, in contrast, are those whose character is shaped mainly by their contemporaries and peers, the process commencing in childhood play and in the earliest school years. Throughout *The Lonely Crowd,* it is clear that Riesman much prefers the earlier inner-directed type, the achiever, whether in business or the arts or whatever, to what William Whyte, in his different terminology, called "the organization man." "The ideal of behavior," wrote Lionel Trilling in a review of this book, "which is indigenous to the social life of the modern child, is the model and perhaps the mold of the ideal of adults, at least of the middle class. We are coming to be a civilization in which overt ambition, aggression, and competition are at a discount. Not, of course, that the sources of natural aggression are drying up or that people no longer seek prestige. But self-aggrandizement takes new forms as the ideals of other-direction become increasingly compelling. Overt ambition gives way to what Mr. Riesman calls antagonistic cooperation, which implies affability, blandness, a lively sensitivity to the opinion of the group, the suppression of asperity. Social differences must be minimized as far as possible. Wealth must depreciate itself, and must seek to express itself not in symbols of power but in fineness of taste. Food is ordered less for the old-fashioned virtues of substantiality and abundance than for the new charms of elegance and artistry." Riesman, as I have said, prefers the inner-directed person of an earlier America, but he recognizes that we cannot simply will him back into existence. He proposes, instead, the cultivation of a greater degree of *autonomy*—a good idea, no doubt, but one which in his 1950 presentation seems rather pale and lacking in concreteness.

The popularity of books like this, and the seriousness with which they were taken, indicates that there would have been new emotions flowing in the Sixties. These books seem to me to foreshadow, sober as they are, academic even, a shift in sensibility—from an impatience with organization to a demand for individuality, from stability to adventure, from form to feeling. We have seen this kind of shift occur again and again in Western culture, most notably, perhaps, at the end of the eighteenth century, but also, more recently, when the Victorian era gave way to the exuberant modern energies of the early twentieth century.

To compare large historical entities with smaller ones, the eighteenth century did have some things in common with the Fifties. Both highly valued a sense of order, both sought and achieved an impressive prosperity. Both distrusted utopian impulses in politics. Both valued elegance highly. Indeed, Napoleon's foreign minister Talleyrand once remarked that no one who had been born after the French Revolution could know how sweet life could be. It is certainly out of a sense of these affinities that the Fifties in fact saw a great rise in eighteenth-century scholarship in the universities, with lavish new editions of Swift and Pope and Horace Walpole, and major studies of Johnson, Burke, and other Augustan heroes. Yet the eighteenth century did in fact issue in romanticism, extravagance of emotion and behavior, and revolution in France. It ended with the visions of Blake, the peasant songs of Burns, and on into the sexual openness of Byron and the narcotic reveries of DeQuincey and Coleridge; the Fifties, too, ended in extravagances of feeling and behavior, the desire for diverse kinds of revolution, and also some genuine creativity along the way.

There are indeed some signs now—not necessarily conclusive—that the old cycle may repeat itself. Romanticism ended in Victorianism. Now, in the early Eighties, neo-Victorian currents are stirring. In the religious and moral appeals to work, the family, and self-discipline, we may be seeing a kind of neo-Victorianism struggling to be born.

If writers like Riesman and Sloan Wilson expressed discontent with organization, routine, and other-directedness, alternative conceptions of the self were available—flowing from the printing presses and the movie screens during the Fifties; and they became powerful influences on behavior beginning in the middle of the decade, particularly among the enormousy enlarged younger population that emerged during the middle years of the decade. The postwar baby boom produced a peculiarly proportioned population during the second half of the Fifties, with a huge cohort of teenagers, raised in circumstances of increasing material prosperity, accustomed to adult deference, and seeking a sense of both individual identity and identity as a generation. Large numbers of them began to find both, outside of the familiar models.

Remember this about Jack Kerouac, whatever else you may think about him and his influence, remember it and honor him for it. He died before the end of the Sixties, but he had no use at all for any of their anti-American frenzies. Some time in the mid-Sixties, Kerouac and Allen Ginsberg, according to eyewitnesses, took part in a reading of poetry and prose in Detroit. Anti-Vietnam emotion had reached new heights of intensity in the circles likely to turn up at such a reading. Ginsberg produced some American flags, which he passed around for burning. That was too much for Kerouac, the French-Canadian from working-class Lowell, Massachusetts. Kerouac rescued what flags he could, folded them carefully, and saved them.

The legend of Jack Kerouac resembles in one respect that of Sherwood Anderson. Kerouac "walked out"—in his case, he walked out on the Columbia football team and became an artist, a most satisfying idea to some people. He did this, just as Sherwood Anderson one day stood up at his desk in a business office and just left—and wrote *Winesburg, Ohio*. The reality where Kerouac is concerned is rather different.

Kerouac's father Leo was a job printer who had been born in New Hampshire and had moved to Lowell. Kerouac got out of Lowell through a football scholarship to Columbia. He was darkly handsome, intense, and dreamy. His dreams were heroic. He thought he derived from an ancient and aristocratic line. He meant to be an Ivy League All-American, and, in fact, he was a talented running back. But he also meant to be a great writer on the model of Joyce. In a freshman game against Rutgers in the fall of 1940, Kerouac was the best back on the field, but he broke his leg in the next game, and was out for the year. He wrote for the student newspaper, he kept an extensive private journal, and he wrote stories in the manner of his current literary hero, Thomas Wolfe.

In the fall of 1941, Kerouac reported to Coach Lou Little for football practice. But many students, including football stars, had begun to enlist in the armed services. On the hot September day when President Roosevelt's "I hate war" speech blared from every radio, Kerouac walked away from Baker Field to enlist. He had a new dream. He would become a war hero.

In a single day in Boston, he enlisted in the Marine Corps and was sworn in, and then he enlisted in the Coast Guard. That night, he got drunk and passed out in a men's room. The next morning, he got out of town and away from the authorities by shipping out as a merchant seaman. When he got back, he joined the Navy. The point of all this is obvious. From the time he dropped out of Columbia in 1941 until he met his ultimate redeeming hero in 1947, Kerouac's life was an unmanageable chaos.

When he got out of the Navy in 1943, he got married for a couple of months and returned to Columbia—but not as a student. He fell in with the Columbia literary and bohemian crowd, which included nonstudents both around the university and downtown in Greenwich Village. He slept in Allen Ginsberg's dormitory room, earning Ginsberg one of his expulsions. Dean Alexander Mac-Knight, a venerable institution, described Kerouac as not welcome at Columbia. He saw a lot of William Burroughs, the heir to the Burroughs business machine fortune, who would write the drug epic *Naked Lunch* (1959). The intense and chaotic atmosphere in this literary-narcotic milieu issued in the weird events of August 1944, with the murder of the homosexual Dave Kammerer, the jailing for manslaughter of the Columbia student Lucien Carr, and the jailing of Kerouac as an accessory.

Kammerer and Carr had gotten drunk and then gone down to Riverside Park along the Hudson River to sit on the grass. Kammerer suddenly became enamored, and told Carr that he would kill him if they did not have sex. Carr stabbed Kammerer with a boy scout knife. Then he threw his body into the Hudson River. Frightened, he visited Burroughs and then Kerouac. Oddly, Carr and Kerouac then went out on the town. The knife went down a subway grating. They went to the movies, looked at some paintings, ate hot dogs and then Lucien turned himself in to the police. His defense was based on repelling a homosexual attack, but he got two years in Elmira. Kerouac spent several days in jail, but charges were not pressed against him.

In 1947, amidst the chaos of his life, Kerouac discovered the Hero—the individual who, unlike Kerouac, could live amid chaos and prove invulnerable to it, who could master it: Neal Cassady. Kerouac signed on as Cassady's bard, the Homer to Cassady's Achilles. But, oddly enough, this Achilles also taught his Homer how to write the kind of prose that made him famous.

Kerouac described the meeting with Cassady, whom he called Dean Moriarty, in the opening paragraphs of *On the Road:*

I first met Dean not long after my wife and I split up. I had just gotten over a serious illness that I won't bother to talk about, except that it had something to do with the miserably weary split-up and my feeling that everything was dead. With the coming of Dean Moriarty began the part of my life you could call my life on the road. . . .

One day I was hanging around the campus and Chad and Tim Gray told me Dean was staying in a cold-water pad in East Harlem— Spanish Harlem. Dean had arrived the night before, the first time in New York, with his beautiful little sharp chick Marylou; they got off the Greyhound bus at 50th Street and cut around the corner looking for a place to eat and went right in Hector's, and since then Hector's cafeteria has always been a big symbol of New York for Dean. They spent money on beautiful big glazed cakes and creampuffs. . . .

I went to the cold-water flat with the boys, and Dean came to the door in shorts. Marylou was jumping off the couch; Dean had dispatched the occupant of the apartment to the kitchen, probably to make coffee, while he proceeded with his love problems, for to him sex was the one and only holy and important thing in life, although he had to sweat and curse to make a living and so on. . . . My first impression of Dean was of a young Gene Autry—trim, thin-hipped, blue-eyed, with a real Oklahoma accent—a sideburned hero of the snowy West.

In her splendid biography of Kerouac, Ann Charters notes that Kerouac slightly cleaned up this first meeting. Cassady had not worn any shorts. He stood naked in the doorway of the tenement, a revelation to Kerouac, a Nietzschean hero appearing unexpectedly in Spanish Harlem.

In Kerouac's Neal Cassady-Dean Moriarty hero of *On the Road*, readers in 1955, especially young readers, discovered something new and powerful, the hero who masters chaos and lives entirely outside the ordinary patterns of middle-class life, a hero of the sexual instincts, but also a hero of courage and daring.

On the Road, furthermore, rediscovers America. It is a mid-Fifties travel book. The characters, moving from place to place and from dive to dive, do see the country in its fabulous variety. *On the Road* has a sort of oral sense of American history: "Bull had a sentimental streak about the old days in America, especially 1910, when you could get morphine in a drug store without prescription and Chinese smoked opium in their evening windows and the country was wild and brawling and free, with abundance and any kind of freedom for everyone. His chief hate was Washington bureaucracy; second to that, liberals; then cops."

Cassady provided Kerouac with his example of a new kind of hero, but he also led Kerouac to the new style of *On the Road*. Cassady was a prolific letter writer and sent hundreds of letters to Ginsberg and Kerouac about his adventures, of working on the railroad, and getting drunk and passing out, of "banging" girls in parks. In February 1951, Cassady sent Kerouac what Ginsberg later called the Big Letter, 13,000 words, written with the "sense of careless freedom" that Cassady got from benzedrine. Kerouac was overwhelmed by the letter, by the style and by the hectic adventures. *On the Road* came into focus, an autobiographical novel with Cassady as its hero, written in the direct stream-of-experience style of the Cassady letter.

One other feature of the Kerouac legend, perhaps not surprisingly, is false. He did not simply "type out" *On the Road*. He had been working on it for seven years, beginning in 1948, the year after meeting Cassady. But in 1951, with the "Big Letter," the book crystallized, and the boy from Lowell, Massachusetts, may well have written a great novel.

Two other figures can be put beside Kerouac's Neal Cassady-Dean Moriarty as alternatives to the familiar modes of social life in the Fifties. One was a literary idea which had a small but perhaps important vogue, and the other became the central image in a kind of vast teenage cult. They had affinities with each other and with Kerouac. In 1957, the novelist Normal Mailer published a pamphlet called *The White Negro*. A year earlier, the movie *Rebel Without a Cause*, starring James Dean, had premiered at the Astor Theater in New York.

Mailer, who was born in Long Branch, New Jersey, arrived at literary eminence after the war via Harvard, Marxism, the Army, and the 1948 Henry Wallace campaign. His best-selling war novel, *The Naked and the Dead* (1948), was written in a conventionally realistic mode, but thereafter Mailer shifted to psychosexual themes and explored original and not wholly successful narrative methods—in *Barbary Shore* (1951) and *The Deer Park* (1955). He was interested in Wilhelm Reich's radical sexual theories, and he clearly was searching for a more autonomous, ecstatic, and even religious self. In *The White Negro* essay, he sought to clarify this conception, which had remained murky in his fiction.

The White Negro or "hipster," he thought, would transcend conventional social roles. He would live in close touch with his senses, and particularly his erotic senses. He was courageous, an adventurer seeking experience beyond good and evil—like Nietzsche's *ubermensch*. The experience sought was intense, extreme. Modernists like Hemingway and Sartre lurked just beneath the surface of Mailer's individualistic and courageous existentialist. The White Negro knows that "in a bad world there is no love nor mercy nor charity nor justice unless a man can keep his courage . . . that what made him feel good became therefore The Good." The White Negro believed in love, but not in love as the search for a wife: it was in love "as the search for an orgasm more apocalyptic than the one which preceded it."

Mailer's White Negro-hipster-existentialist represents, in one direction, a rebellion against his earlier leftist Marxist-Henry Wallace collectivism. But in all of its principal details, it also expresses a rebellion against the Fifties. This ideal figure is precisely not an organization man, not a force for stability, not the father of a family. (Shortly after the appearance of this book, Mailer stabbed one of his wives. The joke that went around was that he had become the White Negro Othello.)

Mailer gave fictional embodiment to his hipster-hero in his character Sergius O'Shaugnessy, the Irishness of whose name reflects Mailer's admiration for the Kennedys, inhabiting the White House and legendary for sexual prowess. In a story that achieved a good deal of notoriety at the time, called "The Time of Her Time," Mailer endeavors to present the cosmic orgasm for which the White Negro was supposed to strive. In this episode, Mailer takes seriously the metaphor "tight assed," as Sergius produces an orgasm in a tight-assed Jewish intellectual named Denise by loosening her up through anal intercourse:

> And she was close. Oh, she was close so much of the time. Like a child on a merry-go-round the touch of the colored ring just evaded the tips of her touch, and she heaved and she hurdled, arched and cried, clawed me, kissed me, even gave off a shriek once, and then her sweats running down and her will weak, exhausted even more than

me, she felt me leave and lie beside her. Yes, I did that with a tactician's cunning, I let the depression of her failure poison what was left of her will never to let me succeed, I gave her slack to mourn the lost freedoms and hate the final virginity for which she fought, I even allowed her baffled heat to take its rest and attack her nerves once more, and then, just as she was beginning to fret against me in a new and unwilling appeal, I turned her over suddenly on her belly, my avenger wild with the mania of the madman, and giving her no chance, holding her prone against the mattress with the strength of my weight, I drove into the seat of stubbornness, tight as a vise, and I wounded her, I knew it, she thrashed beneath me like a trapped little animal, making not a sound, but fierce not to allow me this last of the liberties, and yet caught, forced to give up millimeter by millimeter the bridal ground of her symbolic and therefore real vagina. So I made it, I made it all the way—it took ten minutes and maybe more, but as the avenger rode down to his hilt and tunneled the threshold of sexual home all those inches closer into the bypass of the womb, she gave at last a little cry of farewell, and I could feel a new shudder which began as a ripple and rolled into a wave, and then it rolled over her, carrying her along, me hardly moving for fear of damping this quake from her earth, and then it was gone, but she was left alive with a larger one to follow.

So I turned her once again on her back, and moved by impulse to love's first hole. There was an odor coming up, hers at last, the smell of the sea, and none of the armpit or a dirty sock, and I took her mouth and kissed it, but she was away, following the wake of her own waves which mounted, fell back, and in new momentum mounted higher and should have gone over, and then she was about to hang again, I could feel it, that moment of hesitation between the past and the present, the habit and the adventure, and I said into her ear, "You dirty little Jew."

That whipped her over. A first wave kissed, a second spilled, and a third and a fourth and a fifth came breaking over, and finally she was away, she was loose in the water for the first time in her life, and I would have liked to go with her, but I was blood-throttled and numb, and as she had the first big moment in her life, I was nothing but a set of aching balls and a congested cock, and I rode with her wistfully, looking at the contortion of her face and listening to her sobbing sound of "Oh, Jesus, I made it, oh Jesus, I did."

There we have it, the orgasmic apocalypse that was one of the central motifs of the Sixties: though Sergius is also something of a misogynist. The most powerful emotion in the story is the hostility he feels for the dozens of women he brings to his Greenwich Village studio to introduce them to things devoutly to be hoped for.

The image presented on the screen by James Dean has some elements in common with Mailer's White Negro. A few days after his first major manifestation, *Rebel Without a Cause,* premiered in New York, Dean was dead. On September 30, 1955, he was driving his low-slung Porsche Spyder to a sports car race in Salinas when a college student named Donald Turnupseed made a left turn into his path. Dean had just completed another movie, *Giant,* but it was in *Rebel Without a Cause,* a movie about senseless violence among directionless teenagers, that Dean most powerfully projected the image that made him a national hero to millions of young people. That image was one of a tough but—importantly—vulnerable young man who nevertheless makes the leap out of meaninglessness to courage and authenticity. He is the teenager who becomes more than a teenager, a Mailer-Hemingway hero, but who looks not unlike the face you might see in the mirror. William Zavatsky, who is writing a book about *Rebel Without a Cause,* recalls its effect on him in 1955 when he was an adolescent growing up in Bridgeport, Connecticut:

> I walked out of the movie house that day confirmed in my sense of isolation, but not without taking something precious with me: the feeling that others shared my pain. The image that James Dean projected in *Rebel Without a Cause* told me that I could go it alone, but that I had to know when to reach out, the way Jim reaches out for Judy after Buzz has gone over the cliff in the chicken run. And at the bottom of all these whirling questions was the great one, because Dean, standing on that edge, reminded me of Hamlet facing the nothingness of the sea below the crags of Elsinore. 'Y'know something?' he says to Judy. 'I woke up this morning, you know—and the sun was shining, and it was nice, and all that type of stuff. And the first thing—I saw you. And, uh, I said, "Now, boy, this is gonna be one terrific day, so you better live it up, cause tomorrow you'll be nothing." See? And I almost was.'

Charmingly enough, Zavatsky comments:

> For the next few years, I rehearsed James Dean relentlessly. I let my hair grow out and started brushing it back, and I hunted for the red

windbreaker. It was the only piece of clothing Dean wore in the film
that you could really latch on to. . . . Up and down Main Street, I
poked my face in the windows of the men's shops. . . . Finally I
spotted it—a MacGregor jacket with the same filmy fabric, the same
collar you could wrap around your neck to look as cool as Jimmy. . . .
The summer after I graduated from grammar school, Bridgeport's
annual Barnum Festival brought Bill Haley and the Comets to Harding
High School stadium. *Blackboard Jungle* had opened, with "Rock
Around the Clock" forever cementing the connection between rock
music and teenage mayhem.

Much later, when the Sixties were long over, Mick Jagger
remarked that the great appeal of rock had been that it *separated*
the generations, and made the young conscious of themselves as a
distinct, indeed authoritative, group.

But it all began in the Fifties. Kerouac's Neal Cassady, Mailer's
White Negro, James Dean and his legend—these were new images
of possibility, of ways of being, and they were part of the new
sensibility.

The new sensibility also received support in the work of several
theorists who produced analytical works that had considerable
intellectual impact as the Fifties approached their end.

The emergence of Herbert Marcuse as a public figure in the late
Fifties is one of the curiosities of intellectual history. It occurred
because his own abstruse preoccupations coincided with trends
powerful in that special moment of transition. Marcuse, a member
of the famous Frankfurt school of social scientists and philosophers, leftists who had fled Hitler and come to the United States,
had long been preoccupied with an apparently insoluble contradiction between his two masters, Marx and Freud. On the one hand,
Marx held out to mankind the hope of a utopian conclusion to the
revolutionary process. Man's alienation from work and self would
end. This is the hope that sounds in *The Communist Manifesto* and
in "The Internationale." Marcuse was a Marxist. But Freud was
more pessimistic. Civilization, he taught, depended upon the
repression of the instincts, the sublimation of eros; civilization
depended upon human pain and neurosis. Marcuse did not ask
whether either of these two doctrines were true, could be demonstrated empirically; instead, in the manner of both traditions, he
accepted them and tried for a reconciliation, an intellectual synthe-

sis within the Marxian-Freudian tradition. Moreover, he was not a particularly lucid writer. Even during his vogue in the Sixties, it is safe to say that few of his admirers could actually bring themselves to read him. But he became a theoretician of the Sixties because his "reconciliation" of Marx and Freud—like a theologian's reconciliation of Aquinas and Scotus—coincided with something that was actually happening in the American experience. Marcuse decided that Freud was a Victorian, and that *we did not have to be nearly as repressed as Freud's doctrine assumed.*

In both *Eros and Civilization* (1955) and *One Dimensional Man* (1964), Marcuse's solution to the contradiction between eros and civilization would have been laughable to either Freud or Marx. He argued that technological progress would abolish the contradiction through the spread of leisure. With automation, we would be free, or almost free—and the contradiction between eros and civilization, at the heart of Freud's thought, would be greatly ameliorated if not abolished. "Complete automation in the realm of necessity would open the dimension of free time as the one in which man's private *and* societal existence would constitute itself. This would be the historical transcendence toward a new civilization." A technological utopianism would abolish the contradictions between Marxist and Freudian doctrine. We would have more leisure, more freedom, and more sex. Though this was a sentimental solution to Marcuse's intellectual problems, it was exactly what was happening in the lives of his largely youthful readers and students. They *did* have more leisure, and they certainly did have more sex. Marcuse caught on. It was credit-card Marxism.

But Marcuse's "solution" only raised more difficulties, principal among which was that utopian bliss did not thus arrive. To explain which he drew upon the reverse-spin tactics of the dialectic, in which what seems to be actually is not. In the later development of his thought, in "Repressive Tolerance" (1969), for example, he argues that apparent freedom is actually its opposite, repression—since it prevents those who enjoy it from achieving the "real" freedom which will transform the human condition and usher in the reign of pleasure and virtue. In his earlier "erotic" thoughts of the Fifties, Marcuse found some resonance among the affluent and youthful practitioners of the new sexual freedom, who had little concern with contradictions between Marx and Freud. In his later attacks upon actual freedoms as not "real" freedoms, he legitimized the totalitarian and even criminal components of the New Left. In the history of Marxist and Freudian thought, he is only a ridiculous footnote. He ended his days as a professor at the University of California in San Diego, and as the mentor of the Communist ideologue Angela Davis. His colleagues there remember him as incredibly stuffy and "European," a "Herr Doctor Professor," who clearly knew little about American realities. Perhaps all of his theorizing about eros and freedom and repression was merely some obscure quarrel with himself.

Norman O. Brown also began his intellectual career as a Marxist, but with *Life Against Death* (1959) he announced the storming of utopia not through political-economic but through sexual revolution. Again, as with Marcuse, his theories—however speculative and bizarre—did have some resonance with the greater sexual freedom that had been developing in America throughout the Fifties. Brown abandoned his Marxism, and found his utopian promise in a radical revision of Freud's theory of repression. If Freud had always argued, and especially in *Civilization and Its Discontents*, that civilization required instinctual repression and pain, Brown simply argued that civilization was not worth the pain. Furthermore, in *Life Against Death*, he argued—with impressive scholarship and literary sophistication; many of his pages are entirely brilliant—that what civilization represses is not awareness of eros but awareness of excrement. *Life Against Death* proposes nothing less than the abolition of all repression. It was a book steeped in the Western intellectual tradition—when he worked out his ideas, Brown was a professor of classics at Wesleyan— but aimed at the abolition of Western civilization. As Lionel Trilling wrote in a respectful review: "The concept of repression as used here is specifically Freudian and it refers not merely to the mechanisms at work in the individual person to control or seemingly extirpate his instinctual drives, but also the whole structure of the culture, which is at once the instrument of repression and its fine fruit. And the culture that Mr. Brown has in mind is Western culture—when he gives his book the secondary title, 'The Psychoanalytical Meaning of History,' he refers to the development of Western culture at the behest of repression, of our culture as it is Aristotelian and Cartesian, as it is intellectualized and highly moralized, as it is scientific and instrumental, as it sets more store by the aggressive than by the erotic impulses."

But in this review, Trilling is fascinated by Brown's refusal of the easy way out. Brown does not, finally, refer to society as the primal cause of repression. Brown argues that the infant *as we know it* is the agent of repression, that human nature generates its own repression of its erotic and other bodily impulses. What then? In answer to Freud's pessimism about human nature *as we know it,* Brown cries out for a new human nature—not only an end to the repression of genital sexuality, itself, indeed, restrictive and repressive, but an end to the repression of the "polymorphous perverse" impulses of the infant state. What the infant desires, the adult should freely do. This is indeed taking at face value Wordsworth's famous dictum that "the child is father to the man." Only thus, in the title of *Life Against Death,* can life triumph over death in an "erotic exuberance," but an exuberance that clearly accepts excrement into the "resurrection of the body." One of the central chapters of *Life Against Death* is called "The Excremental Vision." The horror of Gulliver in Book Four of *Gulliver's Travels* when the Yahoos exuberantly fling excrement at each other and at him is a horror clearly not shared by the reborn "polymorphous perverse" human of Brown's vision of liberation.

After *Life Against Death,* Brown, as might have been expected, disappeared into apocalyptic prose poetry of uncertain meaning. But *Life Against Death* was a great hermetic analysis, within the admittedly problematic terms of Freudian doctrine, of one possible dimension of that doctrine. Viewed in its historical context, it was a prophecy a few years earlier of the actual utopian-erotic impulse of the hippie, a legitimation in elegant intellectual terms, of infantile behavior.

Unless you take Freudian doctrines as scientific truths, of course, the whole argument seems a bit silly. Still, reviewing it in the fall of 1955, Lionel Trilling spoke in tones of awe: "But I know that I shall not have done with the book until time and habituation have brought me into a more intimate relation than I yet have with the arguments that Mr. Brown makes for the necessity, the possibility, and the desirability of the change he advocates."

Intellectually, so far as I can see, this is preposterous. But perhaps it explains why Trilling was so passive when the Yahoos assaulted Columbia in 1968 with excrement, both spiritual and physical.

Finally, speaking of doctrine, a largely forgotten book by Paul Goodman called *Growing Up Absurd* (1959) enjoyed a wide vogue and was a moral catalyst as the Fifties drew toward their close.

Before *Growing Up Absurd,* Goodman had published volumi-
nously, but in obscurity. He had written dozens of stories and
poems, reviews and essays, and even co-authored a book on city
planning with his brother Percival, and he had written a novel
called *Empire City.* It had all fallen like a stone to the bottom
of the ocean and been forgotten. I have not, to this day, met anyone
who can tell me what happens in one of his short stories. But
with *Growing Up Absurd,* he suddenly became famous, a presence. *Growing Up Absurd* employed a direct, plain style that
might well be compared with Orwell's, and it dealt with the sense
of distance that was opening up between self and conventional
social role for many sensitive young and even middle-aged people.
The society Goodman described gave its young no world to grow
up in that could reasonably be described in terms of nobility,
honor, community, and faith. Growing up in such a society was to
experience absurdity. Goodman's brilliance was that he used traditional moral and spiritual values to undermine the American society he was criticizing. There was, of course, some irony in this,
since Goodman was a homosexual, who once wrote that "my
homosexual acts have made me a nigger, subject to arbitrary
brutality and debased when my outgoing impulse is not taken for
granted as a right." But Goodman was able to transmute this very
particular discontent, that of the homosexual outsider, into a
general indictment of America in the Fifties, and that he was able
to do so was in large part due to his "plain talk" style.

So far, here, with Mailer, Marcuse, Brown, and Goodman, we
have been focusing on what amounts to a sexual critique of the
Fifties from the Left. But this coincided dramatically with politics,
the Aldermaston Easter Peace March in England, which began in
1960, linking sex and left-protest politics in a way that drew
students by the hundreds from Europe and America. The destina-
tion of the march was the nuclear research facility base at Aldermaston. But as the heterogeneous crowd wound its way along the
roads and lanes, camping out, the reality had little to do with
submarines or bombs. It was a springtime children's march, and
often not-so children's, of pot, guitar music, and easy sex. Many
of my Columbia students included the Aldermaston march in their
European schedule—for the sex and fun. The old leftist slogan of
"solidarity" took on a new left meaning that was sexual. It was a
group fuck-in, a fuck-against-the-bomb—but the bomb was pretty
remote. The same was true of other Sixties "protest"

movements, whether the Gene McCarthy campaign of 1968 or the subsequent protests against nuclear power plants like Seabrook in New Hampshire. For my part, I have always considered it both ridiculous and revealing of the personalities involved that sex required this sort of political "cover."

The sexual apocalypse, the substance of things promised and hoped for by Mailer, Brown, and the rest—the orgasm at the end of the rainbow—did not of course occur. But the Sixties did consummate a general relaxation in sexual matters which even a neo-Victorianism in the 1980s surely will not repeal, since it is so deeply rooted in changing social realities: the independence of women, the tendency to marry later or sometimes not at all, the virtual disappearance of the older sense that sex is sordid and dangerous. This process had been underway at least since the 1920s, and the Sixties completed it.

Nor did the racial apocalypse occur—what Garry Wills was pleased to herald in a moment of prophetic afflatus as *The Second Civil War* (1968). Instead, we moved toward an overdue racial equality through such sober measures as the Civil Rights Act of 1965. The contribution of the Sixties was essentially to inflame the racial issues to a peak of emotional frenzy, an atmosphere which evoked such improbable figures as Huey Newton, H. Rap Brown, Eldridge Cleaver, and Stokley Carmichael. These "spokesmen" would not have achieved any credibility or prominence without the special atmosphere of the Sixties inflating their balloons. Brown blew himself to bits with a home-made bomb in Baltimore. Cleaver has become a born-again Christian. Carmichael and Newton have disappeared from view, as have the Black Panthers and the rest of the cast of characters from the Sixties. We now argue over busing and quotas.

The Sixties affected, often for the better, some of our attitudes, but it is a decade that will live on principally through its songs and its poems. Before 1960, reading the modernist giants like Eliot and Yeats and Pound, a young writer had the sense that writing poetry was an impossible activity. *No one* could write poetry of that power. The poets of the Sixties simply started afresh, loosened the rhythms of verse, appealed to different traditions. They had the courage to make the break, in retrospect a necessary break, and they wrote some poetry that will live.

Looking back on the Fifties, it seems to me that we will see them increasingly as an exciting, intellectually intense, and variegated period, when much that now matters was born. I see the Fifties also as framed by two great deaths, the deaths of two men, who, as we look back upon them, loom more and more important for what they embodied in American history. Senator Robert Taft of Ohio, Mr. Republican and Mr. Conservative, died in the summer of 1953. Secretary of State John Foster Dulles died in the spring of 1959. As we think of the Fifties, once again and in a new way, it will be good to reflect on these two men, quintessentially men of their time. Both embodied an older and thornier Protestantism than we have been accustomed to since, both were highly intelligent, and neither suffered fools gladly. And each of them embodied a theme, the truth of which we are in the process of rediscovering in the Eighties.

The son of a president, Robert Taft thought almost to the end that he some day would be president himself. He had a brilliant record at Yale and stood at the head of his Harvard Law School class. When he ran for the Senate in 1938, his wife, Martha, said to an audience of Ohio coal miners: "He did not start from humble beginnings. My husband is a very brilliant man. He had a fine education at Yale. He has been well trained for his job. Isn't that what you prefer when you pick leaders to work for you?"

Nine times out of ten, that approach would have been a political disaster, but from the beginning of his political career, Taft refused to common-man it. His father had been president and chief justice of the Supreme Court. His family included diplomats, lawyers, judges, members of the state legislature, civic leaders. The Tafts were Ohio, American, aristocracy, and the Taft boys went to Yale. They were men of intellect and property and respected both.

In that Depression and New Deal year of 1938, the voters of Ohio rejected a passionate New Dealer and sent Taft to the U.S. Senate.

Bob Taft was tall, owlish, and wore rimless glasses. He spoke in a flat midwestern accent. Year after year, he fought the New Deal on grounds of unchanging principle. His mind worked like a computer, he had almost total recall of fact and analysis, and he was not a man to challenge in debate at a committee hearing or on the floor of the Senate. He was against the spread of federal power when the entire American articulate class was for it. His welfare bills gave jurisdiction to the states, and they were defeated. "When I say liberty," he wrote, "I do not mean simply what is referred to as 'free enterprise.' I mean liberty of the individual to think his

own thoughts and live his own life as he desires to think and live
. . . liberty of a man to choose his own occupation, liberty of a man
to run his own business as he thinks it ought to be run, as long as he
does not interfere with the right of other people to do the same
thing. . . . Gradually this philosophy has been replaced by the idea
that happiness can only be conferred upon the people by the grace
of an efficient government. Only the government, it is said, has the
expert knowledge necessary for the people's welfare."

This was the assumption he spent his political life fighting. And
he began to draw blood. In 1950, big labor went all-out in Ohio to
defeat the author of the 1947 Taft-Hartley labor reform act, but
Taft won re-election by a wide margin, and gained momentum
toward his goal of the 1952 Republican nomination. He was the
Republican leader in the Senate, Mr. Republican. He had a clear
and independent intellect. He had opposed the Nuremberg war
crimes trials because they violated "the fundamental principle of
American law that a man cannot be tried under an *ex post facto*
statute. . . . In these trials we have accepted the Russian idea of the
purpose of trials—government policy and not justice." This position, intellectually unassailable, earned Taft a chapter in John F.
Kennedy's book *Profiles in Courage,* but it certainly was not
conventional American presidential politics.

Bob Taft had been beaten by Wendell Wilkie for the Republican
nomination in 1940, by Thomas E. Dewey in 1948. The Northeast
still dominated the Republican Party. In 1952, Eisenhower narrowly defeated him in Chicago, but after a meeting at Columbia, at
which the two men agreed on fundamentals, Taft supported
Eisenhower with iron consistency.

Before his final run for the presidency in 1952, Taft characteristically had a thorough physical examination and got a clean bill of
health. In the spring of 1953, however, he went to his doctor for an
exasperating pain in his hip. After a series of tests, the doctors told
him that his case was hopeless. He continued to go to the Senate,
on crutches, and he kept the news of his cancer from his wife, who
had had a stroke, and told his friends that he was going to "fight it."

At New York Hospital, the surgeons performed exploratory
surgery. They found that the cancer was not localized. Nodules
broke out in his mouth and on his chest and back. The autopsy
showed that it had been an uncommon form of cancer which
spreads very rapidly and had in the last days reached his brain.

President Eisenhower wrote in his diary: "Senator Taft's death came so quickly after his first knowledge of any illness that I think it astonished even those of us who had some reasonable early warning of the nature of the illness. . . . On July 21 I called him on the telephone. He was feeling well and said that within one week he was going to leave the hospital and come back to Washington. We discussed a number of matters, including the appointment as assistant secretary of labor of a man named Siciliano. On July 31 he died, never having left the hospital."

John Foster Dulles, one of the great men of the Fifties, also died of cancer, in the spring of 1959. He had been Eisenhower's Secretary of State since the inauguration, and if either Taft or Dewey had won in 1952, he would still have been Secretary of State. He was admired and reviled as the stern embodiment of America's hostility to communism. Dulles was blunt. He did not speak of the Soviets as "adversaries" or "a superpower." He called them "the enemy." But the deepest reason why Dulles was hated by the Left here and abroad was that he considered communism morally evil, and said so. He considered "neutralism" like Nehru's *immoral*, and said so. He believed that the task of America's foreign policy was to advance the cause of freedom everywhere, and said so.

"What we need to do," he once remarked, "is to recapture . . . the crusading spirit of the early days, when the missionaries, the doctors, the educators, and the merchants carried the knowledge of the great American experiment to all four corners of the globe."

His father had been a Presbyterian minister in Watertown, New York, and as a boy Dulles had memorized long passages from the Bible. The family liked to sing "Onward, Christian Soldiers" together, and his boyhood heroes were Paul Revere and John Paul Jones. In 1907, when he was nineteen and a Princeton undergraduate, his grandfather, a lawyer who had been Benjamin Harrison's Secretary of State, took him to the Second Hague Peace Conference. Then there came law school, marriage to a niece of Robert Lansing, Woodrow Wilson's Secretary of State, international legal practice at Sullivan and Cromwell. Presidents Roosevelt and Truman called upon him as a symbol of a bipartisan foreign policy. He attended innumerable conferences in Europe and Asia, backed the Marshall Plan and NATO, got the word "justice" ranked equally with "peace" in the U.N. Charter.

In November 1956, surgeons removed a cancerous growth from

his intestine, and he recuperated. In February 1959, he was stricken with almost unbearable stomach pains, but flew anyway to London, Paris, and Bonn. He could scarcely walk. "If it isn't cancer," he told a friend, "then I feel the trip is too important to put off. If it is cancer, then additional discomfort doesn't fundamentally matter anyway."

At the end of April, he had to resign.

President Eisenhower called a press conference in the Colonial Room of the Richmond Hotel in Augusta. He had difficulty fighting back the tears. His fists were tightly clenched at his sides. "What I have to say," he said, "concerns Secretary Dulles." Eisenhower announced the resignation. He said that Dulles would continue as a consultant. "I personally believe," he went on, "that he has filled his office with greater distinction and greater ability than any other man our country has known—a man of tremendous character and courage, intelligence and wisdom."

While Dulles was dying at Walter Reed, he had a constant stream of visitors—Eisenhower, Nixon, Dulles' family, Secretary of State Christian Herter. Until nearly the end he followed foreign policy closely.

Nixon told me that the last time he saw him, Dulles was running a high fever and was sucking on ice cubes for some relief.

Taft and Dulles are dead. The Sixties are gone, and so are the Fifties. A couple of years ago, I had dinner in New York with Dr. Timothy Leary, the Sixties LSD guru. Leary now takes nothing stronger than a glass of white wine. He was on his way to Princeton, to address a conference of psychiatrists on the subject of the dangers of permissiveness.

Envoi: History Must Be Told

The most influential professor at Dartmouth College during the Fifties was a refugee from Hitler named Eugen Rosenstock-Huessy. He was a Christian-existentialist and taught in the philosophy department, but not in the usual academic way. He was short, barrel-chested, powerfully built, and had a shock of white hair. He had a heavy German accent. He gave rambling lectures that moved between Germanic erudition and current events, but always circling back to the core of his thought. Students taped his lectures. The records still exist. Students packed his classrooms. He had served as a colonel in Von Hindenberg's army during World War I. His patience with student stupidity was limited. Sometimes, in response to a particularly obtuse undergraduate remark, he would advance into the seats, lift the student with his powerful arms, and pronounce, "Pig, you don't deserve to live!"

His primal philosophical insight had occurred at the battle of Verdun. During a panic, he had been forced to execute some German troops. But then, during a lull in the fighting, he had crawled alone out into no-man's land. Suddenly, a bombardment began. He felt not only physical fear, as the executed soldiers had indeed felt, but existential fear. He was a naked worm. He was outside of *history*. There, under the bombardment, he was meaningless, a worm, an insect. Thereafter, all of his intellectual activity, however esoteric, whether he was talking about Christ or Egyptian history, Franklin Roosevelt, Hitler, or Dartmouth College, represented an attempt to get back inside *history,* to see the significance of *real* history, to rise above the condition of a naked worm.

"Anything," he would tell his class, "that has been this way since you were twelve seems to you to have existed since time immemorial. You think it has always existed. You have no sense of history, or why history must be told. You don't know the difference between human history and a scientific diary about a study of rats.

"But history is dualistic. It is not for man the history of spiders, who have been the same since time immemorial. Dartmouth College has not been the same since two hundred years ago.

"Is history a specialized thing, for Ph.D.s or the History Department? Is it about the price of wheat in Lisbon in 1608?

"I don't think so.

"We have to tell what an epoch-making event is. History is those events which make it dangerous, intolerable to live as if we had existed the same from time immemorial. History is time memorialized.

"People must be shocked out of their lives—their lives as of today. History is not the result of yesterday. It is not *The Encyclopaedia Brittanica.* It is not a mere register of facts. A cocktail party does not make the future. But there are events that change life and make the future.

"When your father married your mother, he did not know how it would turn out. She will not be as beautiful now as when he married her, or not in the same way. But unless they acted, not knowing the future, there would be no future for you.

"Memorialized events change life and make history. They surround us.

"Lincoln did not know the result of freeing the slaves. But he changed history. When men do what is demanded of them, the results surround us.

"Moses changed the world. But because of the Cross we cannot ever return to that earlier world. The world was changed again. That is why history must be told.

"The philosopher Nietzsche is regarded as a madman. But in his genius he foresaw the crisis of Western civilization. He acted as a philosopher, despite ridicule, with faith. He did not care about the consequences.

"Gentlemen, I tell you that if only the Marxists had predicted the twentieth-century crisis, well, they would have had the prophecy, the reality of history. But Nietzsche acted in freedom and in intellectual faith and took the risk.

"All freedom exists because of faith, because of the risks that were taken.

"If you believe in the philosophy of the ash can, that everything has always existed and that nothing matters, then I tell you that this country exists now because of innumerable acts of faith. That you exist because of them.

"Do you really think that all of the fighting from Sam Houston to Gettysburg was meaningless? You sit here today because men volunteered, not knowing the consequences, in 1860, and in 1942.

"And, because your parents volunteered.

"And that, gentlemen, is why history must be told."

Notes

It is impossible to list all of the printed sources for a work such as this, but I wish to express particular indebtedness to the following. They will richly reward the interested reader with further adventures in the history and the culture of the Fifties.

Arlen, Michael J. *Exiles*. Farrar, Straus and Giroux, 1970.

Bowles, Jerry. *A Thousand Sundays: The Story of the Ed Sullivan Show*. G. P. Putnam's Sons, 1980.

Boyarski, Bill. *The Rise of Ronald Reagan*. Random House, 1968.

Cuddihy, John Murray. *No Offense: Civil Religion and Protestant Taste*. Seabury, 1978.

Dickstein, Morris. *Gates of Eden: American Culture in the Sixties*. Basic Books, 1977.

Ewald, William Bragg, Jr. *Eisenhower the President*. Prentice-Hall, 1981.

Ewen, David. *All the Years of American Music*. Prentice-Hall, 1977.

Frommer, Harvey. *New York City Baseball: The Last Golden Age, 1947–1957*. Macmillan, 1980.

Greenberg, Clement. *Art and Culture*. Beacon, 1961.

Hamm, Charles. *Yesterdays: Popular Song in America*. Norton, 1979.

Josefsberg, Milt. *The Jack Benny Show*. Arlington House, 1977.

Laing, Dave. *Buddy Holly*. Collier Books, 1971.

Lathem, Earl. *The Community Controversy in Washington*. Harvard University Press, 1966.

Levy, Julien. *Arshile Gorky*. Abrams, no date.

Lewis, Peter. *The Fifties*. Lippincott, 1978.

Marshall, S. L. A. *The River and the Gauntlet*. Morrow, 1953.

May, Rollo. *Paulus*. Harper and Row, 1973.

Miller, Jim, ed. *The Rolling Stone Illustrated History of Rock and Roll*. Random House/Rolling Stone, 1981.

Novak, Michael. *The Joy of Sports*. Basic Books, 1976.

Ritter, Lawrence and Donald Honig, *The Image of Their Greatness: An Illustrated History of Baseball from 1900 to the Present*. Crown, 1979.

Sander, Irving. *The New York School: The Painters and Sculptors of the Fifties*. Harper and Row, 1978.

Schapiro, Meyer. *Modern Art: 19th and 20th Centuries*. Braziller, 1978.

Smith, Walter Bedell. *Eisenhower's Six Great Decisions: Europe, 1944–45*.

In addition, I found it to be a great adventure to read through the popular periodicals of the Fifties, including Time, Newsweek, The New York Times, *and* Variety.

A special acknowledgment is due Michael J. Arlen, Harvey Frommer, S.L.A. Marshall and Walter Bedell Smith, without whose above-cited books the "Camera Eye" interchapters "Ernest," "Almost to Manchuria," and "Overlord," and Chapter Five, "The Boys of Summer," could not have been written.

Index

297